THOMAS P. GORE

Courtesy Harris & Ewing, Washington, D.C.

THOMAS P. GORE

The Blind Senator from Oklahoma

By Monroe Lee Billington

THE UNIVERSITY OF KANSAS PRESS · LAWRENCE · 1967

PREFACE

Although totally blind as the result of two separate accidents during his childhood, Thomas P. Gore rose above that handicap to fulfill his lifelong ambition to be a United States Senator. Active as a young man in Populist politics in Mississippi and Texas before moving to Oklahoma Territory at the beginning of the twentieth century, Gore was elected to the Senate as a Democrat from Oklahoma when that state was admitted to the Union in 1907. Defeated for re-election in 1920, he gained a Senate post for a final term in 1930. This is the study of the political and senatorial career of a blind man known for his independence.

The writing of this work has been a cooperative enterprise. To name all of the persons who have contributed to it would be impossible, but all of them have my thanks, along with those specifically mentioned here. Gaston Litton, former Archivist at the University of Oklahoma, first aroused my interest in this subject and introduced me to the primary source materials. Gore's law partner, J. Roy Thompson, Jr., gave me information on the Senator's early years and personal life. Thomas D. Clark and Edwin C. McReynolds read the manuscript in its entirety, saving me from the most serious errors of fact and interpretation. With appreciation I mention Everett W. Thornton, friend and teacher, whose unwarranted confidence has spurred me in this and other endeavors. My thanks are extended to the editors of these journals for publishing my interpretative essays on Gore, parts of which reappear in this volume: *Journal of Southern History, Chronicles of Oklahoma, Southwestern Social Science Quarterly,* and *Mississippi Quarterly.* A grant from the research fund of the University of South Dakota aided me in the final stages of preparation. This book could not have been written without the assistance of a silent co-author, my wife Mary Elizabeth, who helped in innumerable ways to bring it to completion.

University of Toledo
January, 1967   M.L.B.

CONTENTS

In the midst of bewildering times, I have pursued the path of duty as I saw it. Paint me as I am.
— THOMAS P. GORE.

I. POLITICAL APPRENTICESHIP

MISSISSIPPI WAS THE SCENE of a political revolution in 1875. That year saw the Democratic party make a supreme and successful effort to recapture the important state offices after a decade of Republican and Negro rule. James Z. George and Lucius Q. C. Lamar were the two leaders most responsible for the political turnover. George, as chairman of the state Democratic executive committee, was the guiding genius of the political battlefield, while Lamar, from his seat in Congress, won the sympathy of the nation for the downtrodden southern whites. By turning out the carpetbag regime of Reconstruction days, the old Democratic party was able to control Mississippi politics until just after the turn of the century, when James K. Vardaman instituted another revolution, less spectacular than that of 1875.

The political scene in the state between these two revolutions was far from quiescent. Although the one-party system prevailed, there was much intra-party strife, and the diminishing Republican party still had some influence. Politicians often carried guns when on campaign tours, and in one instance the feeling was so intense at a joint political debate that a group of Democrats appeared with a fieldpiece. Blood was occasionally shed under such circumstances, and qualified voters were sometimes refused admission at the polls by brute force. Ballotbox-stuffing, Negro intimidation, and the cry for white supremacy were common.[1]

Economic conditions in the rural areas of Mississippi contributed to the political rumblings. While agriculture was in a depressed condition and the price of cotton steadily declined, farmers had difficulty meeting payments on their mortgages. As the agrarians came to believe that they could improve their economic plight through political power, conditions in the state became more chaotic. The beginnings of the Farmers' Alliance and the spread of the radical Populist movement contributed to the troubled political scene in Mississippi during the last quarter of the nineteenth century as the long-suppressed agrarians rose in revolt.

1

Thomas Pryor Gore grew into manhood in this economic and political milieu. The second child of Caroline Elizabeth (Wingo) and Thomas Madison Gore,[2] Thomas P. was born on December 10, 1870, in Old Choctaw County, Mississippi, near the small village of Embry.[3] He claimed descent from one Paul Gore, Captain of Horse during Elizabeth I's reign in England, who was given an estate in Ireland by the Virgin Queen. His first American ancestor was supposed to have been James Gore, who moved from Ireland to Frederick (now Montgomery) County, Maryland, about 1756. Four years later this Gore moved with his eight sons to the Spartanburg District in South Carolina. Thomas P. traced his unbroken lineal descent only as far back as 1776, however, when his great-grandfather, Thomas T., was born in South Carolina. His pioneer circuit-riding grandfather, Ezekiel F., was born in South Carolina in 1806 and moved to Pickens County, Alabama, in the 1820's. In 1837 Thomas M. was born there. Continuing the westward migration, Thomas M. moved to Mississippi before the outbreak of the Civil War.[4]

Thomas M. Gore lived on a farm in the poor north-central hills of Mississippi but was a lawyer by profession. As a member of the county court, this farmer-lawyer was involved in the local politics of the area. Young Thomas was more impressed by his father's politics than by his farming. The boy did not like farm chores, and early in life he resolved that politics was to be his career. His father encouraged his ambitions. In fact, from the age of five Thomas' nicknames were "Governor" and "Gov" because his father had visions of his son's some day residing in the governor's mansion at Jackson.

When the Democrats gained political ascendancy at the end of Reconstruction, Thomas M. was elected chancery clerk of Sumner (now Webster) County, and in 1877 the Gore family moved to the county seat, Walthall, to allow the head of the family to give more attention to politics and law.[5]

At the age of ten "T. P." served as a printer's devil for Edgar Wilson, editor of the Walthall *Warden*. While inking and setting type, the lad absorbed the political talk which buzzed around the newspaper shop. After a year in this apprenticeship, he began his political career in a tangible way. In 1882 he served as a page in the Mississippi senate, while boarding in the home of United States Senator James Z. George.[6] During this year at Jackson, Gore firmly decided that nothing would deter him from becoming a United States Senator.

Not long after this resolve crystallized in his mind, an accident impaired one of his eyes. Having bought his brother a toy crossbow for his birthday, Gore decided to shoot it once to be sure that it functioned properly. Finding the arrow lodged in the bow, he tried to loosen it, and in the process the arrow was discharged, striking him in the right eye. In spite of the youngster's being taken to New Orleans for treatment, the eye was completely lost and had to be removed.[7]

The loss of an eye is not necessarily a catastrophic event in the life of an eleven-year-old, but for Gore it was. Three years earlier, as he and a young friend had been playing near the family's grazing work oxen, his playmate had thrown a stick which struck Gore near his left eye. Though the vision of this eye was partially impaired, his parents were hardly aware of the fact at that time; consequently, he received no medical attention after the accident. With the complete loss of the other eye, the boy was compelled to depend upon the injured one, to which belated medical attention was subsequently given. He was able to use his remaining eye enough to play the usual children's games, and he could diagram sentences with a magnifying glass and work mathematical problems on a blackboard, but by the time he was twenty years old he was totally blind.[8]

With darkness slowly enveloping his son, the father suggested that he be sent to the institute for the blind at Jackson, but Gore rebelled at this idea. His father did not insist, and the blind boy attended the school system for normal children. His classmates, his sister, and his mother read his lessons aloud to him. Charles H. Pittman, a distant relative, later came to live in the household, and for reading lessons to the blind youth he received his room and board free for over two years. Constant companions, both boys profited from their joint studies while attending the normal school at Walthall.[9]

An organization which both Gore and Pittman especially enjoyed was the Walthall Normal School Debating Club. The four most active members of the club were Gore, Pittman, Thomas L. Lamb, and W. W. McDowell, who debated political subjects such as the problem of revising the state constitution.[10] Regularly debating as partners, Gore and Pittman spent many hours together cultivating their oratorical abilities.

Gore's interest in politics intensified after he had classes in political economy and parliamentary law. At his suggestion the debating club was organized into a body patterned on the United States Senate.

The students introduced, debated, and passed bills, copying as nearly as possible regular parliamentary procedure. Gore reveled in the debates this arrangement afforded, and the first bill that passed the moot senate was introduced by him.[11] Since there was little other entertainment for the small community of Walthall, the students of the school often performed at "public exercises." Gore invariably delivered one of the major speeches on such occasions, and he was soon recognized as the most promising of the young orators.[12]

As his speaking ability developed, Gore was also invited to speak at country picnics and political gatherings, his "first real public speech" being made at a Farmers' Alliance meeting in the summer of 1888, before he was eighteen years old.[13] The editor of the local paper was so impressed with Gore's Commencement address at Walthall Normal in June, 1888, that he printed it on the front page a few weeks later. Entitled "Excelsior," the speech was indeed a masterpiece of oratory for a young schoolboy.[14]

Gore continued his schooling at Walthall for two more years, the final year being devoted to the "scientific course." After finishing his high-school training and having obtained a license to teach, he assisted his sister in the public school at Cadaretta in Webster County during the winter of 1890-91. For this teaching he received school warrants which he sold at a discount of 10 per cent in order to obtain cash from them.[15]

The Farmers' Alliance had been organized in Webster County in 1887 as the main channel for agricultural discontent in that area. The chief reservoir of leadership for the organization was the prominent Gore family, including A. C. Gore, West Gore, R. A. ("Abe") Gore, the Rev. John E. Gore, and Thomas M. Gore. The Alliance often ran members of the Gore family for various elective posts. The campaigning was always vigorous and bitter, but the Alliance had difficulty in winning votes from the dominant Democratic party.[16]

As T. P. Gore's oratorical ability increased, the Alliance men came to realize that it had a powerful weapon at its disposal. In July, 1891, they chose Gore as their candidate for the state legislature, preferring him to W. T. McKee and A. F. Williams. When it was realized the election was to take place a month before the nominee's twenty-first birthday, Gore had to withdraw from the race. McKee and Williams claimed the right to the nomination, but the convention met again, ignored their claims, and nominated T. P.'s uncle, John E.

Gore. McKee suggested a primary to settle the issue, but the Gore family so dominated the county Alliance that this proposal went unheeded.[17]

Thinking that the best approach to politics was through law, in the fall of 1891 Gore entered the Law School of Cumberland University in Lebanon, Tennessee. He was accompanied by his long-time friend, Thomas L. Lamb, who served as his amanuensis. Both Gore and Lamb received their Bachelor of Laws degrees in 1892. Upon his return to Mississippi Gore was admitted to the bar there. He assisted in his father's law office in Walthall, and practiced throughout the county.[18] But his interest was primarily in politics, not law, and he was soon giving most of his attention to his first love.

By 1892 the Mississippi Farmers' Alliance had been absorbed by the national Populist party, which ran James B. Weaver for President in that year. At their state convention in Mississippi the Populists nominated Gore for presidential elector in the fourth district. He began in Pontotoc County an active campaign which carried him over the entire district campaigning for Weaver and Frank Burkitt, Populist candidate for governor.

Now an unusually fluent speaker, Gore attracted considerable attention in this campaign. After a joint debate between Populists and Democrats at Grenada, Gore being the main attraction for the Populists, the editor of a Democratic newspaper commended the "Blind Youth" as an able and sincere speaker, though he concluded that the Populists had been roundly defeated in the debate.[19] Gore was invariably praised for his eloquence by both Populist and Democratic papers, even though Democratic editors criticized him for not being able to meet the arguments set forth by the opposition.[20] In 1892 the Populists were no more effective at the local level than at the national, and both Gore and Burkitt were defeated. But Gore's speeches in the 1892 campaign were undoubtedly important for the morale of the Populists.

In the following year Gore received little notice in the newspapers. He may have been compelled to devote more time to his law practice, but he may have been working quietly, too, for the Populist cause. The latter assumption seems more likely, for in the spring of 1894, he was one of eight members of the press committee of the People's party responsible for establishing another Populist newspaper. The Cumberland *Mississippi Populist,* designed to be a "middle-of-the-road" Populist organ, was first issued in April, 1894; its supporters hoped for statewide circulation.[21]

By 1894 Gore's reputation as an orator had spread beyond the boundaries of Mississippi. In that year the Populists of Navarro County, Texas, invited him to Corsicana to help them in their furious battle with the Democrats for political control of the county.[22] Traveling to Texas in April, 1894, he spoke throughout the summer, "making converts to Populism every day,"[23] and was partly responsible for the agrarian party's gaining control of the Navarro County government. After having made many Texas friends, Gore triumphantly returned to Mississippi in time to campaign for Populist candidates in his own state.[24]

With Texas friends encouraging him to move west, Gore became dissatisfied in Walthall. Having already induced his younger brother Ellis to study law, Thomas persuaded him to migrate to Texas, where he himself planned to open a law office. Ellis was to be his office assistant while preparing for the bar. The two Mississippians arrived in Corsicana early in December, 1894, and in January, 1895, they took over the law office of Lee Callaway, who had recently been elected county attorney.[25] The venture was not remunerative, however, and after his office assistant was appointed deputy district clerk, Gore returned to Mississippi in the spring of 1895.[26]

With the Populists making a determined effort to capture important elective offices in Mississippi, Gore immediately entered the political arena upon his return to the state. The Populists nominated him for state representative from Webster County, but he did not limit his activities to his own campaign. Perhaps the best orator among the Mississippi Populists, he stumped the state in the interest of his party's ticket, meeting in joint debate the ablest Mississippi Democrats. In fact, the Democrats made it a point to have their best talent available whenever Gore spoke.[27] Earl Brewer, Democratic candidate for state senator, who met him no less than nine times, later recalled that "T. P. Gore was hard to wallop and it took a considerable army from the Democratic party to do it."[28] A Democrat from Winston County called for reinforcements after Gore had visited Louisville. To Senator A. J. McLaurin, Democratic nominee for governor, he urgently wrote: "The 'Pops' are jubilant over the outcome of Gov's canvass, with no one to meet him in this Co[unty]. If you can possibly come fix the time and we will fix the place. Let me hear from you at once."[29]

On at least two occasions Gore and McLaurin met in debate, the first coming as a surprise to McLaurin. When McLaurin appeared in Walthall to address the people of Webster County, Gore requested a division of time. McLaurin declined, remarking that he must not be late in getting to Eupora in order to catch the local train. McLaurin proceeded to speak for about two hours, never alluding to Gore's having asked for an opportunity to speak. This snub aroused Gore. According to the Eupora *Sun*, he leaped to the platform as soon as McLaurin stepped down and within two minutes he "knocked the Senator out of the water high and dry." McLaurin stood with an expression on his face which seemed to say, "Where the h--l were you when the cyclone passed?" He quietly got out of town as quickly as possible.[30] On another occasion Gore "met and scalped would-be Governor McLaurin" at Pittsboro. McLaurin was reported to have been so badly shaken from the experience that he completely forgot to pay his hotel bill and told his hackman that "Calhoun was the d--st Populist county on earth."[31]

As the campaign developed, Gore's speaking engagements increased. On two different tours he spoke a dozen times in less than two weeks. Billed as the "Blind Boy Orator," he was publicized more than any other Populist speaker in the north-central region of the state.[32] The Eupora *Sun* recorded his campaigning in detail and with obvious Populist bias. It reported on one occasion that Gore, after speaking for an hour and a half, invited those in the audience to come forward and shake hands with him. A great rush for the stand was made, even Democrats being eager to shake his hand, many of them confessing their "sins." On another occasion when Gore concluded a speech the applause lasted for twenty minutes. Members of the crowd then rushed to the platform and "lifted him from the stand and bore him aloft on their shoulders from the grounds, amid scenes of frenzied enthusiasm and exaltation."[33] Throughout the campaign he continued to "hurl the brimstone of truth upon the sinning Democracy as Jehovah hurled it upon sinning Sodom." Often his Democratic opponent fled the scene of a joint-debate, leaving the Democrats defenseless against the "consuming fires of Populism."[34]

The Democrats were soon sending wagonloads of people to Gore's speeches to help "yell him down." They were able to do it sometimes, but at other times Gore succeeded, between "intervals of cat calls and the braying of two-legged asses," in converting several who had for years blindly followed in the wake of "the machine."[35]

Throughout the campaign Gore's platform oratory identified him with "the people." He stirred anger and class prejudice, and used wit, sarcasm, and ridicule as weapons against his Democratic opponents. His speeches were often punctuated with cries from the crowd of "Give it to him, Gov!" Sometimes Democratic leaders refused to debate Gore a second time because of his rapier thrusts, and occasionally an opponent complained that Gore took advantage of his blindness.[36]

But most opponents had respect for Gore's ability. After a speech at the Populist state convention in Jackson in August, 1895, the Jackson *Clarion-Ledger,* a Democratic paper, considered the speech the strongest ever made by any Populist. The paper concluded its praise of Gore by saying: "He is a wonderful blind boy, and we are sorry he is not enlisted in a better and more hopeful cause."[37] Many of the survivors of the pre-1900 era have spoken highly of Gore's ability, whatever their own party affiliation had been in the 1890's.

Despite the Democrats' respect for Gore, the Populists were soundly defeated in the 1895 elections, and the Democrats were delighted when Gore lost the race.[38] Evidently Populism in Mississippi was on the wane. Discouraged over the prospects of its future, Gore in December, 1895, moved to Texas once again.

Although Gore no longer lived in his native state, he accepted an invitation from the Mississippi Populists to be a delegate to the St. Louis Populist National Convention in the summer of 1896. The Mississippi delegation was opposed to fusion with the Democrats, but it was compelled to accept the convention's action endorsing William Jennings Bryan for President. When the convention agreed that it should nominate a separate vice-presidential candidate, however, Frank Burkitt was nominated, Gore seconding the nomination. Burkitt later withdrew in favor of Tom Watson of Georgia.[39]

Throughout 1897 Gore was politically inactive. This may have been due to two reasons. From all indications he was struggling to make a living after he and his brother Ellis opened a law office shortly after Gore's return to Corsicana.[40] For 1897 the Gore and Gore law firm was taxed on miscellaneous property valued at only $200, and T. P. later recalled that he "played hide and seek with the wolf" in Corsicana.[41] Also, he may have not given attention to politics because in October, 1897, he was indicted by a grand jury, being charged with seduction and abortion.[42]

Soon after arriving in Corsicana Gore had become acquainted with a blind girl who lived with foster parents, and it was the girl's foster mother who brought the charges against him. After the trial had been continued in November, 1897, and May, 1898, the district attorney requested the court in July to instruct the jury to return a verdict of not guilty because the evidence was insufficient to sustain a conviction. Gore was thus freed after the charges had been highly publicized.[43] Gore later claimed that the blind girl's charge was a political frame-up, although this has been discounted by others.[44] It is true that the Populists nominated Gore for Congress in 1898 and that he was defeated, but there is no evidence to indicate that the trial influenced the election. In all likelihood it did not, for after Bryan's defeat in 1896, the Populist party declined sharply, and the elections of 1898 were generally unsuccessful for the Populists over the entire nation.

Gore had become a Populist as a youth because his father and uncles were Populists. He had grown up at a time when his family and friends were revolting, and it was only natural for him to join these Populists against the Democrats. The young orator had no philosophical reasons for aligning himself with the economically depressed farmers of Mississippi and Texas, and he was too busy orating on economic conditions or attacking the party in power to give thought to basic Populist philosophy. Not philosophically attached to Populism and opportunist enough to appreciate the decay of the party and the movement, Gore joined the Democratic party in 1899.[45] At the Democratic convention at Kansas City in 1900, he supported William Jennings Bryan. The Democrats were quick to realize Gore's oratorical appeal and they used him in their national campaign. Traveling as far north as South Dakota in that year, he preached Democratic doctrine to the farmers of the prairie states.

Shortly after his return from this campaign tour, Gore married Miss Nina Kay, whom he had met four years earlier at a Populist picnic. A native of Palestine, Texas, and one of twin daughters of a cotton plantation owner and country doctor, Miss Kay won Gore's appreciation at their first meeting. Offering to serve his plate, she asked what part of the chicken he liked best. When he answered that the gizzard was his favorite piece, she returned with a plateful.[46] Gore later recalled, "I couldn't get that brown-eyed girl out of my mind;

9

so I married her." The wedding occurred on December 27, 1900, and within a few months the couple were making plans to move to Oklahoma Territory.[47]

As an ardent Texas Populist Gore had been openly critical of the Democratic party and after changing his allegiance to it, he realized that his political fortunes had a brighter future elsewhere than in Navarro County, Texas. Turning his thoughts to the land north of the Red River, Gore foresaw the making of a state. With his wife's encouragement he determined to join those pioneers who were eagerly creating it out of the former Indian lands. Gore saw in the territory an opportunity for a free homestead, a new field for his professional services, and, most important, a new political beginning.

The area north of Texas reserved for the Indians of the United States had long been coveted by white settlers. With cattlemen desiring grazing contracts, with the discovery of a rich vein of coal in the Indians' domain, and with the building of railroads through the lands of the Five Civilized Tribes, increased pressures were placed on the federal government to open the region to non-Indian settlement. Yielding to these forces, government officials in 1889 contracted with the Creek and Seminole tribes to buy over three million acres of their land in central Oklahoma, and the first of several colorful "runs" occurred in that year. In May, 1890, a territorial government was established for these ceded lands, Oklahoma Territory's acreage increasing after each succeeding opening.

By the time Gore became interested in moving to Oklahoma Territory, it was evident that the Comanche-Kiowa-Apache Indian country was soon to be opened for settlement. In June, 1901, the general land office delimited three counties in the surplus Indian lands of southwestern Oklahoma. These counties, designated Northeast Caddo, Northwest Kiowa, and South Comanche, had Anadarko, Hobart, and Lawton named as their respective county seats.

Gore and his father arrived in South Comanche County in late June, pitching a tent in the high prairie grass just east of the Lawton townsite. Years later Gore wrote, "I located at Lawton before there was any Law–ton. There were only two little shacks on the town-site when I located my tent on the Eastern Boundary which was then called 'Goo-goo' avenue. The blue grass [?] was waist high on most of the town-site, particularly where there were 'hog-wallers.' The hardy mesquite occupied part of the town-site."[48] Gore's father had gone along to help the blind man overcome the obstacles that all new-comers invariably face in a frontier area. His wife of seven months, remaining in Texas until permanent housing could be constructed, arrived at Lawton in September, 1901.

Instead of allowing the homesteaders to select their land by a "run" as in previous openings, government officials chose to register the home-seekers and to draw the registration cards from boxes to determine who would receive land. Gore was among the 135,000 applicants who desired one of the 13,000 homesteads available. He failed to draw a land claim in the lottery, but he bought a lot at the corner of Ninth and "B" in Lawton and established his law office there.[49]

Gore was not long in Oklahoma Territory before he resumed political activity. Representing the Lawton area, he traveled to Enid in April, 1902, to attend the territorial convention of the Democratic party. After J. M. Dobson had welcomed the delegates in behalf of the Enid Commercial Club, Gore appeared before Oklahoma Democrats for the first time when he was asked to respond in behalf of the delegates to the speech of welcome. His speech tickled the ears of the delegates ("I would rather be a humble private in the ranks of those who struggle for justice and equality than to be a minion of plutocracy, though adorned with purple and gold"); many said it was the finest piece of oratory they had ever heard.[50] Undoubtedly this speech aided Gore's future political career in Oklahoma.

The Democrats had met in Enid to choose a candidate for territorial delegate to Congress, an office the Republicans had virtually monopolized since the territory was organized. When a deadlock occurred at the evening session, a delegate from Grant County, still entranced by Gore's speech earlier in the day, suggested the smooth-speaking Comanche County newcomer as a dark-horse compromise. Despite the enthusiasm of his own delegation over this suggestion, Gore was not chosen, the nomination going instead to William Cross.

Gore then became the Democratic nominee for the territorial council from the district composed of Caddo and Comanche counties. So confident was he of his own election that he spent most of his time traveling over the territory campaigning for Cross. By stumping the whole territory he was assisting the nominee, the Democratic party, and his own political future. The *Pawnee County Courier* summed up the summer's campaign: "The drawing card of the campaign in

Oklahoma is T. P. Gore of Lawton. The reputation of the blind orator has become such that he is now traveling with Mr. Cross . . . over all of Oklahoma. . . . Great crowds come out to hear the man who handles the English language as did Blind Tom the piano."[51] The speeches and contacts Gore made in the summer of 1902 were undoubtedly helpful in his campaign for the United States Senate in 1907.

Although Cross lost his race to sit with the Fifty-eighth Congress,[52] Gore easily won the race in the eleventh territorial district and sat with the territorial council which met at Guthrie for the 1903-1905 term. The thirteen councilmen who composed the upper house of the territorial legislature were elected for two-year terms, but actually they met for only sixty days during the period beginning on January 13, 1903. Gore was assigned to the committees on the Judiciary, Education, Railroads, Federal Relations, Printing, Quarantine and Animal Industry, and County and County Affairs.[53] Because of his blindness he was allowed to employ a private secretary who could assist him and also be the clerk of the Committee on Federal Relations. His wife served in this position.

Filling his first elective position, Councilman (commonly called Senator) T. P. Gore made minimal contributions to the territorial legislation of 1903. He introduced several bills to amend the Oklahoma statutes dealing with contracts, crimes, and school districts, none of which passed. His bill to make rape and incest capital crimes in certain cases also failed. Two other Gore bills, one requiring railroad companies to construct depots, flag-stations, sidetracks, and switches under certain conditions and one prohibiting ownership of lands in Oklahoma Territory by nonresident aliens, were also rejected by the council. A bill to increase the pay of grand and petit jurors was not reported out of committee. Gore's interest in the financial status of the territory was revealed in a bill which, had it passed, would have provided for the investment of the public building fund of the territory.[54]

Gore appealed to territorial pride when he introduced a bill to declare April 22, anniversary date of the first great "run" into Oklahoma Territory in 1889, a legal holiday in the territory. According to one newspaper of the region, Gore delivered a masterful speech in the council on this bill, and he was highly praised for his eloquence. But the Committee on the Judiciary voted four to one (Gore casting the dissenting vote and filing a minority report) to recommend that the bill be rejected.[55] April 22 remained another working day for Oklahomans.

Not all of Gore's efforts were in vain. A bill appropriating money from the territorial common school fund for school districts in his area was passed unanimously. Other bills introduced by him and accepted by the council included (1) an act to legalize the incorporation of the towns of Walters, Hastings, and Sterling in Comanche County, (2) an act to authorize the town of Temple to construct, own, control, and operate waterworks and fire apparatus, and (3) an act requiring railroad companies to provide openings through embankments and other obstructions for drainage.[56] Obviously Gore's contributions to territorial legislation were meager.

The most important accomplishment of this term of office was that Gore kept himself in the public eye. When his friends encouraged him to run for territorial delegate to Congress, he refused on the grounds that he had not lived in Oklahoma long enough to aspire to that office.[57] The truth is that he was already running for the higher office of Senator from Oklahoma when the territory attained statehood, and he reasoned that an appointment to Washington as territorial delegate would remove him from the political scene in the territory and perhaps hinder his aspirations for the higher post. Admitting that he desired a Senate seat, Gore caused the Oklahoma City *Daily Oklahoman* to assert, "When Gore becomes a senator for Oklahoma the land of the fair god may well rejoice in having one man the equal of the representatives from any state of the union."[58] From the time of his election to the territorial council until 1907, Gore's every public act and pronouncement were designed to garner votes for the election which was inevitable with Oklahoma's entry into the Union.

II. A FIRST-TERM SENATOR

AGITATION FOR STATEHOOD for Oklahoma had begun soon after the establishment of the territory and had increased in intensity proportionate to the growing population. As early as December, 1901, a convention had been held in Oklahoma City which memorialized Congress to grant statehood. A month later David A. Harvey, Oklahoma's first territorial delegate to Congress, introduced a bill in the House of Representatives providing for Oklahoma statehood.[1] Soon after this time bills were introduced to bring about statehood for the eastern part of the present state of Oklahoma, known as Indian Territory.

It quickly became apparent that sentiment was divided on the admission of Oklahoma and Indian territories. Some people favored one state composed of both territories (single or joint statehood), while others preferred two states (separate or double statehood). Both plans with numerous variations had supporters in the two territories during the last decade of the nineteenth century.

Several bills dealing with Oklahoma statehood were introduced in Congress during the period from 1895 to 1901, but they received no serious consideration. In 1896 a bill was submitted providing for the immediate admission of Oklahoma Territory with the annexation of Indian Territory by reservations. This "piecemeal absorption plan" was distasteful to the residents of Indian Territory, and the plan made no headway. Two years later identical bills were introduced in the House and Senate declaring for the union of the twin territories prior to their admission as a single state. This was a logical plan, for the differences between the two sections were numerous and important, and a single territorial government could have harmonized those differences in preparation for single statehood. But because those who opposed single statehood under all conditions were joined by those who wanted to delay it until it was the only alternative, this effort for unification was quashed.[2]

Throughout this period arguments pro and con were made for

both double and single statehood. The Republicans in Oklahoma Territory had a slight numerical advantage over the Democrats and so did not want to be linked with the overwhelmingly Democratic territory to the east. With one exception all delegates to Congress from Oklahoma Territory between 1890 and 1907 were Republicans. They felt that separate statehood would afford them opportunity to control the western area. The Oklahoma Democrats, including T. P. Gore, on the other hand, favored being joined with Indian Territory, thus assuring the Democrats complete control of one large state.[3] Convinced that they would share little in the politics of a single state, the Democrats of Indian Territory were not happy with the prospect of being tied with the territory on their west. There were few Republicans on the east side and their opinions carried no weight. The eastern states of the nation generally favored one state in the Southwest, while Democratic leaders of the South looked with favor upon the possibility of having four more Southern Senators in Washington. Many people in the territories argued that one state comparable to its neighbor Kansas was more desirable than two states the size of Indiana. They also pointed out that the huge state to the south would be more than eight times the size of either of the two proposed small states.

As a matter of fact, the opinions of the people living in the territories had little to do with the final decision. It soon became evident that the leaders in Congress had decided upon a union of the twin territories. The last serious effort to admit Oklahoma Territory separately was made in November, 1903, when Congress met for a brief special session. In the following spring a bill calling for two new states, one composed of Oklahoma Territory and Indian Territory and one of New Mexico and Arizona, was passed by the House.[4] Almost a year later the Senate struck out the sections of the bill providing for the union of Arizona and New Mexico, but accepted the provisions admitting the twin territories as the state of Oklahoma. The House refused to allow Oklahoma statehood without action also being taken in regard to New Mexico and Arizona; a conference committee failed to arrive at an acceptable compromise.

While the national legislature was trying to deal with the problems of statehood for Oklahoma, several conventions were held in which delegates from the territories met to encourage enthusiasm for statehood and to send memorials to Congress requesting action. After

the territorial governor had vetoed a bill passed by the Oklahoma
territorial legislature in 1899 calling for a constitutional convention,
statehood conventions organized by various Oklahoma leaders were
held almost yearly. The last of the several single-statehood conventions was held in Oklahoma City in July, 1905. Over a thousand
delegates and several thousand visitors attended this largest of such
conventions.[5] Gore, a delegate from Oklahoma Territory, responded
to the address of welcome, and then nominated R. L. Williams as
temporary chairman.

This convention drew up a memorial to Congress and sent a committee of twenty to present it to President Theodore Roosevelt requesting that he urge Congress to grant "immediate joint statehood
. . . to Oklahoma and Indian Territories, on their own merits, and
without reference to any right or claim of other Territories seeking
admission to the American Union."[6] Gore telegraphed Congress:
"Power with justice is glory, without it tyranny. Greatest Generals
ofttime [sic] retreat. Earn the gratitude of millions, make us a state."[7]

Roosevelt recommended single statehood in his State of the Union
message in December, 1905. In June of the following year he effec-
tively silenced all opposition to a union of the territories by signing
an enabling act which allowed the people of the two territories to
write a constitution, form a state government, and be admitted to the
Union. The enabling act provided for fifty-five delegates to be selected
from each of the twin territories and two from the Osage Indian
Reservation, the only part of the territory of Oklahoma in 1906 which
had not been placed under county government. The outcome of the
election of delegates held on November 4, 1906, was a surprise to
everybody, including the victorious Democrats. The Republicans did
not expect to carry a majority of the districts, but they had hoped at
least to make a creditable showing. Even this they failed to do. With
112 seats to be filled the Democrats captured exactly one hundred
(although one of the Democrats was elected as an Independent), the
Republicans polling the remaining twelve.[8] The delegates gathered
at Guthrie on November 20 for the first meeting of the Oklahoma
constitutional convention, the gathering being in session periodically
from that time until the final adjournment on July 16, 1907. William
H. ("Alfalfa Bill") Murray presided over the convention and had
considerable influence on the final draft of the constitution.[9]

Although not a delegate to the convention, Gore was at Guthrie during its meetings. Consulting with delegates, making suggestions, lobbying, and giving "sound advice," he proved to be an asset to the constitution-framers.[10] He suggested that the constitution contain a clause prohibiting corporations from issuing stocks and bonds "except for money paid, labor done, and property actually received," as well as one declaring fraudulent stocks and bonds null and void. He also wanted the document to contain an employers' liability clause defining "fellow servants" and making corporations liable in certain instances for injuries or death to their employees. Revealing his antagonism to privilege, Gore remarked, "If we build our constitution and code upon the eternal rock of equal justice, the gates of special interests, though they assail, can never prevail against us. But if we build upon the quicksands of inequality, the winds and waves of special interest will soon overwhelm the splendid fabric of our institutions."[11]

Long before the convention met, newspapers had speculated on prospects for the Senate posts. When single statehood seemed assured, a tacit agreement prevailed among politicians of both parties that each of the territories absorbed into the new state should be represented by having one Senator chosen from the east and one from the west. Besides Gore, Oklahoma Territory Democrats talked of Thomas M. Doyle of Perry and Roy Hoffman of Chandler, both of whom had been agitators for single statehood, and Roy Stafford, editor of the *Daily Oklahoman,* as possible candidates for the coveted seat. From the east side of the state a much longer list of Democrats was available: Pleasant Porter, Creek chief; C. B. Stuart, McAlester; William T. Hutchings, Muskogee; Henry Furman, Ada; Lee Cruce, Ardmore; Robert L. Owen, Muskogee; and prominent statehood convention leaders, C. N. Haskell and William H. Murray.

The most likely vote-getters among the Republicans of Oklahoma Territory were Dennis T. Flynn, several times territorial delegate to Congress, who did not seem eager for the race after the delegate elections foreshadowed a Democratic state legislature; Bird McGuire of Pawnee, who had also served in Washington; Tom Ferguson of Watonga; and national committeeman Cash M. Cade of Shawnee. In the east such Republicans as Clarence B. Douglass, editor of the Muskogee *Daily Phoenix;* Pliny Soper, Republican national committeeman; William Busby, well-to-do coal mine operator of McAlester; Tams Bixby, commissioner to the Five Civilized Tribes; and John R.

Thomas and Charles W. Raymond, both of Muskogee, were discussed. The convention leaders reduced the list of prospects for the Senate seats, however, when they decided to make the two seats available only to non-members, in order to silence those who pretended to see a conspiracy in their allotment of the spoils to one another.[12] By not being elected a delegate to the convention, whether by plan or by accident, Gore was in a position to contend for a Senate seat.

The senatorial races began before the constitutional convention officially ended. In fact the Democratic state primary was held on June 8, 1907, five weeks before the end of the last session. Gore's leading opponents, Roy Hoffman and Martin L. Turner, were able men, and though neither was considered rich, both had at their disposal considerable sums of money which they used freely in their campaigns. Gore mortgaged his home in Lawton for $1,000, and that sum was his total expenditure in this important race.

Traveling around the state in this "cheese and cracker campaign" by "thumbing" his way via trains,[13] Gore drew large crowds with his oratory. He was at his best when on the platform appealing to the rural people of Oklahoma by attacking the trusts, the railroads, and the privileged classes. He promised to let "the people" rule if he were elected. Favoring the initiative and referendum and "another method of selecting Senators other than by the state legislature," Gore had these additional planks in his 1907 platform: adoption of the Oklahoma Constitution; removal of restrictions from the sale of allotments of Indian lands; increased irrigation; regulation of freight rates; reduction of the tariff; taxation on incomes; economy in government spending; abstention from subsidies, militarism, and imperialism; protection for labor and legitimate capital; justice for all and favoritism to none; dethronement of trusts and enthronement of the people.[14] Such a platform could not fail to appeal to many Oklahoma listeners.

Two days before the election the Guymon *Herald*, a Hoffman supporter, published a stinging diatribe against Gore. Calling him a demagogue, the *Herald* said that he was not a Democrat at all, and that he had great audacity to ask the Democratic party for the highest office available in Oklahoma. Referring to him as a "radical socialist," it reminded its readers that he was a virulent Populist before drifting into Oklahoma. "Former Texas democrats," the paper continued, "are inclined to laugh when they hear Gore referred to as a 'demo-

18

crat.' They know him for the [most] malignant and vituperative enemy of the democratic party that ever came to Texas. He abused the Democracy and the Democrats so viciously that his speech is still remembered as the most vindicative [sic] assault ever attempted against the party in that state." The paper quoted from a speech Gore had made in 1896: "The trouble with the democratic party is [that] it is a party of statesmen without statesmanship, of patriots without patriotism, of heroes without heroism. . . . The republicans stand for principles, though that principle may be wrong, and they will always fight you in the open, but the democratic party is Judas like, it will kiss and betray."[15] The fact is that in his Populist ardor Gore did make remarks similar to these. Such propaganda was used to good effect against him, and he found it difficult to live down his Populist background.

The ballot for the Democratic primary was arranged with the candidates of each side of the state grouped together, the voter being instructed to vote for one candidate from each side. Gore won because it had been earlier agreed that the candidate having the highest tally among the western candidates would be chosen, as would the high man in the east, irrespective of his showing vis-à-vis those running in the other division. The total count showed that except for this gentlemen's agreement both Senators would have come from the eastern side of the new state. Robert L. Owen with 48,885 and Henry Furman with 39,113 had more votes than Gore, the leading westerner, with 38,288. Gore led Roy Hoffman, who had 34,358, and Martin L. Turner, Oklahoma City banker, who received 29,210 votes.[16] It appeared for several hours that Hoffman was the winner in the west, but the rural vote came in late to give the election to Gore. Gore's opponents wanted Furman to break the tacit agreement and ask for the nomination at the Democratic convention, but this Furman refused to do. Owen and Gore were made the official Democratic nominees on June 19.

William Jennings Bryan visited Oklahoma City in the late summer of 1907 to praise the Oklahoma Constitution and urge its adoption. He also gave his blessing to C. N. Haskell, Democratic nominee for governor, as well as to Owen and Gore.[17] While Bryan was speaking for the Democratic nominees, several newspapers in Oklahoma pleaded for a Republican legislature to prevent Owen and Gore from going to Washington. But the press was asking too much. The predominance of Democratic delegates to the constitutional convention indicated that the first state legislature would be overwhelmingly Democratic, and this was borne out in the election held September 17. Sixty days after the election President Theodore Roosevelt signed the proclamation declaring Oklahoma a state.[18] Gore was a part of the happy crowd that set off the inaugural uproar in Guthrie on November 16 when the telegraphs clicked off the good news.

The newly elected Democratic governor, Charles N. Haskell, delivered his inaugural address amid joy and shouting, and announced the appointments of Owen and Gore as United States Senators from the forty-sixth state in the Union. The two men left immediately for Washington and were present for the opening of the Sixtieth Congress. When they were not received because they had not yet been elected by the state legislature, they returned to Oklahoma. On December 11 the Oklahoma legislature met in joint session, officially electing the new state's Senators.

Gore had finally reached his coveted goal. From the days of his youth as a page in the Mississippi legislature he had dreamed of being a United States Senator. When he left his native state in 1895 he had vowed never to return until he had been elected to the Senate. Twelve years later he went back with the vow unbroken. Gore considered his election a cherished birthday gift, for only the day before the Oklahoma legislature made his election official he had become thirty-seven years old. The youngest member of the Sixtieth Congress' upper house and representing the youngest state, Gore also had the distinction of being the first totally blind man ever to serve in the United States Senate.

Oklahoma's first Senators, Gore and Robert L. Owen, who was a part-Cherokee Indian, arrived in Washington two weeks after the beginning of the first session of the Sixtieth Congress. As soon as the Oklahomans had become full-fledged members, it had to be decided when their terms would officially end. Placing three pieces of paper of equal size, numbered one, two, and three, into a ballot box, the secretary of the Senate had each of the new members draw out a piece of paper. Owen drew the paper numbered two which, as previously arranged, entitled him to be included among those Senators whose terms of service expired March 3, 1913. Gore drew the paper numbered three, gaining the short term which expired on March 3, 1909.

Representing a newly formed western state whose constitution was in accord with the rising progressive spirit, Gore quickly showed his sympathy for progressive legislation. Two days after being sworn in, acting in his official capacity for the first time, he introduced a constitutional amendment providing for the direct election of United States Senators. Shortly afterwards he suggested a constitutional amendment authorizing an income tax. Although aware that these changes were not imminent, Gore sensed the impact of the progressive era and knew that these or similar changes were inevitable. From the very beginning he aligned himself with those advocating progressive legislation during the early decades of the twentieth century.

Before becoming involved in national issues and while acquainting himself with his new duties, Gore gave attention to his constituency. He introduced a bill to appropriate $150,000 to defray the expenses of the Oklahoma constitutional convention and to reimburse the state for its costs to ratify the constitution and to elect officials. When this bill died in the Committee on Appropriations, Gore sought the services of the Committee on Territories, but again his efforts were in vain. He also proposed that Oklahoma be granted two additional Congressmen and that the eastern district of the state be divided into three judicial districts, making courts more accessible for those required to attend. Repeated and severe drouths made it difficult for Oklahoma homesteaders to meet their financial obligations, and Gore spent considerable effort working to extend the time of payments on certain homestead entries and to grant extension of time to purchasers of lots in the new state. Gore's greatest constituent appeal was made to that large segment of the population which had not yet received land. Consistent with his election platform, he introduced bills providing for the removal of restrictions from the sale of allotments of Indian lands.

The primary problem with which the Sixtieth Congress had to deal was the panic of 1907. Excessive speculation had begun in 1906, making heavy demands on banks. By the beginning of 1907, the resources of numerous financial institutions were strained, and by October business was almost at a standstill. With the national banking system weakened considerably through the growth of trust companies which had extended their business from that of trusteeship to commercial banking, Congress set out to restrict certain practices which it considered responsible for the panic.

Since many banks had failed because they had not protected their deposits with adequate reserves, Gore introduced two bills designed to protect depositors in national banks against losses. Both of these bills were buried in committee as the Republicans, possessing a clear majority in both houses of Congress, attacked the problem of the panic and the currency in their own way. Nelson W. Aldrich of Rhode Island, chairman of the Committee on Finance, introduced a bill in the Senate dealing with the national banking laws; Edward B. Vreeland of New York introduced a sharply different measure in the House. Ultimately combined and known as the Aldrich-Vreeland Emergency Currency Act, these bills dominated the attention of the first session of the Sixtieth Congress. Gore offered several insignificant amendments to the Senate version, but all of them were rejected.[19]

In the debates on the emergency currency measure, Gore criticized the Chief Executive for saluting J. Pierpont Morgan and John D. Rockefeller as deliverers of the country when, in Gore's opinion, they were responsible for the critical financial condition in the first place. He called the financiers "pirates" who had "shipwrecked the prosperity of this country." When Robert M. La Follette of Wisconsin charged that devices were being used to concentrate money in New York and to cripple ordinary business, Gore revealed his own position by praising La Follette: "I trust that he will regard it as not otherwise than a compliment when I say that, in my opinion, he is the best Democrat and the poorest Republican in the Senate and in the United States. If I was a Republican I should be willing to support him for the Presidency; if he were a Democrat I should be willing to support him."[20] This was the first time Gore had praised La Follette publicly, but it was not the last time they were to stand side by side on important issues. The "Fighting Progressive" had the blind progressive's support many times during the next decade.

Since the provisions of the House and Senate emergency currency bills were strikingly different, a conference was necessary to reconcile them. With the compromises being reached, the bill as it finally became law made possible the formation of associations of cooperating banks which were permitted to issue notes safeguarded by certain classes of securities or by commercial paper. The whole association was to be jointly liable to make good the notes, but the only bonds covered by this bill were those of states, counties, cities, and towns. A provision for the creation of a monetary commission was included.

This bill, confessedly a makeshift measure, was coaxed through

Congress only after the failure of the famous La Follette-led filibuster which temporarily delayed its passage and the adjournment of Congress. During the filibuster La Follette held the floor continuously for over eighteen hours, sustaining himself by drinking an egg and milk mixture and eating an occasional sandwich during quorum roll calls. William J. Stone of Missouri at last came to the aid of La Follette, and Stone was relieved by Gore. In his first long speech in the Senate, Gore spent two hours attacking the Aldrich-Vreeland compromise. He regarded this "pernicious measure" as a cross between a financial eagle and a vulture, "related to the vulture in devouring the dead and related to the eagle in devouring the living." He wanted to "pare the beak and the talons of this animal." Desiring to "extract the fangs or to dull the claws of this financial monster," he considered the bill wrong in principle and felt it would prove unwise in policy; he therefore opposed it "root and branch." Believing that the passage of this bill meant the beginning of a new and bad system of currency, he predicted that county and municipal bonds would be made the basis of ordinary currency if it became law.[21]

Before joining the marathon, Gore had laid careful plans with his cohort. He was to be relieved by Stone; afterwards La Follette, rested from his long vigil through the previous night, was to resume. Stone had left the Senate chamber for a rest during the Oklahoman's speech, and when he returned Gore was informed that the Senator from Missouri was present and ready to speak. Gore concluded his speech, turned his sightless eyes toward Stone's seat, and sat down, expecting to hear the Missourian claim recognition. Much to the chagrin of the filibusterers, Stone had stepped out of the Senate chamber after Gore's having been informed of his return. Unaware of Stone's departure, he surrendered the floor when no collaborator was present to claim it. It was a costly mistake, and many suspected that Stone had been called out of the Senate chamber in order to trick the blind man, but this was never proved. A popular rumor had it that Gore had been forced to sit down by a Senator behind him who pulled at his coattails, but Gore later discounted this version of the incident.[22]

Seizing the opportunity, the chairman of the Finance Committee demanded a roll call on the bill. Weldon B. Heyburn of Idaho shouted for recognition when he realized what was happening. When the Vice-President hesitated in the confusion, Aldrich dashed from his seat to the well of the chamber, shook his finger at the presiding officer, and yelled for a roll call. Heyburn continued to clamor for recognition. With the Vice-President's hesitation, the secretary of the Senate, who had previously promised to cooperate with the bill's sponsors if the opportunity arose, began calling the roll. Being the first on the list, Aldrich quickly responded to his name, but the Vice-President declared that it was only fair to recognize the Senator from Idaho inasmuch as the chair's attention had been distracted for the moment. Aldrich insisted that the roll call had begun and that, under the Senate rules, it could not be interrupted after a Senator had responded to his name. This argument being technically correct, the roll call was continued.

Since the *Congressional Record* clearly shows that Heyburn had asked for recognition before the beginning of the roll call, there is no doubt that the filibuster was overcome by doubtful practice. The obstructionists had hoped to talk until general congressional demands for adjournment *sine die* forced the abandonment of the legislation.[23] With this hope lost, the conference report was accepted, and the President signed the bill within a few hours after Gore's fatal error.

After Congress adjourned in May, 1908, the Washington crowd made rapid preparations for the forthcoming elections. When he drew the short term upon entering the Senate in December, 1907, Gore had announced that he would be a candidate for re-election the following summer.[24] The short term was hardly time enough for him to make or lose friends; he was nominated by the Democrats without opposition. Aware that the Oklahoma legislature would undoubtedly be overwhelmingly Democratic again, the Republicans nominated former territorial delegate Dennis T. Flynn as their party sacrifice.[25]

The Democrats met in Denver in July, 1908, to nominate their national candidates. The first day of the convention was consumed with routine business, including the address of the temporary chairman and the announcement of committee appointments. On the next day the chairman of the Committee on Credentials informed the convention that his committee's report would not be ready until the evening session and moved that the convention adjourn until that time. But the delegates, with noisy support from the galleries, were in no mood to adjourn. They had met in Denver for a rousing time and were not to be denied expressing their pent-up emotions. A move that the convention "hear from any . . . prominent Democrat whom the delegates would like to hear" was met with roaring approval.[26] Calls from the floor for Gore were heeded, and the blind orator gave a brief but potent speech. When Gore mentioned the name of William Jennings Bryan, pandemonium broke loose, and for an hour and twenty minutes a Bryan demonstration held sway. If a number of favorite sons had designs on the presidential nomination before Gore's speech, the resultant demonstration dispelled those illusions. The Great Commoner, already a strong contender, received the nomination on the first ballot in the wake of the demonstration.[27]

Perceiving that his own re-election was not in danger, Gore spent the summer making highly entertaining speeches against the Republican presidential nominee William Howard Taft, picturing him as Roosevelt's puppet. On a thirty-day campaign tour for the national ticket, the popular orator traveled widely making speeches. Optimistic for Bryan's chances in November, Gore went as far as Salt Lake City in his efforts to win the West for Bryan.[28] During this torrid campaign, the Senator's services were requested in Ohio, West Virginia, Maryland, and New York. It was "deemed of utmost importance to the party that he fill these engagements."[29] By October a political observer for Gore advised him to return to Oklahoma to campaign in his home state. The adviser favored Bryan's candidacy, but he did not want Gore to place his own re-election in jeopardy; the Republicans had intensified their campaign in Oklahoma.[30] Such fears proved to be unwarranted. Although Bryan carried Oklahoma over Taft by a narrow margin (12,000), the state legislature went strongly Democratic as expected. In January, 1909, by a strict party vote, the legislature officially returned Gore to his Senate post.[31]

When the Senator had an important speech to prepare for use during political campaigns or to present his views in the Senate, he would sit alone in his favorite rocking chair and organize the speech in his mind, often holding a cherished book in his hand while meditating. His speeches were extemporized, with short passages in them being committed to memory, although he developed a habit of holding a piece of paper in his hand which he often appeared to consult as his speech progressed. He seldom used gestures, and he never had his speeches read by another person. When he spoke on the floor of the Senate, he turned slightly in the direction of the Senator being addressed as if to look at him. Gore had the uncanny ability to anticipate a question or remark from another member when he held the floor, often pausing to turn in the direction of a Senator about to speak to recognize him before he had time to rise completely from his seat. If his remarks were not directed toward any particular colleague, the blind orator faced the speaker's desk. With his head tilted slightly backward and with his finger tips lightly touching his desk in front of him as he emphasized his remarks, he spoke out clearly and distinctly in sonorous tones. Even though his hearers might not agree with what he was saying, they were attentive when he spoke.[32]

The Senator's speeches were filled with references to history and literature which were evidence of his wide reading. Not concerned with light or darkness and frequently unable to sleep, Gore often sat for hours while important books were read to him by his wife, his secretary, or any other person available and willing to be pressed into service. If he owned the book being read to him, he sometimes requested that sentences which he considered important be underscored with a pencil. Upon a second reading of the underlined words, he could remember quite clearly the significant portions of any volume. He enjoyed visiting secondhand bookstores and browsing among the volumes, asking his secretary or wife to read occasional passages from books with titles appealing to him. Because of his love of books, he rapidly acquired a large and valuable library.

Gore would not allow the handicap of blindness to present insurmountable difficulties in his personal habits. He bought only white shirts, thus preventing the problem of getting a colored one that might clash with his suit. His wife always bought him socks of the same style and color, avoiding another color problem. The Senator always dressed himself, and when he did not have access to the Senate barber shop, he shaved himself. He carried different denominations of coins in separate pockets to facilitate handling, and he never erred in counting change. On his numerous campaign tours, most of which were made without his wife, Gore carried a large grip with only the essential articles of apparel in it. When spending a night in a strange room, before he retired he would ask to be led to the bathroom, the door of which he requested to be left open. After tapping around the bedroom and the entrance to the bathroom with his cane and placing his grip on a stool at the foot of his bed, he then retired. The following morning he would be fully dressed and ready for breakfast when others of the party called upon him. When dining he would permit no glasses near him on the table for fear of his upsetting them and spilling the liquid.[33]

Gore's eyes were medium blue, the right glass eye matching his left eye almost perfectly. He was a blond with a fair complexion, but his hair prematurely turned silvery white. The six-foot, two-hundred-pound Senator was a figure of striking dignity, with a hurried walk and erect carriage, the ever-present cane swinging from his arm as he grasped an arm of a male secretary who usually accompanied him in the Senate. Gore was undoubtedly an inspiration to hundreds of other blind people who aspired to some measure of success in the world of the seeing.

III. VOTING WITH THE MINORITY

WILLIAM HOWARD TAFT frequently referred to the need for tariff revision in his campaign of 1908, and it was assumed that he meant revision downward from the Dingley rates which had been in existence for twelve years. In his inaugural address the new President referred to that "pressing problem," revision of the tariff. A special session of the Sixty-first Congress opened on March 15 for the sole purpose of such revision. Two days after the session began, Sereno E. Payne, chairman of the House Ways and Means Committee, reported to the lower house a bill which noticeably reduced the Dingley rates on pig iron, machine tools, agricultural implements, lumber, print paper, and sugar, to name only a few of the items included, and was in harmony with the President's campaign speeches. Of more than two hundred amendments attached to this bill in the House, most were in the direction of greater reduction.

Passing the lower house without difficulty in April, 1909, the bill ran into serious problems in the upper chamber, where advocates of a high tariff were in the majority. The boss of the Senate and chairman of the powerful Finance Committee, Nelson W. Aldrich, proceeded to rewrite the Payne bill completely. Aldrich and his associates were a formidable group, although they did not frighten the Republicans from the Middle West, who became their most outspoken critics during the tariff struggle. With the Democratic minority for the most part cheering from the sidelines, the progressive Republicans left their impact on the tariff measure before it became law. Led by Jonathan P. Dolliver of Iowa and Robert M. La Follette of Wisconsin, both powerful orators and aggressive opponents, in the spring of 1909 the progressives were able to carry on an effective struggle.

When Aldrich brought the House bill out of committee with 847 amendments making it nothing more than the strongly protective Dingley tariff with some improvements in detail and classification, the progressives attacked the measure of the "New England Tyrants" in full force. Realizing that they all could not study it in its entirety, the progressives divided it, each taking a certain schedule to study intensively. In smashing speeches they attacked the bill with force and logic. Aldrich, its virtual author, first met these attacks with indifference, later with contempt, and finally with rage.[1] In the beginning he argued that the amended bill reduced rates, but such arguments were without effect in the face of the intensive study and caustic remarks of the progressives.

Although primarily a conflict of conservatives and progressives within the Republican party, the tariff struggle was not strictly that. While most of the Democrats gave tacit support to the progressives, some of them could not refrain from entering into the heated debates. Gore fell into the latter group. Never one to leave the scene of a word-battle, he joined the progressives with vigor. Energetically attacking the tariff bill, he agitated Aldrich and his colleagues with stinging criticism and wit. Of the notorious woolen schedule K, Gore punned that the protectionists were trying to "pull the wool over the eyes of the people."[2]

These tariff debates first brought Gore to national attention, and his "remarkable wit, prodigious memory, and real intellectual force" revealed by them won a good deal of public respect for his ability.[3] During these debates Gore amazed his colleagues with his retentive mind. Citing from memory a long list of New England cotton and woolen manufacturing companies and giving their gross earnings, capital stock, profits, dividends, and surpluses in an effort to show that such corporations were making large earnings and thus did not need tariff walls, Gore reeled off the statistics with such ease that he astonished his listeners, both friend and opponent.[4]

To the tariff bill Gore offered twenty-one amendments, most of which either provided for a reduction of duty on the articles or placed them on the free list. His several amendments providing for reduced rates on such articles as blankets, sugar, and barbed wire for fencing were defeated, as were his amendments placing on the free list items like lumber imported for the use of churches, schools, colleges, or charitable institutions. He also failed to place on the free list cotton thread, flower bulbs, and textbooks for public schools. If Gore had had his way, these and many additional items would have been placed on the free list. He also felt that every worker should be allowed to buy his tools untaxed. "Let us encourage industry rather than dis-

29

courage it," he said, "and if any man desires to toil, desires to add to the Nation's wealth, in God's name, let him toil untaxed."[5]

Gore's amendment to the silk schedule, providing that small percentages of other substances be included by manufacturers in silk cloth, was also rejected. He proposed a tax of six cents per bunch on bananas because he felt that the United Fruit Company had a virtual monopoly on banana importation, but his suggestion was not accepted. Another protective amendment which Gore offered was tabled by the protectionists themselves. He wanted all alien immigrants above the age of fifteen years who could not write at least fifty word in any language to pay a tax of two hundred dollars before being allowed to enter the United States. In offering this amendment Gore pointed out that the tariff walls were being raised higher and higher to protect the American laborer against pauper labor. If the Republican Senators were serious about their supposed protection of the American laborer, he cynically remarked, they would protect him not only from the pauper goods from abroad but from the paupers themselves. Clearly Gore was attempting to embarrass the protectionists, but they nonchalantly tabled his amendment.[6]

Gore introduced a resolution calling for a committee to be set up for the purpose of investigating and reporting to the Senate at the earliest possible date (1) the import prices of various articles of general and ordinary consumption, (2) the wholesale prices of those articles, (3) the retail prices, and (4) the prices of similar articles of domestic production. When an opponent declared that Gore's move was made to embarrass the Finance Committee and that no real good would result, Gore insisted that he was after facts and that this procedure was one way to get them. A few days later he called up his resolution and made fun of Aldrich and his work, provoking laughter from his colleagues and the galleries. But Aldrich had the last laugh. The resolution was referred to the Finance Committee, where it languished. A week before the final vote was taken, Gore offered another resolution which instructed the Finance Committee to arrange and report each schedule of the pending bill as a "separate, distinct, and complete bill within itself" in order for each Senator to be able to vote on each measure without being required to vote for or against the whole bill.[7] This suggestion was not feasible, however, and, objection being raised, was dropped.

On the remaining amendments Gore invariably voted against

increasing duties, for the reduction of duties, and for an increased list of free goods. A comparison of Gore's votes with those of Aldrich on the 129 roll calls on the bill shows that they were on opposite sides 118 times. Only five times did they vote alike, and then Aldrich voted against such insignificant items as the tea tax and the increased pine-apple tax.

Despite the energetic opposition, the protectionists slowly but surely increased the rates of the tariff bill. On practically every roll call they were able to outvote the progressive-Democratic coalition. On the final vote they numbered forty-five, the opposition being able to muster but thirty-four. Stormy conference sessions followed. With the exception of Payne, the Republican conferees were sky-high protectionists; Cannon and Aldrich had seen to this when the conferees were appointed. Time after time the House rates were set aside in favor of those advocated by Aldrich. The final product contained higher rates than the Dingley tariff. The average *ad valorem* rates on dutiable imports contained in the schedule were 50.62 per cent as compared with 44.84 per cent in the act of 1897.[8] The Payne-Aldrich tariff law was a signal victory for protectionism.

After the Supreme Court declared an income-tax law unconstitutional in 1895, several measures and resolutions dealing with the same subject were introduced in the legislature, but none of them had passed. In the course of the debates on the Payne-Aldrich tariff, the progressives made further attempts in this area. Norris Brown, a Senator from Nebraska, and Gore both introduced resolutions calling for income-tax amendments to be added to the Constitution. When these resolutions received no attention, the progressives introduced an income-tax measure as a substitute for the inheritance-tax clause deleted from the tariff bill.

With the progressive-Democratic opposition in temporary majority and threatening to filibuster the tariff to death unless their tax measure was brought to a vote, Aldrich worked feverishly to trade tariff advantages for pledges against the income tax, but a week before the vote was to be taken the income-taxers still had a majority of five. President Taft, agreeing to use his influence to stop the income tax on corporations, sent a speech to the Senate in which he advocated the adoption of his corporation tax as an amendment to the tariff bill and indirectly condemned the income-tax measure by suggesting that a constitutional amendment be drawn up. Upon the completion of the reading of the speech, Gore moved that the President's message be referred to the Finance Committee with instructions to the committee to report a constitutional amendment within two days, but this motion was speedily tabled, and the Taft-Aldrich strategy succeeded.[9] A corporation tax was included in the Payne-Aldrich bill, and the progressive legislators failed in their attempt to add an income-tax law to the federal statutes. Needless to say, Gore was disappointed in the passage of the Payne-Aldrich tariff and the defeat of the income-tax proposal.

The conservative-progressive fight over tariff legislation and the income tax was a portent of what the Taft administration had to cope with for four years. Convinced that Taft had betrayed them, the progressives were out for revenge. From August to December, 1909, many of the administration's leaders tried to restore harmony, but to no avail.

When the celebrated controversy between two members of Taft's official family, Secretary of the Interior Richard A. Ballinger and Chief Forester Gifford Pinchot, broke into the open, the progressives rushed to the support of Pinchot, Taft upheld his Cabinet member, and any chance of harmony was gone forever. When Congress met in December a number of resolutions were submitted, including one by Gore, calling for an investigation of the Interior Department and the Bureau of Forestry of the Agriculture Department. A joint committee to investigate the departments was appointed, and, beginning its work in January, 1910, it was in almost constant session until June. This developed into an almost strictly intra-party squabble, however, and most of the minority members of the Senate, Gore included, refrained from becoming involved in the highly publicized Pinchot-Ballinger controversy.

Throughout the spring of 1910, with Taft defending Ballinger and the progressives shouting for his dismissal, the Senate carried on its less exciting legislative duties. Among the suggestions of the President for legislative enactments were several conservation measures, a proposal to amend the Interstate Commerce Act, a statehood enabling act for New Mexico and Arizona, and a plan for establishing postal-savings banks.

Of these suggestions Congress proceeded to give most of its attention to the problem of the regulation of common carriers. Since the passage of the Hepburn rate bill in 1906, there had been much agitation to strengthen the powers of the Interstate Commerce Commission, and the President himself had expressed a favorable attitude toward these demands. When Congress began dealing with the problem of railroad regulations, the conservative-progressive differences were again in evidence, and Taft cast his lot with the regular Republicans. Written by a committee appointed by the executives of the country's first-class railroads, a "safe" bill was sent to Congress, and Aldrich, a persistent opponent of any real advance in railroad regulation, worked for the conservative measure.[10]

A progressive-Democratic coalition in the House struck out all the sections of the bill contrary to the Sherman Antitrust Act, adding clauses providing for physical evaluation and for long- and short-haul regulations, as well as amendments defining telephone and telegraph companies as common carriers. The Commerce Court was saved only when a progressive amendment to strike it out resulted in a tie.[11] When the bill reached the Senate, Aldrich and Taft opposed adding amendments to it, but this scheme did not succeed. Too many regular Republicans did not dare in an election year to vote for the bill as it came to the Senate. With the help of the Democratic minority and some regular Republicans who would soon be running for re-election, the progressives were able to alter the measure materially before the final vote was taken in June, 1910. This Mann-Elkins Act as finally accepted was a significant advance in railroad regulation.

As a member of the minority and having progressive leanings, Gore happily followed the lead of the progressive Republicans in their drive to strengthen railroad regulatory laws. Agreeing in almost every instance, Gore voted with the Middle Western states' representatives in their opposition to the abuses which the railroads imposed on the farmers of the prairie plains. On the day the final vote was taken Gore offered this amendment to the bill: "Whenever any common carrier, subject to this act, shall bring suit to enjoin or otherwise delay or defeat the collection of taxes due under the laws of any State, such a suit shall take precedence over all other suits pending in such court." Admitting that this amendment ought to be a general statute applying to all suits rather than a special statute applying only to those suits instituted by common carriers, Gore apologized for introducing it. But he thought that the subject was important enough to warrant its being offered at that time. He expressed the opinion that, since "revenue is the breath of life to a state government," the states should not be paralyzed by a slow trial involving railroad taxation. The amendment was rejected by a voice vote.

A few minutes before the final vote was taken later that day, Gore made his first and only speech in regard to the bill under consideration. While voting with the progressives in almost every instance, he had not entered into the discussions of railroad regulation. But he could not refrain from giving his opinion of the bill which the progressives had made acceptable to him. In this brief speech he pointed out that the "vitals" of the original bill were the sections authorizing agreements between interstate carriers without the previous approval of the commission and authorizing mergers and consolidations between competing carriers. He expressed approval of the modifications to these sections effected by amendments.[12]

Aldrich had been able to defeat many of the progressive amendments to the bill by a series of agreements with some of the minority members. Several Democratic members voted with the regular Republicans after being promised by Aldrich that he would give his support to the bill to enable New Mexico and Arizona to become states. Hoping to have four more Democratic members added to the Senate with the admission of these states, the Democrats went along with Aldrich to keep the railroad bill from being too stringent. Gore was in favor of statehood for New Mexico and Arizona and relished the idea of additional colleagues from the Southwest, but his dislike of the railroad abuses was stronger than his desire for more support at this time. He voted consistently with the progressives for their amendments and in opposition to the amendments of the regular Republicans. He voted for the bill in its final form "on account of its general benefits, notwithstanding it contained the clause creating the Commerce Court."[13]

Another measure of importance recommended by Taft and receiving the attention of Congress was designed to establish federal postal-savings banks. An old Populist proposal, the idea was acceptable throughout the country. Banks were to be set up in every post office, where the timid and the poor could deposit their small savings with complete confidence. Forbidding the postal banks from paying more than 2 per cent interest on deposits, it gave them power to invest their deposits in government bonds. The progressive Republicans were agreeable to this last clause, but the Democrats were suspicious. At this time the national banks of the United States held millions of dollars worth of United States bonds drawing 2 per cent interest. On the basis of these bonds national-bank notes had been issued. Aldrich and his monetary commission had decided to propose a central bank of issue for the entire country to replace the old national banking system. But a way had to be found to relieve the national banks of their large holdings of 2 per cent bonds, since the bonds would be practically unnegotiable under the new scheme because the interest rates were so much higher on the current federal issues. A master plan was conceived to purchase the bonds with postal-savings deposits. The progressive Republicans would be forced to support the bill, the national banks would be content, and the future central bank would be almost assured.[14]

A progressive-Democratic coalition was able to limit the investment of the postal funds in 2 per cent bonds to 30 per cent of deposits at the President's discretion, but the bill was still unacceptable to the Democrats. With only one Democratic defection the bill passed the Senate by a strict party vote, 50 to 22, all of the progressive Republicans voting in its favor. Gore voted with the Democrats and progressives on the various amendments, and made only one speech, which came just before the final vote. Setting his views on record, he stated that he had originally planned to vote for the bill because "it would confer benefits and blessings upon the poor of this country . . . too seldom . . . the direct beneficiaries of our legislation." But by the time the final vote was imminent, he had realized what the bill actually contained. He said, "I believe that this measure is a Trojan horse and that a central bank will be found within its hollow sides, armed for a destruction of those whom it professes to befriend. . . ."[15] Refusing to go along with the Republican plan for a central bank, Gore voted against the postal-savings bank and hoped for the day when the Democrats would be able to put their own currency reforms into effect.

The congressional elections in November, 1910, were encouraging to Gore. The Democrats had gained control of the House, and the progressive Republicans, routing the regulars in numerous contests, definitely held the balance of power in the Senate. Taft had tried to conciliate the progressive wing of his party by promising to ask for a revision of the tariff, schedule by schedule. When the President made his recommendations, however, he did not ask for such a revision, but rather for a reciprocity agreement between Canada and the United

States. The Democratic House liked the reciprocity proposals, for the bill was not strongly protective.

The progressive Republicans of the Senate, favoring reciprocity in theory but not the Taft treaty, were able to delay the passage of the reciprocity measure in the last session of the Sixty-first Congress. When it was apparent that the measure would not pass, Taft surprised the legislators and the country by calling Congress into session in April. This session saw an incongruous situation in which many Democrats backed the administration on the reciprocity measure while a large number of regular Republicans opposed it. The progressive Republicans, too, generally disliked the measure.

Gore joined with his fellow Democrats to favor the measure. He refused to vote for any amendments which would tend to imperil the final passage of the bill. Revealing his strongly anti-protectionist philosophy, he planned to vote for a bill no matter what form it assumed if it reduced a single duty on a single article. Remarking that he favored "perfect free trade" between the United States and Canada, he announced that free trade had contributed much to the prosperity of the United States. Believing that the farmers had been the victim of special privilege and protective duties in the past, he wanted to do all he could for them by reducing duties and enlarging the free list. The Middle Western progressives, who lived nearer Canada than did Gore and whose constituents would feel the effects of free trade more than his own, pointed out that such trade would be damaging to agriculture and the businesses of the Midwest. Gore simply replied, "So long as Canadian wheat will feed the hungry, so long as Canadian lumber will shelter the homeless, why should we refuse to accept the blessings placed at our door by Him who fashioned the universe itself?"[16]

Aware of the peculiar situation of his agreeing with many regular Republicans who were supporting the bill and opposing the progressives with whom he had voted in the past, Gore remarked, "I am as willing to progress with the standpatters when they progress as I am unwilling to stand pat with the insurgents when they for the moment stand pat."[17] When the progressives and a few Democrats in favor of a high tariff tried to amend the bill to make it as unpalatable as possible, Gore voted against every one of their amendments. Proposing an amendment himself to place on the free list such items entering the United States from Canada as flour, meal, dressed meats, packinghouse products, and farm implements, he quickly stated that his amendment was of less importance than the bill as a whole and that he would withdraw it if it appeared the amendment would hinder the passage of the final bill. So, when the bill passed the Senate in July, 1911, Gore and many of his Democratic colleagues joined the Republicans faithful to the Taft administration. Those opposing it were the progressives whose constituencies would directly compete with the lower-priced Canadian products and the protectionists who wanted no infringement upon the tariff act of 1909.

Ironically, Canada refused to accept the plan. In an election in which the reciprocity treaty was the sole issue, the Liberal government, which favored the agreement, was defeated. With the Conservatives in control of the government and with Canadian nationalism rising, the manufacturing interests were able to repudiate reciprocity.

Taft had blundered by calling for the special session of Congress without securing assurances from the Democrats that the session would be limited to consideration of reciprocity. The opposition was quick to take advantage of this and proceeded to arrange a Democratic-progressive coalition for the purpose of revising the tariff, schedule by schedule. This group quickly pushed through a series of tariff bills, the first of which was a farmers' free list bill, placing on the free list numerous articles purchased by agricultural producers.

Gore tried to extend the free list to include items dealing with wood pulp and certain types of paper, but his amendment was rejected. He also failed in his attempt to place on the list additional imports from Canada, such as several kinds of fresh meats, canned meats, extracts of meat, lard, tallow, wheat flour, corn meal, plows, tooth and disk harrows, and other kinds of farm implements. Had this third suggestion been accepted, the President would have been given the power to make reciprocal trade agreements with other countries of the Western Hemisphere, if any of them desired to establish commercial union with the United States. The free list bill included many items giving compensation to Gore's large farm constituency, but he steadfastly insisted that he favored the bill, not because it aided the farmer, but because he opposed in principle the entire protective tariff system.[18]

The free list bill was followed by the passage of bills reducing the duties on the woolen and cotton schedules. La Follette led the fight in the Senate to secure the passage of these measures. Although not agreeing with La Follette on reciprocity, Gore assured the Wisconsin fighter of his full support in the battle to reduce duties on cotton and woolen goods. Gore had little to say about the cotton schedule, but he attacked the notorious schedule K of the Payne-Aldrich tariff. Favoring "emancipation" from that schedule, he worked to reduce its duties. He eased his attack only slightly by admitting that the reductions should be made gradually in order to give industries time and opportunity to adapt and adjust themselves to changing conditions. So vehement was his language toward the existing schedule that his opponents called him unfair and unreasonable.[19]

The efforts exerted in behalf of the tariff measures accomplished nothing. After manipulating the Senate into accepting them, La Follette and his followers were disappointed to see the President veto all of them on the ground that they were not scientific but political.

During this year the progressives made another effort to pass a resolution calling for the direct election of Senators. Gore had long been an advocate of this progressive step but did not participate in the debates on this issue, which lasted for over a month in the spring of 1911. When the final vote was taken Gore voted his progressive leanings, but many Southern Democrats were frightened into voting nay by the alleged threat to white supremacy when the Sutherland amendment, which gave the national government the power to alter state election laws, was accepted. The resolution did not receive the required two-thirds majority when it came to a vote in February, 1911.[20]

Direct election of Senators had been publicized by the so-called Lorimer affair. After William Lorimer was chosen as United States Senator by the Illinois state legislature, it was shown by a state investigation that $100,000 had been contributed to his campaign by large Chicago corporations.[21] After four Illinois legislators confessed in court that they had received large sums of money in return for their votes for Lorimer, a progressive-sponsored resolution to inquire into the corruption passed the United States Senate early in 1910. But an investigating committee dominated by regular Republicans reported that Lorimer had received a majority without the bribed votes and that therefore he was a duly elected Senator. The progressives continued their attack despite this subtle rationalization, but they failed to pass a resolution declaring that Lorimer was not legally elected. Public criticism of the Senate for its defeat of the resolution relating to the direct election of Senators and for its retention of Lorimer was adverse. A year later the resolution for direct elections was passed, and Lorimer was unseated.[22]

Throughout the Lorimer affair Gore had remained silent, but in every instance he cast his votes with his Democratic colleagues who followed the lead of the progressive Republicans. His was a vote against influence and corruption of the "moneyed interests." He felt that with direct election of Senators the state legislatures would be protected against the suspicion of scandal, so that future Lorimer cases would be avoided.[23]

Gore's major achievements as a minority member of the Senate were in the field of Indian affairs. Representing the youngest state in the Union, which only a few years before had been reserved for the Indian wards of the United States, Gore spent a great deal of time and energy handling the many matters relating to Oklahoma's large native population. He introduced scores of bills and amendments giving relief to individual indigent Indians, providing for protection of the Indians and their lands in legal controversies, and providing for the proper distribution of their funds. Bills reimbursing the Five Civilized Tribes for lands allotted to freedmen, removing restrictions from the sale of allotments,[24] and opening the rolls of the various tribes (so that unenrolled descendants of enrolled members could be added) were common among Gore's legislative duties during these early years.[25] By his action substantial sums of money were appropriated for Indian schools in Oklahoma and per capita payments were made to individual Indians out of the various tribal funds.

Gore's best-known act on Indian matters was his fight against the so-called McMurray contracts. In 1905 J. F. McMurray, an attorney in McAlester, Oklahoma, had sent representatives to several thousand members of the Chickasaw and Choctaw tribes securing contracts to represent them in the forthcoming government sale of their tribal property. With over thirty million dollars of valuable coal and asphalt Indian lands to be sold, McMurray had a 10 per cent fee written into the contracts. If the President had accepted the agreements, the McMurray firm would have netted over three million dollars.

Various factors combined to delay presidential action on the contracts, and when McMurray's persistence was brought to the attention of the Oklahoma delegation in Washington in 1910, Gore set out to prevent the contracts from being approved. He was convinced that the government would deal with its wards in a protective way and that they did not need legal representatives in the disposal of their lands. In effect, Gore saw McMurray as attempting to be the legal representative of the Indians who needed no representation. In a letter to the Attorney General, Gore pointed out that there was only a remote possibility the Indians would need legal assistance of a private nature, and even then expert legal talent could be obtained in their behalf for not more than 0.1 per cent of the total value of the land sales. He urged the Attorney General not to approve the contracts, because they were "illegal, unnecessary, unjust, and unwise."[26] In April he telegraphed the President expressing the hope that the McMurray contracts would be rejected.

At the same time Gore was pushing through the Senate a bill which would provide that all contracts affecting tribal money and property of the Five Civilized Tribes must receive the approval of Congress before becoming valid. In June he introduced a resolution, favorably reported by the Committee to Audit and Control the Contingent Expenses of the Senate, which authorized the Indian Affairs Committee to ascertain whether the employment of private counsel or agents in connection with the sale of the Indian lands was necessary, and, if so, if a 10 per cent fee was reasonable. Included in this resolution was a clause expressing the sense of the Senate that no contracts relating to the sale of Indian lands should be approved until the report authorized by the resolution had been made.[27]

Except for the Oklahoma delegation, few of the officials in Washington showed concern about the McMurray contracts. Chafing over a conference report on the deficiency appropriation bill which omitted his amendment providing that Congress approve all Indian land sale contracts, Gore made a desperate effort to block the contracts. On June 24, 1910, he stated on the floor of the Senate that on May 6 a representative of McMurray had called on him to inform him that it would be to his financial advantage to withdraw the bill requiring congressional approval of Indian contracts. According to Gore, this person had suggested that $25,000 to $50,000 might be made available if Gore would not oppose the contracts further.[28] Gore told the Senate that at the time he had been approached he had told several persons of the proposed bribe but that nothing had been done about it; for these reasons he was bringing up the subject on the Senate floor. He charged in his startling speech that a powerful lobby had exerted pressure to get these contracts for McMurray and ended by saying that if the contracts were approved, their supporters would be fully aware that there was money available to pay for that approval.

The charge made front-page news and spurred the legislators into action. The day after Gore revealed the attempted bribery, the Senate appointed a committee to investigate and report whether any Senator had been connected with the Indian contracts or whether any improper attempts or efforts were made to secure the passage of a statute affecting the approval of Indian contracts.[29] No money was set aside for the functioning of this committee, however, and a similar House committee, appointed on the same day, came to have the responsibility of the investigation. The House resolution provided for open hearings and for the evidence of them to be presented to Congress.

The House committee began its investigation in August, 1910, primarily concerned with the facts relating to the Indian contracts and Gore's charge of attempted bribery.[30] The committee held meetings in Muskogee, McAlester, Sulphur, Pawhuska, and Tulsa during the entire month of August. In November the hearings were resumed in Washington and continued at intervals through January 10, 1911. The arguments of the attorneys for both sides were completed two days later. Gore was present or was represented at most of the hearings and was given equal privileges with members of the committee in examining and cross-examining witnesses. The committee, subpoenaing every person whom Gore requested as a witness, made a special effort to obtain all possible evidence touching the McMurray contracts. One hundred sixteen witnesses were examined, as were numerous contracts, documents, and other related papers.[31]

The committee majority and minority reports were presented to the House on February 28, 1911. The majority of the committee reported that the evidence proved that one Jake L. Hamon had, indeed, approached Gore with an improper proposal respecting the contracts, but that this had been done without McMurray's knowledge.[32] The committee considered the terms "fraud" and "bribery" too strong, but it believed that stronger language than "undue influence" should be used to characterize McMurray's attempts to get Chief Green McCurtain and his son D. C. McCurtain to support his efforts to obtain contracts with the Choctaw Tribe. McMurray was exonerated from the charge that he had a part in the attempted bribe, but the committee censured him for his dealings in Indian contracts

41

and recommended that the contracts not be approved.[33] A one-man minority report, more favorable to Gore, suggested that the evidence did implicate McMurray in the attempted bribery.

Despite the fact that McMurray was exonerated, Gore's purpose in revealing the offer of a bribe had been achieved. By focusing publicity on the contracts he was able to show that they were of little or no value to the Indians. The McMurray contracts, both tribal and individual, had been killed beyond all possibility of resurrection.

The controversy over the McMurray contracts thrust Gore into the national limelight. He was praised by editors throughout the country for his fearlessness and uprightness in revealing the fact that Indian contracts were means for easy money. There was even a boom launched in Oklahoma to advance him as a presidential candidate, but this hardly went further than the red-ink headlines of the *Daily Oklahoman*. Gore himself made political capital out of the publicity. He was quoted as saying he realized that he was "taking his soul into the jaws of hell, and his political future into the balance," but he felt it was his duty to protect those who needed protection.[34] His final statement on the subject was: "I did my duty as I saw it. I do not calculate upon consequences either personal or political to myself. I shall never do so when my duty is involved or when the welfare of my constituency is at stake."[35]

Gore's interest in his Indian constituency did not end with this episode. Throughout his public career, he worked for the Indians' welfare. Amendments designed to protect Indians who owned valuable zinc, coal, and asphalt lands but who were not qualified to care for them were attached by the Senator to appropriation bills. With his colleague Robert L. Owen he argued for more liberty for the native population of Oklahoma. To this end he and Owen requested the investing of more authority in the Commission for the Five Civilized Tribes.

During his first session in the Senate, Gore introduced and secured the adoption of an amendment to an appropriation bill setting aside $300,000 to aid in the establishment and maintenance of rural free schools in the heavily Indian populated eastern part of Oklahoma. This was the beginning of appropriations which lasted for nearly twenty years and totaled almost six million dollars before the lands of the native people became subject to taxation. Gore was proud of his part in providing facilities for the education of Indian children, many of whom were later to make contributions as responsible citizens to the state and nation.[36]

One of Gore's longest Senate battles related to the Mississippi Choctaws. After the signing in 1830 of the Dancing Rabbit Creek Treaty (which cleared the way for the removal of the Mississippi Choctaws to Oklahoma) by the government and these Indians, conflict had arisen between Mississippi and Oklahoma over appropriations for the Choctaws. When appropriations were made for the Mississippi Choctaws, the Senators from Oklahoma contended that the term "Mississippi Choctaw" referred to the Choctaws who had moved from Mississippi to Oklahoma, while the Mississippi Senators insisted that it included those Choctaws and their descendants who did not choose to leave Mississippi under the treaty arrangement.

Senator Owen, of Indian descent himself, had spent a number of years dealing with the legal problems of the Mississippi Choctaws, and he was peculiarly qualified to deal with these disagreements when he was in the Senate. Mississippi's John Sharp Williams was also a lawyer of sound training, and for several years the Senate periodically witnessed legal sparring between Owen and Williams, with James K. Vardaman and Gore adding oratory and emotion to the fray. The disagreements were not limited to Indian appropriations when these four men crossed swords. Word battles occurred over such questions, for example, as whether the Choctaws remaining in Mississippi had a right to share in the profits of the sale of the Choctaw lands in Oklahoma.[37] Sometimes the Mississippi Senators won, and at other times the Oklahomans were the victors. The success of Owen and Gore in handling Indian affairs gained the applause of the chairman of the Choctaw-Chickasaw Treaty Rights Association, who on behalf of both tribes expressed his appreciation.[38]

Gore's contributions in Indian matters were not as significant as Owen's, but his efforts must not be underestimated because of the work of his part-Indian colleague.

IV. NEW FREEDOM POLITICS AND
LEGISLATION

EVENTS PRECEDING the presidential election of 1912 turned the Democratic preconvention maneuvers into an all-out struggle for control of the Democratic party. The congressional elections of 1910 resulted in a virtual Democratic landslide in all sections except the Pacific Coast. The House became overwhelmingly Democratic, and the Democrats captured enough Senate seats to assure them and the insurgent Republicans control of the upper house. The 1910 victories seemed to reflect approval of the principles of William Jennings Bryan, and progressive Democrats throughout the nation expressed confidence regarding the coming presidential campaign. When Bryan announced that he would not seek a fourth nomination, it was apparent to all Democrats that control of the party was at stake in the months preceding the National Democratic Convention.

The liberal wing of the party attached itself to the rising star of Governor Woodrow Wilson of New Jersey. William F. McCombs, William G. McAdoo, and Walter Hines Page were leaders in the move to raise Wilson to the highest office in the land. Establishing headquarters in New York these men propagandized for Wilson during the summer and early fall of 1911. Oklahoma's Senator Gore publicly expressed his hearty accord with the "Wilson for President" movement. After carefully canvassing the political situation, he had concluded that the Governor was the only prospective candidate who could carry both New York and New Jersey, which he believed would be necessary for a Democratic victory; therefore, he announced a full year before the convention that he favored Wilson for the nomination. Though he later admitted that he joined the Wilson ranks because he thought it was a shrewd political calculation,[1] at the time he observed of Wilson: "In respect to legislative policies, he is abreast of the times. He is in harmony with the spirit of enlightened and rational progress, and yet he is wise enough to know that 'too swift arrives as tardy as too slow.' "[2]

By the late fall of 1911 a number of other persons, including

44

Josephus Daniels, Albert Burleson, Thomas J. Pence, and Louis Brownlow, had aligned themselves behind Wilson's candidacy. These four men and Gore met with Wilson in Washington in December, and they agreed that additional headquarters to be managed by Daniels and Pence should be set up in Washington.[3]

As a close friend of McCombs, the general manager of the Wilson campaign, Gore gave valuable preconvention advice. When the Democratic National Committee met in January, 1912, to select a city in which to hold the nominating convention, following Gore's suggestion McCombs was able to get Baltimore named as the site. Gore and McCombs favored Baltimore over New York City because they did not want Wilson's candidacy to have the appearance of being Tammany-dominated.[4] When Byron R. Newton, publicity agent for preconvention activities, clashed with McCombs, he was discharged, and McCombs accepted Gore's suggestion for a replacement. As the preconvention struggle intensified, the sickly McCombs leaned more heavily on Gore. "It was to him, more than any other person," Mc-Combs recalled, "that I turned in the most difficult moments."[5]

As Wilson's campaign gained momentum a counter-campaign developed. Gore's role became that of spokesman to the press to reassure the public of Wilson's uprightness. In January, 1912, when the Wilson managers were doing their best to bring Wilson and Bryan together politically, the New York *Sun* published a letter written by Wilson to Adrian H. Joline in 1907 expressing an uncomplimentary attitude toward the Nebraskan. Writing that he would like to "do something at once dignified and effective to knock Mr. Bryan once for all into a cocked hat," Wilson had agreed with Joline's opinion that Bryan's proposal for government ownership of the railroads was socialistic. The publication of this letter was well-timed, as one of the bitterest anti-Bryan and anti-Wilson newspapers in the country endeavored to drive a wedge between the Commoner and the Governor. The object of the newspaper's printing the letter was apparent to most observers. Gore's comment was accurate when he said that it had "two designs, both sinister. First—to put Wilson and Bryan asunder, to divide progressive Democrats and conquer them. Second—to inflame the animosity and resentment of Mr. Bryan's faithful friends and followers and cause them to desert Wilson."[6]

A week after the publication of the Joline letter, the Wilson candidacy, apparently recovering from the thrust of the *Sun,* received another blow that for a time threatened to thwart Wilson's presidential ambitions permanently. George Harvey, editor of the conservative *Harper's Weekly* and an early advocate of Wilson's candidacy, disliking the New Jersey Governor's alliance with the young progressives, tried to wreck Wilson's prospects. Implying that the Governor was ungrateful for his magazine's support and financial connections, Harvey published a misleading announcement stating that Wilson had suggested that Harvey's support was injurious to his candidacy.

When this announcement appeared in the January 20 issue of *Harper's Weekly,* Wilson's opponents rejoiced. Exploiting the Wilson-Harvey break unmercifully, the conservative papers of the country outdid themselves in attacking Wilson as an ingrate for refusing to accept Harvey's support. Assisting the Wilson managers in their attempt to prevent these attacks from becoming effective, Gore jauntily declared the whole incident "a bubble, not a billow."[7] He defended Wilson by intimating that the critics of the Governor should be willing to tell the public frankly whether their candidates would accept a financial obligation similar to the one the Governor declined. "I would rather see Governor Wilson defeated and his heart an open book, 'that all who run may read,' " he declared, "than to see him triumphant with a skeleton in his political closet which had been concealed from the eyes of a confiding people."[8] He also helped ease the situation by persuading Francis G. Newlands of Nevada, himself a possible presidential candidate, to declare his support of Wilson. This unhesitating support on the part of Gore and other Democratic leaders was quite effective in rehabilitating the Governor's political fortunes.

The preconvention Wilson campaign in Oklahoma was fostered and organized by Gore with the assistance of "Alfalfa Bill" Murray.[9] J. Robert Gillam and Washington Sorrel, president and secretary respectively of the state organization, established Wilson clubs in strategic towns, including Oklahoma City, Tulsa, Enid, Guymon, Shawnee, Ardmore, and Muskogee.[10] Progressive newspapers, led by the *Daily Oklahoman,* lent their support to the Wilson boosters. But a number of the state's political leaders, notably former Governor C. N. Haskell, were behind the candidacy of Champ Clark, Speaker of the House of Representatives. Of the Democratic leaders in the state, sentiment was about evenly divided between Wilson and Clark. For fear of offending the adherents of other candidates, Gore based his advocacy of Wilson on the alleged fact that he was the only candidate who could marshal the independent vote.[11]

In January, 1912, Gore arrived in Oklahoma to give finishing touches to the campaign organization. Abstaining from making an open fight for his candidate, he nevertheless traveled extensively throughout the state in an attempt to rally his friends for Wilson. When it was rumored that Clark's managers had threatened Gore with political annihilation if he spoke for Wilson in Oklahoma, Gore denied that his opponents had issued the ultimatum. To prove that he had not been intimidated, Gore delivered a speech in Oklahoma City on February 9, but he spoke concerning the general Democratic situation and his remarks regarding Wilson were mild. At the same time he defended his right to freedom of speech and presidential choice.[12] The Republican Muskogee *Daily Phoenix* refused to allow the Democrats the appearance of unity, and four days later published the contents of the purported threatening letters from the Clark men to Gore. But Gore negated any effect this move might have had by his actions at the Oklahoma Democratic convention two weeks later. With the county conventions selecting a majority of Wilson delegates for the state convention, thus asserting that the Gore faction would have complete control of the meeting, he generously suggested that the Oklahoma delegation to the Baltimore convention be evenly divided between Wilson and Clark.[13]

Clark's Oklahoma manager, Scott Ferris, accepted the offer, but when the convention met, the other Clark adherents, who had been assured of the support of candidate Judson Harmon's followers, determined to fight for control of the convention. Gore called a caucus of Wilson delegates on the eve of the convention, at which time his followers voted to regard the Gore-Ferris agreement as binding.[14] With the Wilson men in control of the convention, the Clark instructions were defeated by a comfortable margin (314½ to 285½). The two factions then agreed to divide the delegation, with the provision that if either Clark or Wilson withdrew from the national convention contest, all the delegates would vote for the other candidate.[15]

These developments indicated that the rift in the Democratic ranks as publicized by the Republican press was real. Gore shrewdly healed the breach by insisting that the national delegation be divided evenly. With apparent victory in his hands, Gore was aware that Wilson might not win at the convention. Success in carrying all Wil-

47

son delegates to the convention would then be a Pyrrhic victory. By dividing the votes he saw that he had nothing to lose and everything to gain. If Clark ultimately won the nomination, Gore's support for Wilson would be less distasteful to Oklahoma leaders because he was generous enough to allow half the delegation to vote for Clark. He himself would be running for re-election within two years, and he prudently foresaw that support of a doubtful nominee in 1912 would not help him in his own coming campaign if he alienated important political leaders of his state.

Gore's campaign activities for Wilson before the Baltimore convention did not end with his efforts in Oklahoma. Determined to carry the Midwest in the primaries, McCombs sent Gore in March on a hurricane tour of Wisconsin. But Gore did more than speak; he helped organize an active publicity agency, and from Milwaukee he directed the organization of a campaign which reached to the smallest precinct in Wisconsin. The national headquarters contributed heavy financial support and vast quantities of literature to that state's organization. These efforts were not in vain; twenty of the twenty-four Wisconsin delegates to Baltimore were pledged to Wilson.

When the Democratic National Convention met on June 25, 1912, Wilson's future as a presidential candidate did not look bright. Without campaigning Champ Clark had led Wilson by substantial majorities in most of the Democratic primaries and state conventions. With only 248 pledged delegates to Clark's 436, Wilson and his followers were disheartened, but they were determined to fight.

The convention was riotous from the first day. The Wilson delegates (including Gore, who was a delegate-at-large from Oklahoma) supported Bryan in his revolt against conservative Alton B. Parker of New York as keynote speaker. The Clark men voted for Parker, however, and the judge delivered his speech. At the beginning of the second day, the Committee on Credentials reported that it had not yet completed its labors and would not be ready to report on its efforts until 8 P.M. The chairman of the committee suggested that the convention not recess until that time, "for I know those present would like a display of oratory."

Of the eight who "displayed" oratory, Gore was one. In a rousing speech typical of those made on such occasions, he loosed his oratorical powers on the receptive Democratic ears. Attacking the Republican party as one which "taxes the toys and joys of childhood;

48

taxes the tools in the hands of the toiler; taxes the rags upon the back of the beggar; taxes the crust upon the lips of the hungry; taxes not only the necessaries and comforts of life, but taxes the cerements and the monuments of the dead," he appealed to the convention crowd. He also cast humorous aspersions at the Republicans. Suggesting that all articles in the United States be given two price tags, one including a tariff and the other not, he advanced the plan that all who favored a protective tariff pay the higher price, while those who believed in a low tariff or no tariff be allowed to buy the articles at the lower price. "That law is bound to give universal satisfaction," he announced, "because under its operation it shall be done unto every man according to his faith."[16]

In the meantime, Bryan had prepared a resolution pledging the party to nominate no candidate under obligation to "J. Pierpont Morgan, Thomas F. Ryan, August Belmont, or any other member of the privilege-hunting and favor-seeking class." The resolution demanded that delegates Ryan and Belmont, whom Bryan considered the handmaidens of Wall Street, be expelled from the convention. Bryan's brother called together several Wilson leaders, including Gore, Luke Lea, Cone Johnson, Jerry B. Sullivan, Harvey Garber, and Henderson Martin, all ardent Bryan men, to get their opinion of the proposed resolution. They unanimously agreed that it was too harsh if not entirely unwise.[17] When none of them volunteered to introduce the resolution, the Great Commoner himself took the step, causing an uproar in the convention. Only after the provision expelling Ryan and Belmont had been struck out was the resolution accepted by the convention.[18]

During the night of June 27 and the morning of June 28 the nominations for President were made. Wilson was nominated by John W. Wescott at 3:25 A.M. after a Wilson demonstration of one hour and fifteen minutes. The nomination was seconded in several brief speeches, one of them by Gore. Although praising Wilson highly in the speech, Gore stressed the importance of the cause and principles for which the candidate stood. "The proud, arrogant and omnipotent Republican party is today stranded, broken between the rock of Taft stand-pattism on the one hand and the whirlpool of Rooseveltian radicalism on the other," he concluded. "There must be and there will be a progressive party in the United States. Shall that party be the Democratic party or shall it be the Roosevelt party?"[19]

49

Besides Wilson and Clark, two other candidates of importance were nominated, Governor Judson Harmon of Ohio and Representative Oscar W. Underwood of Alabama. At seven o'clock in the morning on June 28 the first ballot was taken. The four highest candidates were: Clark (440½), Wilson (324), Harmon (148), and Underwood (117½). When the afternoon session began, the lines were tightly drawn for the impending battle. The nervous and sickly McCombs was in charge of the Wilson forces. A. Mitchell Palmer represented Wilson's interests on the speakers' platform, with assistance from William Hughes of New Jersey and Thomas J. Pence of North Carolina. A. S. Burleson was in command of the Wilson delegates on the convention floor, assisted by Gore and McAdoo.[20] When little change in the votes came during the next eight ballots, the Wilson men knew that the knockout blow was being prepared. On the tenth ballot New York's Tammany boss, Charles F. Murphy, cast his state's ninety votes for Clark. This gave the Speaker 556 votes, well over a simple majority, and was the signal for the Clark landslide. The Wilson managers, McCombs, Palmer, McAdoo, Burleson, and Gore, scurried over the convention hall pleading with the Underwood delegates not to give their votes to Clark. North Dakota and Oklahoma refused to switch from Wilson to Clark. When the vote of the Oklahoma delegation was called for, "Alfalfa Bill" Murray, collarless and in his shirt sleeves, waved his arms and roared, "We do insist that we shall not join Tammany in making the nomination."[21] The tenth ballot continued without further significant change in the voting.

On the next ballot the Underwood men knew that they held a trump card. Clark's nomination could be prevented by their holding to their hundred-odd votes, and they were well aware of it. Playing for a deadlock between Wilson and Clark, they hoped that their candidate would be in the favored position as a compromise candidate. They were not ready to bargain with the Wilson or Clark forces; they wanted nothing less than the Presidency. The Wilson men, on the other hand, realized that they had to deal with the Underwood delegates if they were to win the nomination. Skillful maneuvering on their part may have been the decisive factor in Clark's defeat.[22] McCombs, Gore, and T. W. Gregory held long conferences with the Underwood leaders and promised that if Wilson should be put out of the race at any stage, they would use

50

their influence to deliver the Wilson delegates to the Alabamian. The Underwood men in return agreed to remain loyal to their candidate. In this way a solid anti-Clark block was formed, and the Missourian ultimately lost the nomination by the deft and persuasive arguments of the Wilson forces.

Slowly but surely the Wilson votes increased as the numerous ballots were held. On the fourteenth ballot Bryan indicated his support of Wilson. On July 1, Thomas Taggart, Democratic boss of Indiana, startled the convention by casting that state's twenty-nine votes for Wilson, previously given to favorite son Thomas R. Marshall. When Iowa transferred fourteen of its twenty-six votes from Clark to Wilson on the thirtieth ballot, for the first time the Governor led the Speaker on the tally sheet. The delegations from Vermont, Wyoming, and Michigan followed quickly, leaving the ranks of Clark and joining those of Wilson. On the forty-third ballot Roger Sullivan of Illinois released his delegates and Wilson gained fifty-eight additional votes, enough to give him a majority of the convention. With the two-thirds rule in effect, the Wilson forces still needed more votes, however, and these were forthcoming when Virginia and West Virginia joined their growing ranks. Wilson now had 602 votes, Clark 329, and Underwood 98½.[23] The Underwood men knew that the end was in sight, and John H. Bankhead went to the platform and withdrew Underwood's name. The Harmon men, too, were released and in the end Wilson received a total of 990 votes. At 3:30 in the afternoon of July 2, amid wild confusion and tumultuous joy, the chairman of the convention pronounced Woodrow Wilson the Democratic nominee for President of the United States.

Hardly had the convention excitement subsided before the Wilson leaders began to make plans for the election in November. The most perplexing business was that of reorganizing the Democratic National Committee. Daniels, Palmer, Burleson, and Gore conferred several times, finally agreeing that McCombs should be recommended as its chairman. Wilson plainly distrusted McCombs, who was becoming increasingly more difficult to deal with, and insisted that McAdoo be made vice-chairman.[24] When the national committee met on July 15 in Chicago, McCombs and McAdoo were chosen as previously agreed, with a strong executive committee to support them. This committee consisted of original Wilson supporters who had been active in the preconvention campaign: Daniels, Palmer, Burleson, Gore, Joseph E. Davies, J. A. O'Gorman, Daniel J. McGillicuddy, Robert Ewing, James A. Reed, W. R. King, William Saulsbury, and R. S. Hudspeth.[25] Wilson had almost entirely ignored the old guard politicians who had customarily led in the management of Democratic presidential campaigns in selecting this so-called "veranda cabinet."

Early in August the Democratic organization's headquarters were established in New York City. Gore, impressing his fellow workers with his organizing genius during the preconvention campaign, was named chairman of the national Bureau of Organization. When the Senator took charge he found the party machinery in a state of "utter dilapidation," and not until October was efficiency restored.[26] He organized the campaign so well that it was possible to reach the personnel of the smallest precincts.[27] In a pamphlet giving detailed instructions to local workers on how to form Wilson and Marshall clubs, Gore urged the establishment of these clubs throughout the country and supplied them liberally with campaign literature and buttons.[28] The organization bureau distributed 760,000 packages of campaign material to an estimated 360,000 different individuals. Some 3,300,000 pieces of printed matter were sent directly from Gore's office, and about 2,500,000 were sent from the general supply room by order of his bureau.[29]

In an effort to unite all factions in the progressive Midwest and to counteract Roosevelt's popularity in that region, Joseph E. Davies, secretary of the national committee, was chosen to head the Democrats' western office in Chicago.[30] In September Gore and Burleson moved their headquarters to Chicago as a further unifying factor. From that vantage point Gore saw that his hierarchy-type organization kept even the most humble precinct workers on the job.

As the campaign progressed it became apparent to all observers that Taft was a weak contender and that the battle was a struggle between Roosevelt and Wilson, both running on progressive platforms. By failing to draw progressive Democrats away from Wilson, Roosevelt's campaign failed, and the results of the November election gave Wilson an electoral college landslide. Equally significant was the fact that the Democrats would control both houses of Congress for the first two years of the new administration.

Assured of a majority of seventy-three in the House and six in the Senate, the Wilson leaders laid their plans from November to March with pleasant anticipation. Most of their conferences centered around Cabinet choices and the program for the next session of Congress. Gore conferred with Colonel Edward House in November, when he expressed his favorable opinion of Bryan as a possible Cabinet member. In the same month he conferred with colleagues concerning control of the Senate Finance Committee so that "reactionaries, like [Thomas S.] Martin, will not be able to block progressive legislation."[31] The following January the Senator was in conference with the President-elect on two separate occasions, the first being for three hours on January 8, when he and Hoke Smith met with Wilson to discuss Cabinet posts as well as a program for the Congress.[32] Rumors were that Gore would be given a Cabinet position, and it was generally believed in Oklahoma that the Senator could have one if he desired it.[33] There is no indication, however, that he cared to give up his Senate post. On the contrary Gore had attained the height of his ambition when he reached the Senate, and he had no desire to leave it at a time when his influence was obviously increasing.

At the call of newly inaugurated President Wilson, the Sixty-third Congress met in extraordinary session on April 7, 1913, to revise the tariff. A major tariff reduction had not been made for over half a century, and the Democrats were determined to reverse the protective trend. The bill which Oscar W. Underwood, chairman of the Ways and Means Committee, presented to the House in April had not been written hastily. It was drawn from the three Democratic tariff bills which Taft had vetoed two years earlier. In addition months of hearings and investigations had been held before the special session convened. By no means a free-trade tariff, the Underwood bill aimed at moderate protection by placing domestic industries in a genuinely competitive position with regard to European manufacturers. The House also added a provision for a graduated income tax.

As a member of the Senate Finance Committee, Gore approved of the bill when it was reported from that committee to the Senate. He had been a member of the subcommittee which dealt with the income-tax provisions of the bill, but his contributions were limited to his approval only. In fact, Gore had very little to do with this the first of the New Freedom measures. Voting on about two-fifths of the roll calls, he showed little interest in the bill, making only his traditional just-before-the-final-vote speech in which he expressed regret that the free list was not longer but approving of the fall of the "temple of protection."[34]

When it appeared in May that the tariff was running into difficulty owing to the revolt of the Far Western Democrats who opposed the free-sugar and free-wool provisions, Wilson announced that he would consider no compromise. On an important test vote in May, the Senate refused to instruct the Finance Committee to hold more hearings on the bill. Gore supported the President on this hurdle on the tariff issue. When the final vote was taken in September, the administration forces had the situation well under control and the Senate passed the tariff bill, the only Democratic defections being the two Louisiana Senators, who opposed free sugar. The New Freedom legislation thus had a satisfactory beginning.

The next important objective on the Democratic reform schedule was in the field of banking and currency. As soon as the previous presidential election had been completed, plans were being laid for hearings on currency legislation. A bill was being prepared providing for a decentralized banking system, which, at Wilson's insistence, included a general supervisory board. In January, 1913, a tentative draft of the bill had been completed. For six weeks a House subcommittee held hearings on the bill, listening patiently to many bankers and businessmen who advocated a strong and highly centralized reserve system in private hands. The framers of the bill, including Carter Glass of Virginia, chairman of the House Banking Committee, then went over it again, revising and improving its technical provisions at the suggestion of the bankers.

The Glass bill had been kept secret while it was in preparation, but when the press proclaimed what the measure contained, the progressive element of the party was up in arms. The issue at stake was the fundamental character of the proposed banking system. The progressives flatly refused a bill which was hardly more than a decentralized version of the old Aldrich plan. They insisted on outright governmental control over the reserve system and governmental issue of the currency. A serious rift was apparent in the party in May and June because the progressives refused to allow the banking system to be privately controlled. The thought of a "reform" administration's advancing such a bill repelled them. Robert L. Owen, chairman of the Senate Banking and Currency Committee and Gore's colleague from Oklahoma, was progressive in outlook and opposed the bill. The showdown came in June after the President held several conferences with Glass, Owen, and McAdoo, the Secretary of the Treasury, who had proposed that the system be established in conjunction with the Treasury Department. The President announced that he would insist that the government have exclusive control of the Federal Reserve Board and that Federal Reserve notes be obligations of the United States.[35]

In June Owen and Glass introduced identical measures in the two houses. After a bitter struggle between Glass and the members of his committee who felt the bill was not progressive enough, the measure was at last accepted by the lower house in September. The following month the bill was reported out of the Senate Banking Committee, passing the upper house in December. Gore took no part in the long struggle over this currency legislation. Because he favored its speedy passage, he remained silent during the debates until the day of the vote. On that day he spent fifteen minutes reviewing the Democrats' achievements in regard to the tariff and currency.[36]

Gore supported the remaining planks of the New Freedom platform, but his support was limited. Although voting "right" on many amendments to the Clayton antitrust bill, he was paired with Republican Isaac Stephenson of Wisconsin when the final vote was taken in the Senate in September, 1914. A Chautauqua tour prevented him from voting on the amendments or being present for the final roll call on the bill to create a Federal Trade Commission, but he was again paired with Stephenson and would have supported the measure had he been present. He made no remarks in the Senate on either of these two important pieces of legislation. His support of the Federal Trade Commission is revealed, however, by the fact that he introduced and had accepted a Senate resolution requesting the commission to investigate certain practices of the Standard Oil Company.

The New Freedom social-justice measures also received Gore's approval. Although not participating in the debates on the child labor law or the La Follette seamen's bill, it is safe to assume that Gore voted yea when the voice votes were taken on these measures.

He agreed with many leaders of the social-justice movement that restrictions should be placed on the ever increasing number of immigrants entering the United States. He reasoned that the wages of American laborers were being reduced as a result of the influx of illiterate foreign laborers being hired at a cheaper rate. Favoring the literacy test which Wilson opposed, Gore voted for the Burnett general immigration bill. As a member of the Immigration Committee, he had been in conference with Wilson while this bill was under consideration, but the President was unable to convince the Senator that the literacy test should be removed.[37] The President had to resort to the veto to keep the bill from becoming law.

Because the New Freedom campaign had stressed the equality of men and Wilson had appealed for Negro support, the new administration early ran into racial problems. In the end the Wilson administration abandoned its plans for aid to the Negroes, but not before Gore had become involved. Traditionally the office of Register of the Treasury had been filled by a Negro appointee. Eager to gain some recognition for Oklahoma in the patronage appointments, Gore urged Adam E. Patterson upon the President for the position. At the President's suggestion Secretary McAdoo discussed the Muskogee Negro with Gore and interviewed Patterson himself. Finding him satisfactory to both Oklahoma Senators, McAdoo recommended the Negro for the presidential appointment.[38] James K. Vardaman and John Sharp Williams, who felt that the appointment of a Negro to the position was "perfectly illogical,"[39] prepared to prevent the confirmation of the appointment. When Vardaman stated he would do "everything in my power" to defeat the appointment, Gore requested him to be content only to vote against the confirmation rather than marshaling significant opposition against it. Vardaman replied, "I feel a great deal more interested in defeating Patterson's confirmation than I do in the passage of either the tariff or the currency bill."[40] Not only was Patterson's appointment prevented, but the Mississippians were so powerful in their opposition that the Oklahomans were forced to break tradition and ask for the appointment of a person other than a Negro. Having been promised the patronage plum if they could agree on one man, they promptly recommended Gabe E. Parker, a Choctaw Indian. McAdoo, Wilson, and the Senate accepted the recommendation, and Parker began his duties in October, 1913.[41]

Woman suffrage was another of the great social-justice objectives of the progressive movement. When an amendment to the Constitution proposing suffrage for women was voted down in March, 1914, the National American Suffrage Association published its first blacklist, naming nine United States Senators and nine Representatives in Congress "whose opposition to woman suffrage is so powerful as to constitute the greatest obstacle to federal legislation that the women have to face."[42] Gore was included in this list; he had voted against woman suffrage.[43] He had not participated in the spring debates on the suffrage, but he had voted with other Southern Senators who wanted to continue state control of suffrage qualifications. Some of the Senators who voted against the suffrage amendment did so because they felt that it forced equal suffrage upon the states against their will; Gore may have agreed with this reasoning. Whatever his motives for voting against woman suffrage, whether the infringement upon state rights or opposition to the weaker sex in politics, he reversed his position later when the issue reappeared. Thereafter he voted and spoke for the extension of the suffrage until it was finally accepted by Congress.[44]

In August, 1912, Congress voted to exempt American vessels engaged in coastwise shipping from the payment of tolls when passing through the Panama Canal. In October of the same year the British Foreign Office protested these exemptions, stating that the law had the effect of violating the Hay-Pauncefote Treaty of 1901, which promised equal rates for all nations. The British suggested that the matter be arbitrated. In a three-hour conference in January, 1914, with the Senate Foreign Relations Committee, the Chief Executive requested repeal of the exemptions as the beginning of a campaign for better relations with the British government. Wilson's stand was interpreted by many to mean that he was showing partiality to the railroads, but he persistently held that the exemption was a direct contravention of the Hay-Pauncefote Treaty and that the domestic situation had no bearing on his stand on the subject.[45] When he was reminded that the Democratic platform of 1912 approved of the exemption, the President wrote, "I feel that no promise made in a platform with regard to foreign affairs is more than half a promise."[46] The legislators held the promises of the platform in more esteem and were reluctant to break the campaign pledges.

57

Finding significant opposition, Wilson made a personal appeal to a joint session of Congress to support his request for repeal of the exemptions. After a bitter three-week struggle, the House on the last day of March passed the bill to repeal the exemption. The fight was longer and more rancorous in the Senate. While the intra-party conflict was in progress, Gore, who favored the President's recommendation but who was also aware that it violated the recent platform, polled the delegates to the Baltimore convention on the tolls question. Of the 1088 delegates, 867 replied to his questionnaire, 702 stating that they were opposed to American ships being exempted from the tolls payment, even though it was recommended by the platform which they had approved. Thirty-eight of the polled delegates were noncommittal, and 127 favored free tolls for American coastwise shippers. Many of the delegates confessed that they had no idea the "miserable little joker" was in the platform.[47]

Gore's one speech in the Senate on the subject revealed his support of Wilson's position. Admitting the danger of breaking the sanctity of platform pledges, Gore argued that the platform was also against subsidies, and the exemption policy was a form of subsidy granting a virtual monopoly to the American coastwise vessels. To Gore the heart of the question was, "Shall we exempt the people and tax the ships or shall we exempt the ships and tax the people to maintain this canal?" Placing the treaty obligation above the platform, he stated that he would cast his choice with the people and accept the consequences.[48] In defense of the President, who was being charged with inconsistency as the entire nation became interested in the subject, Gore simply replied, "I have no doubt that the present Chief Magistrate of this republic would rather be right than be consistent."[49] When a vote was finally taken in June, 1914, the administration forces won handily enough. Naturally, Gore supported the affirmative.

It may have been that Gore gave little attention to the better-known New Freedom legislation because of his work in the field of agricultural legislation. When the Democrats organized the Senate in the spring of 1913, Gore was appointed to the position he desired above all others: chairmanship of the Committee on Agriculture and Forestry. In this position his major responsibility centered around the annual agricultural appropriation bills allocating money for the Department of Agriculture and other purposes.

Working behind the scenes on many other pieces of legislation, Gore found himself the Senate floor leader when agricultural appropriations were being considered. Explaining, defending, amending, discussing, and voting on them, he was tireless in his efforts to secure adequate appropriations for the Department of Agriculture for each fiscal year. He presided over scores of hearings relating to agriculture appropriations. In order to illustrate his part in agricultural legislation, I have chosen a few representative instances from the multitudinous details to which Gore gave tedious attention.

Gore was primarily responsible for setting aside $10,000 to maintain automobiles, motorboats, and motorcycles to serve the Agriculture Department for the year 1914-15. Many Senators had misgivings about the value of motor vehicles, one Senator stating he had never ridden in a horseless carriage and did not plan to. Gore was persistent in his efforts despite the number who preferred mules and horses to mechanical vehicles in government service, and the amendment was accepted.

The problems of halting grasshopper and boll weevil plagues and animal diseases, including Texas fever, hog cholera, and foot-and-mouth disease, received the attention of the Agriculture Committee chairman. The spread of foot-and-mouth disease was particularly vexing. In December, 1914, Secretary of Agriculture David F. Houston urged Gore's committee to seek an emergency appropriation to cover the expenses necessary for the eradication of a new outbreak of this disease throughout the country. Houston explained the reason for the need of immediate action on the part of the Senate: "While up to the present we have had sufficient funds to meet the expenses actually incurred, these funds will not last much longer, and it would be disastrous to delay or to interrupt the work."[50] Officers of the Bureau of Animal Industry presented statistics to the Agriculture Committee regarding the recent outbreak of the disease. With these facts in mind, Gore introduced a bill providing $2,500,000 for this emergency which he rushed through the Senate. Insisting that the need was highly urgent, he asked that there be no debate on the bill. The Senate cut the appropriation to $1,000,000 and sent it to the House. After the bill died in a House committee, Gore attached an amendment to the next agricultural bill putting aside $2,500,000 to be used in the event of any future outbreak of foot-and-mouth disease.[51]

As chairman of the Agriculture Committee Gore did not forget that he came from a predominantly rural state. He attempted over a period of several years to improve farming conditions near his home in Oklahoma. At his suggestion a field station was established in 1915 at Lawton for the study of dry-land farming practices, and he later explored the possibilities of a system of irrigation for the area.[52]

Gore was also interested in bills providing for the uniform grading of grain. When a bill proposing federal inspection of such grading failed to pass the Senate, he offered a substitute, prepared under the direction of the Department of Agriculture, which would establish uniformity among the grades and allow the government to supervise the enforcement of grading standards but leave to the various states the right to maintain inspection machinery. This substitute met the fate of the original bill.[53]

With the outbreak of war in Europe, Gore introduced a measure which, if it had not succumbed in committee, would have established a cotton-credit guaranty system. He proposed to pledge the faith and credit of the government to assist in moving the fall crop and thus avert the loss of half a billion dollars to cotton growers. Had it passed, every bank after filing a bond and making a satisfactory financial showing to the Secretary of the Treasury would have been entitled to receive a guaranteed certificate of credit. This system, according to Gore, "would afford relief to every producer of cotton, however limited his assets or resources."[54] Reminiscent of the Populists' sub-treasury plan advanced in the late nineteenth century, this system would allow farmers to hold their cotton until a satisfactory market price was available. But since it did not appeal to many colleagues, Gore's plan for assisting the farmer did not succeed.

Gore was an advocate of improved agriculture through the application of cooperative principles of farming. He defended farm demonstration work when it was attacked by Northern Senators. Porter J. McCumber criticized it as a sop, stating that little or no benefit was derived from it. Gore reminded the North Dakota Senator that many Southern farmers, especially Negroes, were not as far advanced as the Northern farmers. Many parts of Texas, Mississippi, and Louisiana had been practically revolutionized through this work, he said, and when it was suggested that the work be

60

discontinued in Oklahoma, a storm of protest had been raised.[55]

Gore took a minor though active part in the passage of the Smith-Lever agricultural extension bill, which created a generous grant-in-aid system in behalf of agricultural education through university and governmental extension work in farm villages. He also approved of the Smith-Hughes Act creating a federal board for vocational education to administer the grant-in-aid system, which generously subsidized state efforts in the teaching of commercial, industrial, agricultural, and domestic arts.

Another aspect of the movement to improve agricultural conditions was the growing demand for rural credit reform. During the first decade of the twentieth century it had become apparent that the commercial banking system on which the farmer depended was not adapted to his needs, that the financial machinery enjoyed by other classes of borrowers was inadequate for the farmer, and that the farmer's rate of interest was higher than the rate paid by railroads, municipalities, or industrial corporations.[56] All three major parties endorsed rural credits in the national conventions of 1912, and President Wilson expressed the need for reform in this field in his inaugural address. Agitation for a scheme that would reduce the farmer's rate of interest thus grew rapidly after the Democrats took office in 1913.

Keeping in mind his farm constituency, Gore not only expressed his support for the theory of long-term credits at low-interest rates for the farmers but also set out to make that theory a reality. Securing an amendment to the 1914 agricultural appropriation bill approved on March 4, 1913, he made possible the creation of the United States Rural Credit Commission, which was given the power to investigate and study in European countries cooperative land-mortgage banks, cooperative rural credit unions, and similar organizations and institutions devoted to the promotion of agriculture and the betterment of rural conditions.[57]

Two weeks after President Wilson took office he appointed Gore as a member of this commission to go abroad to study European agricultural systems and conditions. Other duties hindered him from making the European tour, but he wholeheartedly supported the project. Senator Duncan U. Fletcher of Florida was made chairman and John Lee Coulter (agricultural expert of the United States Census Bureau) secretary.[58] In conjunction with the Southern Commercial Congress, this United States Commission and an American Commission (consisting of sixty-seven persons representing the various provinces of Canada and the states of the United States) sailed from New York in April, 1913, for a three-month tour of Europe.

The general plans of these groups were arranged in advance by the International Institute of Agriculture at Rome, Italy. One or more of the members of the United States Commission visited Italy, Hungary, Austria, Russia, Germany, Denmark, Belgium, Holland, France, England, Wales, Scotland, and Ireland. In each country, the minister of agriculture, cooperating with the officials of various important agricultural organizations, arranged detailed programs. Two methods of work were followed. The first was in the nature of hearings which took the larger share of the visitors' time. Experts presented statements of the services performed by governments and by voluntary agencies in the various forms of agricultural cooperation. The second method of investigation was the inspection by the committee members of cooperative institutions themselves, including conferences with the officials in charge. The United States Commission dealt only with the question of credits, while the larger American Commission investigated the other forms of agricultural cooperation as well. Although Gore did not make the tour, he signed the commission's report and studied it in order to learn how the problem of rural credits was handled in European countries, which according to him were 150 years ahead of the United States on this subject.

From the data gathered in Europe, Senator Fletcher framed and introduced in August, 1913, a bill to establish a system of privately controlled land banks to operate under federal charter. With the approval of both the President and the Secretary of Agriculture, this bill was revised by a joint subcommittee of the House and Senate banking committees which reported it in May, 1914, with an additional provision requiring the government to furnish capital for the land banks, to buy their bonds if private investors failed to do so, and to operate the system.

This measure, called the Hollis-Bulkley bill, set off a controversy in Democratic circles when the clause for government support was made public. Wilson and Houston held that this would be special legislation for a particular group and not in the tradition of New

Freedom principles. The spokesmen for the bill disagreed. They were convinced that in the farmers' attempt to gain independence from private bankers, a rural credits system without governmental support and sponsorship would never succeed. When the House agrarian leaders proceeded to introduce the bill despite Wilson's opposition, the administration leaders worked to cut short a possible revolt in the party. Carter Glass received a letter in which Wilson stated, "I have a very deep conviction that it is unwise and un-justifiable to extend the credit of the Government to a single class of the community."[59] The President declared that he would gladly approve the measure without the governmental aid provision, but hinted that he would veto it if the "radical propositions" were included.[60] The Southern agrarian leaders were angered at this development, but they yielded to the pressure and temporarily halted their agitation for rural credits.

While guiding the 1916 agricultural appropriation bill through the Senate, Gore submitted Fletcher's original rural credit bill of 1913 as an amendment. This amendment did not survive the difficult road through the committee, however, and was never reported. In February, 1915, McCumber offered a rural credits amendment without warning the administration leaders. Gore did not know what the amendment contained, but as chairman of the Agriculture Committee he accepted it with the understanding that it would be carefully considered in conference with the House. On this basis the Senate agreed to an amendment providing for the establishment of a bureau of farm credits in the Treasury Depart-ment. After a conference with the President on the subject, Gore expressed hope that the farm-credit legislation would be retained in the agricultural bill when it finally passed. But the House conferees insisted on drastically revising the McCumber amendment, and Gore voiced objection. At last concluding that the subject required further study, the conferees rejected the original amend-ment.

At Gore's insistence a substitute for the McCumber amendment was included in the bill. This new amendment created a joint committee composed of twelve members (three members from the agriculture and banking committees of each of the two houses) which was charged with the responsibility of preparing and reporting to Congress by January 1, 1916, a bill providing for the establishment of a system of rural credits adapted to American needs and conditions. This joint committee on rural credits began work in March, 1915, and on January 3 of the following year submitted a report of its subcommittee on land-mortgage loans, together with the draft of a proposed bill. Two days later Henry F. Hollis of New Hampshire introduced the bill in the Senate. Believing that the short-term credits which had been provided for in the Federal Reserve Act were not adequate for farmers and emphasizing the need for a system of long-term loans at low rates of interest, with the amortization method of payments, Gore lent his support to this bill.[61] The bill passed both the Senate and the House in May without significant opposition and was signed into law by the President in July, 1916, with a number of interested guests present, including the members of the United States Rural Credits Commission.[62]

The culmination of several years of effort on the part of the agrarian leaders, the Federal Farm Loan Act established a system composed of twelve federal farm loan banks capitalized at $500,000 each, the essential function of which was to provide credit for farmers at a low rate of interest on a long-term basis. This act, called the "Magna Charta of American farm finance,"[63] was a distinct victory for the agrarian leaders and represented their major achievement under the Wilson administration before this country's entry into World War I. During his entire career in the Senate, it was the most important single piece of constructive legislation which was favored by Gore and in which he had a significant part.

V. THE NEUTRALITY CONTROVERSY

SENATOR GORE had more than his share of callers requesting his support for appointments to federal offices when the Democrats regained political power in the spring of 1913. When he allegedly thwarted the efforts of Robert A. Rogers of Oklahoma City to become Wilson's Secretary of the Interior, Rogers' proponents, who stood to gain by the appointment, conspired to ruin him politically by an attack on his character. In April, 1913, the press carried a story that Gore had been accused of making improper advances to Mrs. Minnie Bond in a Washington hotel room.[1] Six months later, in the district court of Oklahoma City, Mrs. Bond filed suit for $50,000 damages against the Senator as a result of the scandal and for injuries received in the alleged assault.

A trial was held the following February in which the plaintiff testified that she had invited Gore to her hotel to talk about the possibility of her husband's receiving the post of Collector of Internal Revenue under the new administration. There, she charged, he attacked her. The defendant contended that he had been tricked into going to a hotel room by the plaintiff, who had told him that her husband was there when he actually was not. He branded Mrs. Bond's charge as "an infamous lie." The defendant's attorneys held that J. R. Jacobs (in whose room the purported attack occurred), E. A. Harp, T. E. Robertson, Kirby Fitzpatrick, and J. R. Bond were all disappointed office seekers and that the allegation was the result of a conspiracy to smear the blind Senator.[2] The facts as they came out during the trial supported the defendant's position. It took a jury of nine farmers, a grocer, a banker, and a broker only two and one-half minutes for a vote completely exonerating Gore. So overwhelming was the verdict that the jury stated: "Had the defendant at the conclusion of the plaintiff's evidence announced that he desired to introduce no evidence and rested his case, our verdict would have been the same."[3]

The nature of the charges, the prominence of the parties involved, and the determined efforts of each side made the Gore-Bond controversy a topic of conversation and printed commentary all over the nation. It attracted more attention in Oklahoma than any other political event since statehood. Beginning with the New York *Times*[4] and extending to the lowliest Oklahoma weekly, the press agreed that Gore's vindication was fully warranted.

Gore had charged during the trial that the conspiracy was instigated to bring him into disrepute and wreck his chances for renomination in the Oklahoma Democratic primary in August, 1914. If this was true, the attempted character assassination boomeranged. Not only did he have the solid backing of the press in Oklahoma but also the sympathy and support of most of the voters. The people of Oklahoma were convinced that the cheapest of political tricks had been instigated with the sightless man as the victim. Politically, it was good medicine. Basking in the sunlight of the dismissed damage suit, Gore rode to a three-to-one primary victory over Judge Samuel W. Hayes, who had resigned from the Oklahoma supreme court to make the race. Receiving a majority in every county in the state, the incumbent had a total vote of 86,975 to his opponent's 28,891.

Hayes had no effective issues against the triumphant Senator. The judge tried to manufacture an issue by accusing Gore of being a "rural confidence man" who did nothing for the farmers of Oklahoma,[5] but this made no dent in Gore's strength. The revelation that the Senator was absent for a large number of Senate roll calls was equally ineffective. His opponent's contention that the blind man's humor and oratory did not necessarily make him a good Senator showed the lack of pertinent issues.[6] Detained in Washington because of his interest in an Indian appropriation bill, Gore did little campaigning in this race. Depending almost entirely on campaign literature, he publicized the fact that he had the blessing of President Wilson.[7] With the approval of the administration and with the result of the recent trial still effective, Gore was unbeatable.

A few days before the general election in November Woodrow Wilson sent this day-letter to Gore: "May I not extend through you to the Democrats of Oklahoma my cordial greetings and good wishes on the eve of the election and express my confident hope that they will make a splendid showing at the polls."[8] Wilson's hope was realized; the Democratic ticket won handily, if not overwhelmingly. The heated campaign for governor turned the voters out in record numbers, further increasing Gore's majority in the Senate race. Running well ahead of the ticket, he carried all but three counties, winning over Republican John H. Burford by a majority of nearly 50,000, to become the first popularly elected United States Senator from Oklahoma.[9]

From its beginning in March, 1913, the Wilson administration was faced with the problem of dealing with revolution-ridden Mexico. Refusing to recognize the precarious military dictatorship established by Victoriano Huerta, Wilson injected moral considerations into the realm of international law. This stand on moral principles conflicted a number of times with legal technicalities, and before 1917 Wilson had maneuvered his country into a number of embarrassing situations. Throughout the period Senator Gore stood behind his President in each succeeding crisis. When Wilson went before a joint session of Congress in April, 1914, accusing the Huerta government of deliberately insulting the United States and asking for power to use armed force to obtain redress, the Senate passed a resolution justifying the employment by the President of the armed forces of the United States in Mexico. Viewing the crisis from the President's point of view, Gore supported the resolution, although he continued to stress the value of moral persuasion rather than military force.[10]

After a series of complicated activities culminating in the murder of several Americans by the Francisco Villa gang in northern Mexico in January, 1916, another serious crisis was reached between the two countries. This massacre evoked a demand in Congress for intervention, and a resolution was introduced to authorize the President to use the military forces in Mexico. Foreseeing the possibility of large-scale conflict, Gore introduced a resolution in the Senate authorizing the President to enter into negotiations with Mexico with the view of establishing a neutral zone along the northern border of Mexico. This zone was to be jointly policed by the governments of the two countries until order was restored and the lives and property of American citizens were made secure, after which the forces of the United States would be withdrawn from Mexican territory.[11] Impractical though the scheme was, it revealed Gore's growing pacifistic tendencies.[12]

Gore's pacifism was exemplified in a more concrete way with

the beginning of the First World War. Upon the outbreak of open hostilities in Europe in the summer of 1914, this country became involved in a controversy over preparedness. Should the United States, several thousand miles away from the conflict, remain isolated from Europe and refrain from military preparation? Or should a neutral nation prepare for the eventuality of being drawn into that war? Would the very preparation for war tend to involve this nation in conflict? These and similar questions the American people and its leaders were forced to face as the European war spread.

Unequivocally repudiating war, many persons in the progressive tradition not only opposed military preparation but favored disarmament. These progressives assumed that wars were mainly economic in cause, and they hated the evil because they believed that bankers with money to lend, munition-makers with vast profits to reap, and industrialists with markets to open were the chief proponents and beneficiaries of war. Concentrating largely on economic and social justice at home, progressivism in the minds of many had come to be tantamount to isolationism. A sizable number of the progressives thought of America as a nation with a unique mission: to exemplify for the world a triumphant democracy conquering social and economic injustice.[13] Pacifism was a logical corollary to this philosophy. How could domestic reform be achieved if the nation were plunged into a costly war? With this reasoning many of the progressive leaders were opposed to preparedness.

Definitely aligning himself with the progressive-pacifist group, Gore generally refused to support the President's defense program. He favored a navy "adequate to defend our shores against attack," but could see no value in increasing the standing army or spending money for other military preparations.[14] As an advocate of "naval preparedness only," Gore opposed almost all other military measures which would cost American taxpayers. In fact, opposition to spending money for anything except agricultural needs beneficial to his constituents became almost an obsession with him. His conservative economic opinions and theories were expressed freely in the days before America's entry into the war as well as after. This passion for conserving the taxpayers' money became so strong that it was a chief characteristic of his senatorial career from this time forward.

Although publicly declaring that he favored naval preparedness, Gore failed to vote at all on proposals for founding naval academies on the Pacific Coast and near the Great Lakes, increasing the number of new battleships and battle cruisers, or establishing a shipping board for the purpose of creating a naval auxiliary and naval reserve.[15] Gore opposed on the grounds of economy various bills and amendments concerned with building up the strength of the Coast Artillery Corps, doubling the pay of National Guardsmen, increasing pensions of families of men in service, and compensating government employees who enlisted in service. In considering growth in army and naval appropriations in the spring of 1916, Gore reminded his Democratic colleagues that they had promised taxpayers to practice economy and that he did not like to see this pledge broken.

Consistent with his stress on economy and not because he believed in a large military establishment, Gore favored an increase in the number of cadets at the United States Military Academy. With almost two hundred vacancies in the academy constantly, Gore felt it was a great waste of money to have the facilities available but not used. Expressing his distaste for the system of senatorial and congressional appointments of cadets to West Point, he suggested that the President be given the power to fill vacancies.[16] But too many of his colleagues wanted to keep this instrument of patronage, and his amendment was rejected.

The controversy over preparedness was only one aspect of the larger problem of neutrality facing the United States. From the time the President issued a proclamation of neutrality in August, 1914, until the United States entered the war in April, 1917, the Wilson administration was involved in a struggle both at home and abroad centering around the maintenance of American neutrality in time of war. Resulting from Germany's reliance on the submarine as an important factor in the fight with Great Britain and her allies, a particularly perplexing problem arose over the arming of merchant ships and luxury liners of belligerent powers and the right of neutral Americans under international law to travel on them.

Secretary of State William Jennings Bryan held that if this country were to remain strictly neutral it should not allow American citizens to travel on ships of belligerent nations in time of war and thus involve America in incidents with the belligerents. On the other hand, Wilson believed that it was not compatible with American rights to warn citizens of the United States against exercising freely the right to travel on whatever vessel they chose.

Because of Wilson's stand the administration declined to inform American citizens that they took passage on ships of belligerent nations at their own risk. When in May, 1915, a British luxury liner, the *Lusitania*, was sunk without warning, resulting in the death of 128 Americans, Wilson sent several sharply worded notes of protest to the Germans. Disagreeing with Wilson's position and fearful of American involvement in the war, Bryan resigned from the Cabinet.

Following a series of conferences with Bryan,[17] Gore revealed his opposition to Wilson's policy on January 5, 1916, when he introduced two bills relating to travel on ships of belligerents. Had they been acceptable they would have (1) prohibited the issuance of American passports for use on such ships, (2) withdrawn protection from American citizens who persisted in traveling on those ships, (3) prevented vessels of nations at war from entering ports of the United States if they transported American citizens, and (4) prohibited American vessels and those of other neutral nations from transporting American citizens as passengers along with contraband of war.[18] Admitting that American citizens had the legal right to travel on any passenger vessel they chose, Gore stated that they did not have the moral right to do this, since the risk of involving this nation in war was enhanced by their action. He felt that the legal right should be suspended so that no American citizen could "run the risk of drenching this Nation in blood merely in order that he may travel upon a belligerent rather than upon a neutral vessel."

Finding a number of his colleagues supporting the President's stand on the rights of American citizens, Gore attempted to embarrass them by introducing two resolutions which, if they refused their support of them, would show what he felt was their inconsistent position. In view of the British blockade, which had been interfering with American trade in noncontraband goods, he offered to give the President power to halt the exportation of contraband to those nations interfering with noncontraband neutral commerce of the United States and to prohibit national banking associations from making loans to such countries.[19] He recognized and favored the rights of belligerents under international law to interfere with the shipment of contraband goods, but he pointed out that American citizens had equal right under the same law to engage in innocent commerce with neutral nations and that no belligerent power had the authority to abrogate that right. Arguing that the principle of protecting citizens engaged in neutral commerce in noncontraband goods was on a par with that of upholding their rights to travel on warring nations' ships, Gore stated, "It will be interesting to see whether those who insist that every American citizen should have the right to travel on a belligerent rather than a neutral ship at the peril of engulfing the country in a sea of blood will be equally insistent that American citizens should be protected in their immemorial and sacred right to ship noncontraband goods on neutral vessels."[20]

Gore's reasoning evidently made an impact on some of his associates. As he worked in February to get the Senate to take a stand on Americans traveling on ships of belligerents, it was apparent that his position was gaining supporters. Confused by the State Department's wavering position with regard to the subject of the status of armed merchant ships and actuated by the knowledge that a strong effort was being made to get Senate action on the subject of travel on them, William J. Stone of Missouri, chairman of the Senate Foreign Relations Committee, requested a conference with the President. Senate Majority Leader John W. Kern, Hal D. Flood, chairman of the House Foreign Affairs Committee, and Stone met with the President late in the afternoon of February 21 to discuss recent events and the prospect of Senate action in regard to American rights.[21]

At the White House conference Wilson reiterated that he would hold Germany to strict account if a submarine sank without warning an armed ship upon which American citizens were traveling. He expressed his willingness to go to almost any extreme to support the principle of American rights to travel on the high seas. He is represented as having declared that the State Department would sever diplomatic relations with Germany if this principle were violated again. A loyal Wilson supporter up to this time, Stone lost his temper, banged his fists on the table, and shouted, "Mr. President, would you draw a shutter over my eyes and my intellect? You have no right to ask me to follow such a course. It may mean war for my country."[22]

By the time the President's position was made known to Congress by the conferees, Germany had stated publicly that it would not

71

recede from the position it had announced on February 10: on the last day of the month German submarines would begin attacking armed merchant ships without warning. On February 23, unprecedented panic was provoked in both chambers of Congress. Many of the legislators were convinced that the President actually desired to enter the war. The Democratic members of the House Foreign Affairs Committee hurriedly met and agreed to demand immediate action on a resolution which had been previously offered by Representative Jeff McLemore of Texas warning Americans against traveling on armed ships of belligerent nations. Speaker Champ Clark and Majority Leader Claude Kitchin favored the resolution, but they prevailed on their colleagues to delay action on it until a conference with the Chief Executive could be held. On the afternoon of February 24 Gore attempted to introduce in the Senate a concurrent resolution but was unable to obtain unanimous consent to do so. This resolution was designed to express the sense of the Congress that American citizens should "forbear to exercise the right" to travel on armed vessels.[23]

When the President was informed of the threatened revolt against his foreign policy, he decided to fight his critics in Congress who, he felt, were trying to wrest from him the control of foreign affairs. In an open letter addressed to Stone on February 24 Wilson made it painstakingly clear that he would do his utmost to keep the country from going to war. But he made it equally clear that he could not consent to the abridgment of the rights of American citizens in any respect. Stressing that he was doing his best to serve the interests of peace, he pointed out that if expediency were once allowed to take the place of principle, the door would inevitably be opened to further concessions.[24]

Early the next morning after this letter was written, three Democratic leaders in the House—Clark, Kitchin, and Flood—called on the President to inform him of the sentiment in Congress. The President was told that the McLemore resolution would carry overwhelmingly if it were brought to a vote soon. Wilson declared that he would stand by his announced policies despite congressional resolutions. When the Congressmen asked what would be done if American lives were lost as the result of an armed ship's being torpedoed, Wilson insisted that he would break relations with the Central Powers. Quizzed further, the President admitted that the next step, logically, was war. American intervention in the war might have the effect of bringing it to an end sooner than otherwise, the President answered to a question put to him by one of the Congressmen in regard to the effect of American intervention. Wilson emphasized at this conference, however, that his policies were those of peace and not of war.[25]

When the conversation at the conference held on the morning of February 25 was made known to Gore, he was more than ever convinced that war was imminent. As a result of the two conferences on February 21 and 25,[26] he introduced in the Senate on the afternoon of February 25 his concurrent resolution which expressed the sense of Congress that United States citizens should not exercise their rights to travel on armed ships.[27] Admitting before he presented this resolution that he did not expect it to prevail, Gore expressed his belief that if it did by chance pass both houses of Congress, President Wilson and Secretary of State Robert M. Lansing would take cognizance of it.[28] When the Senate delayed action on the resolution, Gore appeared unperturbed. The day after it had been introduced, he stated that the discussion created by it throughout the nation had accomplished his purpose: to give unofficial warning against travel on armed ships.[29]

Despite Gore's outwardly casual attitude toward the fate of his resolution, as long as it and the McLemore resolution remained unconsidered, an unstable situation existed. In a very real sense, whether the President or the Congress controlled the nation's foreign policy depended upon the outcome of these resolutions before the Congress. After working to bring the straying Democratic members into the administration's fold and when he was certain of a favorable vote, Wilson wrote a letter on February 29 to Edward A. Pou of North Carolina, acting chairman of the House Committee on Rules, in which he demanded politely but firmly that Congress act on the McLemore and Gore resolutions.[30] Wilson informed the press that the way to avoid war was to have the American people stand solidly behind the Executive in his handling of the armed-ship negotiations. His opinion was that the resolution of warning would lead toward war rather than away from it.[31]

The debate on the Gore resolution began on March 2. As soon as the Senate roll call was concluded, Stone made a short speech in which he called attention to the international situation and explained the immediate problem confronting the upper chamber. Admitting his own differences with the President, he stated that he nevertheless desired to bring the Congress to support the President in the conduct of diplomatic questions. In order to define more clearly the attitude of Congress, he suggested that action be taken immediately on the pending resolution. Following Stone, Henry Cabot Lodge and John Sharp Williams expressed their favorable opinion of the President's stand, the latter criticizing the Congress for interfering with the State Department's negotiations and hampering the President.

Gore obtained the floor when Williams was seated, defended his position, and explained his reasons for introducing the resolution. Reiterating that he realized an American citizen had the technical right to travel the high seas, he stressed that in the interest of all Americans that right should be temporarily withdrawn. Since the issuance of passports was discretionary with the State Department, he said, the Secretary would undoubtedly observe any injunction sent to him by Congress. Thus, this resolution would accomplish the end the Senator had in view when he introduced two bills in January, 1916, which would have *required* American citizens to refrain from traveling on armed ships. But what about the people traveling on belligerent nations' ships who had pressing business abroad? Gore's answer: let them travel on ships of neutral nations. To the argument that it would be a loss of dignity to warn Americans off armed ships, Gore noted that neutral Sweden had taken such action and had not lost international respect.

Further defending his action, Gore related a version of a conference which had been reported to him by "the highest and most responsible authority" at which the President was purported to have told certain Senate and House leaders that if Germany insisted upon her position the United States would insist upon hers; that it would probably be followed by a state of war; and that a state of war might not be of itself an evil, since the United States by entering the war might be able to bring it to an end by midsummer and thus render a great service to civilization. Gore emphasized as he made these startling remarks on the Senate floor that he did not know whether the report he had heard was true, but it came to him in such a way that he feared it might be true. And if this were even conceivable he felt that, discharging his duty as a Senator, he could not withhold whatever small service he might render to avert the catastrophe of war. Reiterating that he had no desire to interfere with diplomatic relations or negotiations, Gore stated that he was not willing to see this nation involved in war over an insignificant technicality.[32]

Gore's reference to "a conference" between the President and certain legislators and his charge that the President had indicated a desire for war at that conference set off speculation concerning a secret rendezvous which has come to be called the "Sunrise Conference." The Senator's confused remarks plus his and his associates' faulty memories have helped perpetuate the myth of a secret meeting. Gore's remarks in the Senate on March 2 and his subsequent remarks and writings on the subject indicate that he had confused information which he had received concerning the two conferences of February 21 and 25. The statements quoted by the Senator on March 2 which he attributed to the President are obviously a somewhat exaggerated account of remarks made at the conference of February 25.[33] Yet Gore implied that Senators Stone and Kern were at the meeting to which he was referring, and the only meeting these men attended together was the one on February 21. In the heat of the controversy, with the President and the legislators misunderstanding each other's motives, inaccurate reports of the President's remarks, perhaps too readily accepted as true by Gore and others, were easily exaggerated by rumor. In the light of the circumstances Gore's confusion concerning the conferences is understandable. It is now clear that the conference held on the morning of February 25, 1916, with press coverage on February 26 and March 3, was the so-called "Sunrise Conference."[34]

On March 3 the Senate again considered the Gore resolution, which had been dismissed for other matters after the brief debate the previous day. McCumber offered a substitute for the Gore resolution which was nothing more than the original, but the author had reworded it to try to make it more acceptable to some of the President's supporters. As soon as the substitute was read, it was immediately moved that the Gore resolution and all substitutes for it and amendments to it be laid on the table. At this point Gore rose to a point of personal privilege and modified his resolution. Striking out the heart of it, he substituted these words: "The sinking by a German submarine, without notice or warning, of an armed merchant vessel of her public enemy, would constitute a just and sufficient cause of war between the United States and the German Empire."[35]

After this shocking "amendment" had been presented, virtual chaos resulted as numerous Senators clamored for recognition while Vice-President Thomas R. Marshall rapped for order. When Wesley

L. Jones of Washington asked if it was too late to offer an amendment, Marshall announced it was "too late to offer anything." Gore called for the regular order and the roll call began. James P. Clarke of Arkansas made the point that the resolution could not be considered in its amended form until the following day except by unanimous consent, since it was an entirely new resolution. The Chair did not sustain the point of order. Borah asked for a parliamentary inquiry, but Marshall ruled that the roll call must proceed since Henry F. Ashurst of Arizona had answered to his name. The new Gore resolution was then promptly tabled by a vote of 68 to 14, Gore himself voting in favor of tabling.[36] Several Senators later confessed they did not know what the amendment contained because of the confusion prior to the vote.

If it is true that Gore was simply attempting to help preserve American neutrality by introducing his resolution, why did he suddenly amend the resolution, making it a virtual declaration of war on the part of the United States if American lives were lost through submarine attack? He had indicated earlier that the purpose of his original resolution was to discover indirectly whether the loss of American lives on a ship of war was sufficient cause for a declaration of war, and thus his move was not inconsistent with his primary motive.[37] By amending his resolution, Gore was actually reversing its meaning so that it became a parody on the President's stand that no American right should be surrendered, no matter what the cost. The administration's stand was practically the same as that expressed in the amended resolution: an infringement upon American rights would mean a virtual declaration of war by the United States. (Wilson had used the term "strict accountability" in regard to German submarines' taking American lives.) Many charged that Gore's opposition to Wilson was so violent that he amended his resolution for no other reason but to embarrass the President, since the altered resolution was in fundamental accord with Wilson's announced position.

Gore considered his move to amend his resolution a shrewd one. He knew that his original resolution did not have a chance to pass at the time Wilson requested a vote of confidence by demanding a vote on it. A majority of Senators were loyal to the President and would not vote against him on this important issue. Knowing that Wilson's followers did not want war even though they supported the President's position, Gore thus had them express that point of view by voting to table the amended resolution. Actually the tabling of the *amended* resolution was no victory for anyone, since no one really believed that the loss of an American life on an armed ship was just cause for going to war. The only satisfaction the administration could claim was that it was able to muster enough votes to kill the original resolution even though it did not get an opportunity to prove it.[38] Wilson had asked for a vote on the Gore resolution; instead, he got a vote tabling a resolution epitomizing his own policies. He did not win a victory on the question at stake, nor did any clear-cut expression of sentiment of those voting emerge. If Wilson was the victor, it was by default.[39]

No such shallow triumph was reported by the press at the time. Firmly behind the President in his effort to quash the resolution, many newspapers declared in blaring headlines after the Senate's tabling action that *the* Gore resolution had been overwhelmingly defeated.[40] If it was pointed out that the resolution had been amended to become an entirely new resolution, such a statement was far down in the article or even placed in the column "continued on the next page."[41] Wilson's opponents hardly had a fair hearing as the press of the land rallied to defend its popular leader. Taking its cue from the press, the public at large expressed negligible interest in Gore's parliamentary tactics. The vote was accepted by the American people as a resounding victory of the executive over the legislative branch of the government; no longer was the Congress to interfere with matters within the President's jurisdiction.

Throughout the armed-ship controversy, several influential newspapers had kept to a minimum the strength of the President's opponents by attaching to them a pro-German label. Chief among these was the New York *World*, which obdurately concentrated its attack on a supposedly powerful German lobby in the spring of 1916. On March 7 the *World* in large headlines claimed it had documentary proof that a German lobby had spurred the legislative revolt against the President. The National German-American Alliance, said the *World*, was the driving force behind the Gore and McLemore resolutions as evidenced by documents the *World* had procured from the office of Alphonse G. Koelble, president of the United German Societies of New York. This sensational exposé added a colorful climax to the spring controversy. Gore scoffed at the charge: "There is nothing easier to say than that Senators and Congressmen have been influenced by a German lobby. This argument proves nothing except the absence of any other argument. It would be just as easy to say that the paper making the charge has been bought, bribed, corrupted, and debauched by the American owners of British ships . . . [and] bonds, by a pro-British lobby in the United States."[42]

Actually the *World*'s "documentary" evidence proved to be nothing more than a few stolen papers, some of which were marked confidential, their true meaning unclear because of their incompleteness. Upon close scrutiny it became evident to unprejudiced observers that the only sinister attribute of the documents published by the *World* was the means by which they had come into the paper's possession![43] Gore's own background was Anglo-Irish and the southwestern state which he represented contained a negligible number of people having ties with the German fatherland. There is no evidence whatever that Gore was in sympathy with the German cause, even though adverse propaganda pointed out how his position assisted that government, and newspapers quoted the sympathetic reaction of the German press to his resolution.[44] It is true that both German and Allied propagandists were working in this country and it is possible that Wilson's antagonists were subconsciously influenced by German propaganda. On the other hand, it must be remembered that the majority in the country was leaning toward the British side (as, indeed, Wilson may have unconsciously been doing) and, therefore, any leader who was trying to be strictly neutral would be strongly criticized. Gore was honestly trying to be neither pro-German nor pro-Allies.

Although definitely not a pacifist in the sense that he opposed war under any circumstances,[45] Gore was one of those progressives who tended toward isolationism. But he opposed involvement in the European war for another reason. By this time an economic conservative, he had pledged himself to reducing government expenses and saving the taxpayers' money, and he knew that a declaration of war would bring havoc to the Treasury. Pacifist-progressive tendencies, opposition to militarism, obsession with saving the taxpayers' money, and a fear that the President desired war forced Gore in the spring of 1916 to advocate suspension of what he considered a trivial right in order to lessen America's chances of becoming a part of the European conflict. Although it is now known that Wilson was not trying to maneuver this country into war in the early months of 1916, at the time it was not so apparent, and Gore's stand must be understood in the light of what was then known.

Disregarding what was behind Gore's clash with the President, it is a fact that the position of the State Department was legally unsustainable. The old rules of international law were outmoded in the era of the submarine, and such vague terms as "defensive" and "offensive" armor could not be applied. The administration was clinging to the principle of defending American rights on armed ships because it had waited too long to warn its citizens off these ships. By its silence, it had allowed its citizens to believe that they had a legal right to be protected by the United States while traveling on belligerent vessels.[46]

Gore did not relent in his stand for neutrality after the open clash with the President. In May, 1916, he introduced a concurrent resolution to pledge Congress and the people of the United States to support all efforts of the President to maintain "even-handed and undiscriminating" neutrality and to facilitate the establishment of a permanent peace.[47] Whether done in sincerity or to embarrass the President, such action on Gore's part indicated his desire for neutrality.

At the outbreak of the European conflict, the President in a speech to the Senate had proclaimed: "Every man who really loves America will act and speak in the true spirit of neutrality. . . . We must be impartial in thought as well as in action."[48] As the speaker of those lofty sentiments seemed to be drifting toward the side of the Allies in action as well as thought, Gore attempted to adhere to them.

The first indication of a rift in a heretofore solid friendship between the President and the Senator, the armed-ship controversy was a portent of their future disagreements and ultimate complete break. It was also the first of several events which led to the Senator's defeat in his bid for re-election in 1920.

VI. FIGHTING A WAR AND A
CONSTITUENCY

"I DO NOT DESIRE to go as a delegate to the St. Louis Convention. The honors conferred upon me by the democracy of Oklahoma equal my aspiration and surpass my deserts. I should feel myself as ungrateful and greedy as a monopolist if I should seek to corner still further favors."[1] With these words Senator Gore absented himself from the Democratic National Convention of 1916, which had no difficulty in choosing Woodrow Wilson as its candidate for a second term. But Gore was not indifferent to the pre-election activities which followed. Traveling widely over the United States, he campaigned for the national ticket with peace and progressivism as his major themes. He lauded the Democrats' domestic achievements and described the "blessings of peace due to President Wilson's wise leadership."[2] Under the direction of the National Democratic Speakers' Committee, Gore was sent in late October to California, generally conceded at that time to be a stronghold of progressivism. Punctuating his speeches with innocuous sarcasm and sly humor, Gore continued to dwell upon the subjects of peace and progressivism. He campaigned widely in the Pacific Coast state, attempting to show that the Democratic party was the progressive party by pointing to its legislative accomplishments of the past three and one-half years.

The election of 1916 was one of the closest in the electoral college this country has ever witnessed. When the returns were in from the East and Midwest, it looked as if the Republican candidate, Charles Evans Hughes, would be the next President of the United States. But as the Far West returns began pouring in, Wilson's total rose. With all but California reported, it became apparent that whoever carried that state with its thirteen electoral votes would win. The election remained in doubt for three long days. At last California was officially placed in Wilson's column, and by an electoral vote of 277 to 254 the President was re-elected. He had carried California by less than 4,000 votes.

Many factors joined to give Wilson the razor-thin victory. The labor vote, the women's vote, and the Socialist vote were large blocs which may have swung doubtful states to Wilson.[3] Many theories have been advanced for California's going Democratic. Hughes's purported snub of progressive Senator Hiram Johnson has been said to have lost the election for the Republican candidate. Progressive irritation at the Republican party in general has also been advanced with some basis. Oklahomans proclaimed that the oratory of their Senator easily swayed a few thousand doubtful votes for Wilson; thus, they gave Gore credit for carrying California and insuring Wilson's re-election. Though later admitting that he had "received more credit than I deserved in 1916 for carrying California for Wilson,"[4] at the time Gore did not minimize the impression that his campaigning was of distinct importance in the election. Since many factors influenced the California voters, no one of them can be singled out for that state's going Democratic, but it is undoubtedly true that the promises of continued peace, prosperity, and progressive legislation made by numerous Democratic orators had effect on the California voters. To that extent Gore must be given some credit, for he preached that Democratic theme with gusto and at length in California.

After the Democratic victory in November, 1916, the President stepped up his peace crusade, but events in Europe hindered progress. The Germans intensified their submarine campaign following the American presidential election, and on January 31, 1917, they announced that after February 1 their submarines would sink without warning all ships, neutral as well as belligerent, traveling in the war zone around the British Isles, France, Italy, and the eastern Mediterranean. This pronouncement resulted in a breach of diplomatic relations between the two countries, even though Wilson continued to talk of peace.[5] At the same time he steadfastly refused to ask Congress for authority to arm American merchant ships.

When Wilson received word of the Zimmermann note in which the German Minister to Mexico was instructed to propose an alliance with Mexico if Germany and the United States went to war, Wilson at last went before a joint session of Congress on February 26 to ask for authority to arm American merchant ships. The House quickly acted upon the President's request, but the Senate's noninterventionists found it unacceptable. By filibustering until the session expired on March 4, they were able to prevent a vote from being taken. After the Senate adjourned without passing the armed-ship measure, Wilson indignantly declared, "A little group of willful men, representing no opinion but their own, have rendered the great Government of the United States helpless and contemptible."[6] Wilson then made plans to arm American ships by executive order.

During the month of March several American merchant vessels were sunk without warning, resulting in heavy loss of life. Calling the Congress into special session on the evening of April 2, the President advised the legislators that the actions of the Imperial German Government were nothing less than war against the government and people of the United States.[7] Two days after Wilson made this world-must-be-made-safe-for-democracy speech, the Senate voted 82 to 6 for a declaration of war against Germany; on April 6 the House concurred with a vote of 373 to 50; on the following afternoon the President signed the resolution. The United States and Germany were officially at war.

The participation of Senator Gore in the events between the presidential election in November, 1916, and the declaration of war in April, 1917, was almost nil. Although attending the first part of the second session of the Sixty-fourth Congress from December 4 through December 22 when a recess was taken for the Christmas vacation, Gore contributed virtually nothing. When the session reconvened on January 2, 1917, Gore was in his seat, but on January 3 he failed to appear because of illness. This illness removed him from the national scene until April 11, seven days after the Senate action on the declaration of war.[8]

These facts are particularly important, since Gore's political opponents in every election in which he was involved after this time charged that he was a member of the "little group of willful men" who filibustered the armed-ship bill to death and that he voted against entering the war. These charges have become so general that many writers when giving a brief sketch of Gore or when casually mentioning him in connection with some other event inevitably state that Gore was one of the "willful twelve" or one who voted against the war declaration.[9] Having become ill with a serious circulatory infection during the Christmas holidays, Gore was delirious by February 5 and remained unconscious until the middle of March.[10] Rather than taking part in the filibuster as charged, Gore was totally unaware that a controversial bill was pending or that a filibuster was in progress. Nor was he present when the vote for war was taken on April 2.

The six who voted against the war declaration were Gronna, La Follette, Lane, Norris, Stone, and Vardaman.[11]

Not all of the misunderstanding revolving around Gore's stand on war can be attributed to his opponents. The Senator himself has added to the confusion. Of the eight members absent on April 4 all but Gore sent official word that had they been present they would have voted for war.[12] Later Gore announced that he opposed the declaration and would have voted against it had he been there. But "opposed" and "voted against" are not the same, and this distinction has caused some writers to err. In all likelihood the Senator would have voted as he indicated, but there is the possibility that he would not have done so even though he often afterward declared what his action would have been. Having been ill from January to April, the Senator was completely out of touch with national and international affairs. Pivotal events having direct bearing on the United States' entry into war happened during those three months, changing many people's opinions in regard to entry into war. Gore himself could not have known positively how he might have voted under such changing conditions. Had he been aware of all events during those months he might have changed his position as did a majority of the American public. After all, he both favored and voted for the resolution declaring war against Austria-Hungary in December, 1917.[13]

Of the several momentous war measures passed by Congress in the spring and summer of 1917, the application of the selective service law touched Americans in the most obvious way. In his war message on April 2, the President had implied that the volunteer system, the American military policy generally used for raising manpower in past wars, was to be abandoned. With Secretary of War Newton D. Baker preparing the American public by campaigning for a change from the past policies of this country, the majority of the populace and its representatives were prepared for a selective service bill when the first one was presented in Congress on April 21.[14]

But Senator Gore was not of this group. Believing conscription to be an aspect of military despotism, he favored the draft only as a last resort. He feared that in its "unique attempt to substitute democracy for military despotism in Germany" this country by installing conscription would incur "the risk of substituting military despotism for democracy in America."[15] He believed that the young men of America were not being given a chance to prove that the traditional volunteer system would continue to function, and he disliked having to think of them as being forced to join the armed services through a selective service law. Bluntly expressing his sentiment in a telegram to the Oklahoma City *Daily Oklahoman* on the day of the vote on the draft bill, Gore made his position clear: "I am not quite convinced that an army of conscripted slackers (I dislike the word) would excel either in valor, efficiency, or patriotism an army of patriotic volunteers. Why should we brand the American boy as a conscript without affording him the opportunity to earn the glory of an American volunteer? Are we the degenerate sons of heroic sires? Let us give patriotism a chance before resorting to Prussianism."[16]

Voting against the bill to establish the selective service system, Gore began in April, 1917, a series of negative votes on the draft which placed him at odds with the administration and his constituents.

When a bill to draft eighteen- and nineteen-year olds was introduced with the administration's blessing, Gore rebelled vocally. To him the drafting of eighteen-year-olds was "shocking to the sensibilities" and "makes one think of robbing a bird's nest." When it was apparent that the bill would pass, the Senator tried to amend the bill "to prevent so far as possible the sending of men to serve abroad before they attain the age of 19."[17] The bill passed the Senate without Gore's amendment by a vote of 75-0, but it was unanimous only after Gore changed his original vote. When it appeared that Gore's was to be the only negative ballot, several of his colleagues urged him to withhold his opposition in order to make the vote unanimous, thus impressing the enemy with the Senate's unity.[18] At the completion of the roll call the Senator announced that he was unwilling to be the only member to prevent a unanimous roll call in favor of the measure. But because he had not yet been convinced that events justified the drafting of boys of this age group, he stated that it was impossible for him to favor the measure. He asked permission to be excused from voting and this request was granted.[19]

In his opposition to the draft, Gore thought that he was appealing to the patriotism of his constituency. But the propaganda for a conscripted army advanced by the War Department was quite effective. The young men of the nation were generally convinced that it was more patriotic not to volunteer but rather to be drafted so that the leaders could determine where and how each man could best serve his country. Gore's appeal to patriotism and his language about "conscripted slackers" reacted against him. Indeed, so acceptable was the administration's selective service law that Gore's very appeal to patriotism came to be interpreted as unpatriotic on his part. While Gore was equating patriotism with the volunteer system, the people of Oklahoma were equating it with support of the Wilson policies. Influenced by the *Daily Oklahoman,* which came to question the Senator's loyalty and integrity, a majority of the Oklahoma press and electorate began to interpret Gore's votes as direct affronts to the popular President.

As Gore continued his independent path throughout the summer of 1917, more and more Oklahomans opposed him. The opposition became stronger when Gore suggested that no money be appropriated to transport drafted men to Europe unless they first volunteered for overseas duty. This amendment was perverted by the press in Oklahoma to mean that Gore wanted to prohibit the shipment of food and clothing to American soldiers overseas and to withdraw financial support from them. According to a survey of 225 Oklahoma newspapers, not a single editorial column openly supported the Senator after he purportedly took this stand. A breakdown of the survey indicated that 112 papers were criticizing the Senator, 108 carried no editorials, and five, though not agreeing with him, apologized for his actions.[20]

Opposition to Gore became more outspoken and bitter as additional newspaper space was devoted to his stand in the summer and early fall of 1917. He received more attention in the papers than did all the other members of the Oklahoma delegation in Washington combined. It was observed in the Drumright *News* that "Oklahoma is getting more and more ashamed to claim Senator Gore as her own." In the Stigler *Beacon* it was written, "His studied opposition to the president is becoming embarrassing." The editor of the *Beacon* called the Senator a demagogue who was "positively dangerous" to the country. The Sayre *Headlight* and the Afton *American* hinted that Gore was a sympathizer if not a member of the discredited I.W.W. The Eufaula *Indian-Journal* punned, "With all his brazen talk and misrepresentation of this country, it does seem to us that the United States and Oklahoma . . . have been Gored enough." The Binger *Journal* referred to him as "T. Parasite Gore." Another paper headlined "620 More Days of Gore" and periodically announced the number of days remaining in Gore's Senate term. The editor of the Healdon *Herald* stated that the next person he would support for governor of Oklahoma would be "anti-German, anti-Gore from Dan to Beersheba and no halfway measures or promises accepted. And we'd be greatly interested in a statement from the gubernatorial candidates as to just how they stand with reference to the Kaiser's right-hand man in America, T. P. Gore."[21]

Continuing its influential attack, the *Daily Oklahoman* editorialized: "It will be remembered of Senator Gore that he wanted Americans to get off the seas, that he wanted this country to stop sending munitions to the allies, that he opposed the selective draft, that he would have voted against the war had he been present when the vote was taken, that he objects to sending American soldiers to Europe and he is against the Liberty bonds. But in every other respect Brother Gore is one of the most implacable enemies of autocracy."[22]

The irony of the whole controversy during August and September, 1917, was that Gore insisted he was voting the true sentiment of the people of Oklahoma. He contended that his mail was more than twenty-to-one in favor of his position on the subject of conscription and that 90 per cent of it throughout the summer had approved of his opposing the several war measures.[23] Opposition was generated, he believed, by the press of Oklahoma, which he called the "subsidized mistress of plutocracy." He held that the criticism of his actions was largely limited to a few politicians "who seem to be dazzled by the splendor of power."[24]

Gore continually stirred the burning embers of opposition by sending sarcastic telegrams and writing impassioned letters to Oklahoma. After he received a telegram from S. P. Smith, editor of the Konawa *Chief-Leader,* who expressed the Konawa homeguard's disapproval of the Senator's voting record, Gore wired Smith: "Thanks for your telegram. I enjoy a good joke. Your message reminded me of the ass in the fable that was masquerading in a lion skin. He was cutting a great swath among the other animals until he undertook to roar. Selah." Smith replied: "You are quite welcome to the telegrams. I think we shall be able to send you some more good jokes real soon. In fact, from the way they are going, I am afraid you are going to laugh your fool self to death."[25]

When Alger Melton, chairman of the Oklahoma Democratic National Committee, telegraphed Gore requesting that he resign or represent the people of Oklahoma respecting war legislation, Gore wrote a long letter in which he defended his position and voting record. But he harmed his own cause by disturbing already ruffled feathers in writing to Melton: "I acknowledge no dictator; I obey no boss. . . . I shall not . . . do obeisance to a would-be boss. You will pardon me therefore, if I decline to permit you to dictate my official conduct." To the demand that he step down he further alienated good will by offering to resign and to ask for a vote of confidence if President Wilson and all those who voted for the war and the draft would do the same. "Till you arrange the referendum," he smugly concluded, "I must continue to discharge my duty as I see it."[26] Believing that the state's large rural element was on his side, Gore was confident that a popular referendum such as he suggested, improbable though he knew it was, would be in his favor. Obsessed with the idea of a popular vote and continuing to antagonize his opponents, he introduced in August, 1917, a joint resolution in the Senate proposing an amendment to the Constitution requiring a popular vote before a declaration of war could be made by Congress.[27]

On its front page on August 31, 1917, the *Daily Oklahoman* quoted Mike Donnelly, commissioner of accounting and finance in Oklahoma, as saying that "because Gore is opposing Wilson's war policies every man, woman, and child in Oklahoma should sign a petition calling on him to resign." At the urging of the paper to act on this suggestion, thousands of people signed hundreds of petitions requesting Gore to step down from his Senate post. These resign-or-work-with-the-administration petitions, often drawn up and signed in mass meetings, came from all over the state. The only consolation Gore had in receiving them was that many of his supporters countered by sending him petitions requesting that he not resign.[28] Although never giving an inventory of the strength of his opposition, Gore reported that he had received letters and petitions endorsing his position from all but three of the state's seventy-seven counties.[29] Certainly some of the grass-roots areas defended the Senator, but the overwhelming majority of Oklahomans believed that Gore had assumed an arrogant, unpatriotic attitude during the controversy. At least one preacher of importance delivered a sermon against him. In a diatribe lasting over an hour, a presiding elder of the Oklahoma City district of the Methodist Episcopal Church, South bitterly denounced Gore and placed him in a category with Benedict Arnold. At the height of the controversy the city of Enid changed the name of its community park from "Gore" to "Wilson."[30]

With emotion taking precedence over reason, rumors—some founded on legitimate misunderstandings, others deliberately misconstruing the facts, and still others wholly baseless—were quick to receive attention and publication. The rumor which probably hurt Gore more than any other was the charge that he believed that the selective service law was unconstitutional and that young men should resist the draft. In reply to a constituent's request, Gore had quoted in a telegram the exact language of the law in regard to people exempt from the draft because of religious tenets. The anti-Gore press deliberately misconstrued this statement, the *Daily Oklahoman* blazing in a tall red-ink headline: "GORE WIRES AID TO ANTI-DRAFT AGITATORS."[31] It was charged that Gore was circulating literature to the effect that the draft law was unconstitutional, that those drafted under it were being subjected to unlawful imprisonment, and that citizens were not obligated to obey it. The rumor so garbled the meaning and facts of the telegram that the constituent's name was even corrupted from "Capirs" to "Cappers." With so few news outlets in Oklahoma willing to give him a hearing, Gore had much difficulty quashing the charge that he had encouraged draft resisters. Whenever he had the opportunity, he made his position unequivocally clear: he did not think the draft law unconstitutional; he did not think that those who were selected under the draft act were being subjected to unlawful imprisonment; he did not believe that any citizen should disobey the draft law or any other law.[32]

When the *Daily Oklahoman* reported that Governor R. L. Williams had requested Gore to resign, the Governor denied the report. In an open letter to Gore the Governor wrote, "I don't agree with your position on the war, but I am writing you this letter to advise you that I am trying to preserve all official propriety, and that I never gave out any interview to be placed in the *Oklahoman* or any other paper relative to your resigning. Personally, I feel very kindly toward you and I regret that you have taken the extreme position on the war question that you have."[33]

Gore, of course, had no intention of resigning, and those opponents who knew him well were aware of this fact. This did not deter them from contributing to the popular clamor. The *Daily Oklahoman* on September 16, 1917, in a widely circulated Sunday edition ran huge headlines which read: "Gore—He won't resign, but He'll repent." The second and smaller headline read: "Adroit and opportune Before, He has fed and fattened on Sympathy, but now he is withering in contempt, the most conspicuous object of condemnation Oklahoma has ever known, for political judgment has failed." Then followed a damning article by Walter Ferguson, editor of the Cherokee *Republican,* in which Gore was attacked on the lowest level. Purely political in nature, this article undoubtedly reinforced the doubts of many who were trying to retain their objectivity but who were being influenced by the increasing bulk and intensity of propaganda against him.

Gore was perplexed by the controversy raised over his voting record. Of the voluntary system of recruiting an army he wrote, "One's wisdom might possibly be questioned for voting to stand by so ancient and so sacred a tradition, but it would hardly seem to lay his patriotism open to impeachment."[34]

Considerable opposition to Gore was founded not so much on his disapproval of any particular measure but in general on his not agreeing with the President. This attitude Gore was unable to comprehend. Puzzled when he was criticized for opposing the President, the Senator pointed out that democracy thrives on disagreement and that absolutism would develop if the legislators were obligated to give up their views without question in order to agree with the Chief Executive. Gore refused to be intimidated by the opposition of what he termed the "President-worshipers." "The doctrine that the President can do no wrong," he wrote, "would be as deadly to democracy as the ancient doctrine that the king can do no wrong was fatal to human liberty. . . . I never shall bow the knee and place my hands in the hands of [a] mortal man and pledge myself to be his man." He refused to support what he considered "shortsighted and inconsiderate legislation" simply to curry favor with the President or to escape the criticism of the press.[35]

The Republican Muskogee *Daily Phoenix* estimated at the height of the controversy that 75 per cent of the Oklahoma voters were opposed to Gore.[36] The Senator claimed that the opposition was actually limited to the press and his political opponents. The truth lies somewhere between the two extremes. Certainly the paper's estimate is too high, judging from the friendly petitions and letters Gore received, but Gore did not understand conditions in Oklahoma when he made his statement regarding the situation there. He most certainly would have been defeated if an election had been called in the fall of 1917.

Although the furor over Gore's position receded after October, 1917, it intermittently flared up from that time until his defeat in 1920. When the Senator attended a state Democratic party convention in Oklahoma City in September, 1918, he was not invited to speak. A resolution requesting him to address the convention had been prepared, but it was withheld apparently because the sentiment was so strong among the delegates against his anti-administration voting record.[37] The Oklahoma press interpreted Gore's failure to appear on the platform as a definite, albeit deserved, snub of the Senator by the Oklahoma Democrats.

Gore's voting habits were not altered as a result of the opposition engendered in Oklahoma because of his votes in 1917 regarding the draft. In the spring of 1918 he voted against an amendment providing for universal military training, continuing to express his disapproval of compulsory systems of military service. Re-emphasizing his opposition to militarism, Gore paraphrased Scripture: "What would it profit a nation like our own if it should extinguish militarism everywhere and lose its own democracy?" To the perennial charge that his stand was not looked upon with favor by President Wilson, he replied, "I have made it a rule to obey my own duties as a Member of the Senate of the United States. Any other rule of action would be fit only for a toothless suckling at the breast of power."[38]

Gore further strained his relationship with his constituency by his stand on military pensions. Having opposed the drafting of men with dependent families until "stern necessity" required it, he did not favor giving pensions to dependent families of soldiers. Gore predicted that once pensions were given to families who had members in the armed services the practice would never end. He could see no logic in granting a pension to a family *before* a soldier gave his life for his country. "Shall we then withdraw the $50 a month from his dependent family after he dies? Is this a precedent for a universal pension of $50 a month?"[39] When he was charged with wanting to starve the family of a soldier who was at the front imperiling his life in defense of his nation's honor, Gore replied, "That is not the issue as I conceive it to be. I know of no alchemy by which you can convert into cash the tears of a wife or widow. I do not know how to translate the orphan's tears into the coin of the realm. I do not know the market price of a sigh or a sob."[40] Here again Gore's constituents failed to see the reasoning behind his actions. They only saw this as more evidence of his antagonism toward the administration.

Gore's opposition to war legislation did not end with strictly military measures. Finding many of the emergency measures distasteful, he questioned on innumerable occasions their constitutionality and their infringement upon basic freedoms. When a bill was introduced providing for the punishment of any person who by word or act favored the German cause, Gore wondered aloud in the Senate chamber if such a measure would conflict with freedom of speech. When William Borah of Idaho declared it would not, Gore quizzed him specifically on the exact boundaries of this bill. Finding himself trapped by Gore's questions, Borah attempted to dismiss the misgivings with, "I do not understand that the Senator from Oklahoma is uneasy about himself." Gore retorted, "No. I cherish some lingering respect for the charter of our liberties."[41] Gore joined Senators Johnson of California, Vardaman of Mississippi, and Hardwick of Georgia to oppose this stringent act, and he was clearly one of the bill's most effective opponents, but there was never any doubt about the Senate's passing what became the Sedition Act of 1918.[42] Believing that the bill providing for censorship of the press went "hand in hand with despotism," he argued that even in wartime this freedom should not be restricted. "A free press is a palladium of liberty," he remarked. "The censorship matter strikes at the very foundation of one of the privileges of a free democracy, and I must oppose it on that ground."[43]

Gore also voted against government control during wartime of the nation's major transportation and communication facilities.[44] He contended that government operation of these facilities would decrease the efficiency and increase the cost of service.[45] Although supporting and voting for the espionage bill, Gore soon expressed regret for having done so, "because it has already been used or abused to throttle freedom of speech and freedom of the press."[46]

Gore's voting record was not entirely anti-administration. He voted for the war-risk insurance act which provided insurance for American soldiers, along with compensation, allotments, and allowances for their families. He also voted for an amendment which doubled soldiers' pay, as well as for a civil rights act for soldiers and seamen. Gore himself introduced an amendment to the National

Defense Act providing for a larger number of officers of high military rank in the medical corps of the regular army. He also supported such measures as the preferential shipping bill, the so-called trading-with-the-enemy act, and the bill to draft subjects of the Allied countries residing in the United States.

As a member of the Senate Finance Committee Gore helped prepare the war-revenue acts, and he voted for almost all of the major appropriation bills, aggregating more than $35,000,000,000.[47] He considered of prime importance in winning the war the bill setting aside $640,000,000 for the developing of an air force.

Although supporting these measures, Gore disagreed with administration leaders on how the war should be financed. He advocated greater taxes to meet increased expenditures, while the administration forces leaned toward borrowing. Opposing the majority report on the first war-revenue measure because of this difference, Gore nevertheless voted for the measure in its final form. But he was repelled at the idea of companies such as Bethlehem Steel, Du Pont, and United States Steel making huge war profits and then lending money to the government at interest. He felt that government with its absolute taxing power should get the money by taxes rather than through loans. He declared, "I would like to demonetize war. I might almost say, and say in no invidious sense, every dollar of war profits is dripping with blood and tears."[48]

Opposed to deficit spending, the Senator favored taxing the extra profits of the giant corporations. With farmers having their products artificially controlled, the idea of businesses and industries making huge profits from war contracts and lining the pockets of the already wealthy population was disgusting to Gore. If the Senator had had his way, a high flat rate—he failed to mention a specific figure—would have been established rather than the graduated scale of taxation on war profits which the Senate ultimately accepted. Gore favored the pay-as-you-go plan because, he contended, war profits must be taxed while they are being earned; they cannot be taxed after the war is over.[49] But Gore's economic theories were not considered valid by his associates, and his opinions often carried little weight. He had to be content to vote for measures more acceptable to others than to himself.

Gore also favored placing a prohibitory tax on beverage liquors and was instrumental in getting such a tax adopted. By this tax the nation could reduce drinking, save foodstuffs used in making the liquor, and gain revenue at the same time. He felt that taxes on war profits (collected his way), liquors, and incomes were adequate to raise the extra revenue needed for war, and in theory he opposed all other methods for raising war revenue.[50]

Foreseeing that a war debt of an unbelievable amount would be placed on this country if it did not pay for the war as it went along, Gore stressed time and time again that he did not want to pass a great debt on to future generations of Americans. His desire to keep the nation out of debt brought renewed criticism when he voted against a measure to give $100,000,000 to European countries for relief of their starving peoples.[51] He insisted he was not trying to be obstreperous when he cast this vote; he had voted for various loans to those countries and would vote for more, but consistent with his economic conservatism he refused to vote for an outright gift.

Ever mindful of the cost of the war, Gore introduced a resolution to create a select committee on economy and retrenchment to study appropriations and expenditures and to recommend the omission of unnecessary appropriations. When this resolution received no attention, he voted for an amendment offered by his colleague, Robert L. Owen, creating an auditing committee on expenditures in order to keep a strict account of government expenditures. Believing that those expenditures should be cut to an irreducible minimum, Gore was conscious of the millions of dollars wasted because of haste in time of war. Consistent with his retrenchment stand, he opposed paying government employees time and a half for overtime, and he voted for an amendment requiring government employees in Washington to do eight hours of work for eight hours of pay. He considered overtime work unusually inefficient and believed it a great waste to pay government employees for eight hours when they worked only seven.

Claiming to have originated the slogan "Draft money as well as men," Gore favored the various Liberty and Victory Loan drives and participated in some of them. Before the Southern Commercial Congress in New York on October 17, 1917, he said, "It is as much a public duty to buy bonds as to pay taxes. The man with the pocketbook must stand back of the boy with the bayonet. It would be almost as great a disaster to lose this liberty loan drive as to lose a battle in France."[52] On April 27, 1918, in a patriotic address at the Academy of Music in Brooklyn under the auspices of the Liberty Loan Committee of the City of New York, Gore was partially responsible for over $2,500,000 being subscribed to the Liberty Loan at that evening meeting. Substituting for Secretary of Agriculture David F. Houston at the final Liberty Loan mass meeting at Washington, Gore further showed his patriotism and support of the war by appealing for the buying of more bonds.

Gore may not have favored the nation's entry into the war in 1917 and his actions and comments during the war may have caused honest questions to be raised about his position, but he was not traitorous or even unpatriotic. He was obviously out of step with the times in his stand on such measures as the draft, but he cannot be impeached for that or for insincerity. He often failed to grasp the reality of the war situation when he cast his votes, but he refused to sacrifice his convictions for public favor. Wishing to bring the war to a successful conclusion, he trod his own independent path toward that goal.

VII. FOOD AND AGRICULTURAL LEGISLATION IN WARTIME

AMERICA'S ENTRY into World War I meant many things to many people. To the young men of the nation it meant that thousands of them would shortly be called into the armed forces of their country. To industries it meant greater output in order to supply the United States and its allies with munitions, machinery, and equipment. To the food-growing farmers it meant greatly increased production.

Secretary of Agriculture David F. Houston took the lead in making food help win the war when he invited all state commissioners of agriculture and presidents of agricultural and mechanical colleges to confer with him on plans for increasing the food supply.[1] Over sixty-five officials representing thirty-two states east of the Rocky Mountains met in April, 1917, to discuss the entire agricultural situation actuated by the emergency of the war. A similar conference for the states west of the Continental Divide was held at Berkeley, California. Making plans to stimulate agricultural production as much as possible during the war period, these experts laid out a comprehensive program divided into four main categories: production and labor, distribution and prices, economy and utilization, and effective organization.[2] Their undertaking called not only for expansion within the limits of existing law but also for additional legislation. On the basis of suggestions received at the two conferences, Secretary Houston submitted to congressional leaders proposals for increasing the production, improving the distribution, and promoting the conservation of farm products and foods.

In May President Wilson asked for legislation giving him extraordinary power over the entire food supply of the country. Although stating that the powers which he requested were strictly temporary and would disappear when the emergency had passed, the President asked for supreme authority over the whole category of foodstuffs from raw product to the finished article.[3] Requesting the right to regulate business relationships as well as the kinds and amounts of foods that should be consumed, he also desired broad powers relating to the problems of hoarding, manufacture, sale, and use of food-stuffs.[4] An inventory of the nation's food supply was high on the President's list. On the basis of the recommendations of Houston and Wilson, Congress set out to legislate on food output and food control.

Presiding over hearings in April and May, 1917, Gore, as chairman of the Agriculture Committee, directed most of his attention and efforts during the spring and summer of 1917 to the problems of food production and control.[5] The Senator was in complete accord with the President's request for a food survey, and in May he introduced a bill authorizing a food census. Opponents of the survey, led by James A. Reed of Missouri, believed that food investigators had no right to require farmers to reveal the amount of their stored foods. Because of this opposition, the question was debated many hours in the Senate and House before a similar House bill was ultimately accepted in August, 1917.[6] Gore worked hard for this recommendation of the President.

Except for the food survey the Senator generally did not agree with the President's wartime recommendations concerning food legislation. A sign of their differences appeared in May when the self-reliant Senator, without conferring with the President, introduced a resolution which he thought conveyed ample powers to the Chief Executive for the erection and operation of a rather complete system regarding food supplies.[7] When Wilson's attention was called to Gore's independent action, the President wrote to the Senator, "We are in danger, I fear, of multiplying unrelated pieces of machinery."[8]

The Senator's open opposition to administration-sponsored food legislation first appeared when the contents of the so-called Lever food control bill were fully known. Although favoring the purposes and objectives of the legislation, Gore concluded that the bill dele-gated unconstitutional powers to the Chief Executive, and in a conference on June 14 he informed the President of his position. At the President's suggestion the Senator agreed to take the bill out of committee to allow debate on it.[9] Thus, on June 15 Gore reported the administration bill back from the Agriculture Committee. The committee had been evenly divided on the measure, and compromise was impossible without eliminating many of its features. It was returned to the floor without amendment or recommendation to allow a detailed study by the entire Senate. Announcing that he could not support the measure unless it was materially amended, Gore delegated George Chamberlain of Oregon to take control of the measure on the floor. By divesting himself of any responsibility for the bill, Gore was able to oppose it without feeling obligated to follow the administration's wishes.

As originally drawn, the Lever food bill delegated broad powers to the Chief Executive on food production, distribution, and regulation. Its principal provision authorized exceptional powers to a food administrator not only over food production but also over many businesses in the nation. The debates in Congress brought out clearly the power which the bill would have placed in one individual's hands. Gore feared for the life of the business of the country if one man were given such wide authority. "One of the vital assets of the country in war time is its business," he asserted, "and nothing must be done to disturb it."[10] He remarked that the food administrator might become "a blood clot on the brain of business."[11] The section of the bill requiring businesses to secure licenses from the food administrator in order to operate repelled Gore. "To require a free man in a free country to take out a license to transact business when he should be encouraged to transact business runs counter to my view of first principles as well as of sound public policy," he declared.[12]

Gore not only objected to the wide powers relating to business to be invested in the food administrator, but also opposed virtually unlimited power over food regulation and production. Opponents of the bill pointed out that, as originally drawn, the measure gave the food administrator authority to regulate what should be served on the tables of the nation's households. Gore declared his opposition to one man's being able to tell another man that he must eat round steak even though he preferred sirloin or to eat neck steak after he ordered T-bone. Nor was the Senator willing to give one man the right to compel a farmer to plant a particular crop against the farmer's wishes.[13] Section one was so broad, Gore pointed out, that a farmer could not get a mortgage on a "stocking-footed mule or a calico pony" if the food administrator chose to forbid it.[14] Gore admitted that such powers might never be exercised, but this did not lessen his opposition. When an associate attempted to calm Gore's fears by declaring that no sane man would undertake to exercise them, Gore provokingly stated that he thought it was unwise for a body of sane men charged with responsibility to confer upon a person powers which no one but an insane man would attempt to exercise.[15]

As soon as the administration had decided on a plan for attacking the problems of food production and control, the President asked Herbert Hoover to serve as food administrator. Hoover had gained wide and favorable publicity serving in a similar capacity in several European countries. When it was apparent that the bill was to run into significant opposition, Wilson suggested that Hoover set up his office and organization to operate in an extralegal capacity until the food bill became law. Without legal authorization Hoover organized a voluntary food administration largely at his own expense.[16] Having completed his organization and his program for handling the wartime food situation, by June Hoover was prepared to take charge of regulations officially as soon as legal power was given to him.[17]

Hoover's fame as a practical economist was recognized by Gore, but this did not keep the Senator from attacking him. When Hoover expressed surprise that the food control measure gave him as much power as the opposition claimed, Gore charged that both Hoover and Wilson were advocating the passage of a bill which neither had read.[18] When the food administrator at one point complained because the Senate was delaying action on the food bill, Gore reminded his colleagues and Hoover that the Senate was acting under a unanimous consent agreement which provided for a vote on the bill at a certain date. The debates were not delaying the bill, he asserted. "Possibly Mr. Hoover had been too busy revising upward the dining-car menus," Gore suggested, "to have his attention called to this order of the Senate."[19]

Further revealing his dislike for the administration's plan to deal with the food situation, Gore referred to the members of an agricultural advisory committee as "alleged" farmers. To emphasize this charge Gore gave brief biographical sketches of the men which revealed that they were wealthy ranchers or large plantation owners. Contending that these twenty-four men on the committee selected by Hoover and Houston were not representative of the six million actual farmers in the United States, Gore, although not reflecting on the character of the committee members, indicated disapproval of their having power over agriculture during wartime.[20]

When it was charged that a lobby was operating against the food control bill, Gore offered a resolution to revive the Lobby Committee, expressing regret that the administration forces did not ask for its adoption. Such an act would have delayed the measure even longer, and perhaps this was Gore's real motive for offering the resolution. The President's remark that legislators who delayed the passage of the food bill were laying themselves open, whether unwittingly or not, to the charge of aiding and abetting speculators and others who might hold personal interest above the interest of the United States in the war emergency was interpreted by many as meant primarily for Gore, Reed, and their associates.[21]

Gore's opposition to the food control bill was believed by the Oklahoma press to be part of a scheme by the Senator to oppose everything suggested by the President relating to the war program. The reaction of the editor of the Enid *News* to the Senator's stand on the food bill was somewhat typical of those papers friendly to Gore: "We have never thought of Senator Gore standing in with the speculators in the food control problem. It is not like Senator Gore to do this. He is not of that sort, and we are loath to believe it yet. But it is getting to a place where we must have more explanation from him or we shall soon doubt his intentions." Other papers broke with Gore completely, criticizing him unmercifully for his position on the food bill. The Clinton *Messenger* editorialized, "Senator Gore of Oklahoma is blind morally, mentally and physically."[22]

When he learned that a group of Oklahoma oil producers objected to the inclusion of petroleum under the regulatory provisions of the food bill, Gore supported the protest wholeheartedly. He believed that oil was the last industry which should be subjected to governmental control and interference. Of the proposed law, he wrote for the benefit of the group, "It is virtually a business dictatorship. I do not think Mr. Hoover's genius, however great, would be a substitute for the accumulated business experience of six thousand years or for the business talents and energies of a hundred million people."[23] But the oil producers, like many other Oklahoma groups who disapproved of the Senator's conduct, were embarrassed by Gore's approval. In reply to his telegram and reversing their decision as a result of his support, they informed him: "If the careful and capable councils of the Administration determine to include our business within its proposed scope of dictatorship, as you call it, we will welcome the change and rely confidently upon the wisdom of the Administration to conduct the business for the good of all. . . . Candidly we resent your apparent effort to ensnare oil producers into seeming support of your antagonism to the wholesale Administration program of food control by meaningless platitudes relating to the oil industry."[24]

Gore repeatedly insisted that he had no quarrel with the President, but he did not aid his cause by making statements such as this: "Some seem to imagine that it [the food bill] comes to us in the handwriting of Divinity; that it would be a blasphemy and a sacrilege to lay our hands on the bill; and that [if we did] the wrathful lightnings of an offended Heaven would come down upon us as they did upon the presumptuous man who laid his hands upon the Ark of the Covenant."[25] Nor did he allay misgivings concerning his stand when he theorized: ". . . assume that . . . one day [there might] come to be the Chief Executive of this Republic, a man of dictatorial, of domineering disposition, a man of vaulting ambition, and that we should at the same time . . . have a subservient Congress, made up of drivelling sycophants, made up of fawning court favorites, made up of White House parrots. . . . It is in perilous times of that kind, should they ever come, that we need . . . an inviolate Constitution, to protect us against subservience of a Congress that might be willing to lick the dust at the feet of such a dictator."[26] Gore insisted that he was thinking of a hypothetical situation and that he was not referring to Wilson or the Congress of which he was a member, but obviously his statements were applicable to the situation confronting him. The administration leaders were not happy with his biting tongue or his studied opposition to the food control bill.

As the food measure made its slow way through the Senate, its opponents were strong enough numerically to write several of their amendments into it. They were able to strike out part of the sections which carried broad powers over production and consumption as distinguished from distribution. They were also able to remove the provision controlling farm financing, as well as the section giving Hoover the power to commandeer farmers' seed. As amended, the bill allowed the government to commandeer private property only for public uses connected with common defense.[27] But when Senate and House conferees gathered to reconcile their

100

differences on the bill, the Senate representatives often yielded to the demands of the delegates from the lower house, and several of the opposition-sponsored amendments were rejected in conference. Such action infuriated Gore. When the bill was being considered in the Senate in its final form, he accused the Senate conferees of receding too readily on amendments he favored. This charge caused Chamberlain to strike back at Gore's opposition. If Gore would tattoo "recede" on the foreheads of Senators who receded, commented the Oregonian, the word "obstruct" could be imbedded on the forehead of the Oklahoman.[28] President Wilson agreed that Gore had used "obstructionist" tactics, and thanked Chamberlain for making his remarks. "It is time that we put an end in the most emphatic way to the sort of tactics that have been indulged in," concluded the President in his note to Chamberlain.[29]

Gore denied deserving the obstructionist label. He reminded Chamberlain and the Senate that he had turned the bill over to friendly hands because he did not want to be liable to the suspicion of mismanagement or of an attempt to kill the measure under the false show of friendship. "I did not use the stiletto; I did not fight from ambush; I fought in the open field," he remarked, defending his action. Voting for the various amendments because they made the bill less disagreeable to him, the Senator did not admit that his actions constituted obstruction. "As a Senator of the United States ... I shall discharge my full duty as I see my duty," he declared. "I shall accept full responsibility. . . . I shall not be driven from the path of duty either by the threats of power nor decoyed from that path by the smiles and blandishments of power."[30]

Whether Gore deserved the obstructionist label lies in the definition of the term. That he was one of the most outspoken opponents of the bill there is no question. Because of his antipathy toward it he delegated an administration-approved member of the Agriculture Committee for the task of steering the bill through the Senate and then promptly led the opposition to it. To those who backed the administration such action appeared to be obstruction; to Gore it indicated fair play on his part and the exercise of his due prerogatives.

The Lever food control act as it was finally accepted and signed into law in August, 1917, was a far-reaching piece of legislation, giving the President wide powers for regulating food production, distribution, and prices. Section 14 of the act empowered the President to fix a reasonable, guaranteed price for wheat. On August 11, 1917, by virtue of this authority Wilson set a minimum of $2.00 per bushel for No. 1 northern spring wheat at Chicago.[31] Similar relative prices were established at other wheat centers of the nation.

When it became apparent that the fixed price was not only the minimum but also the maximum figure, Gore went into action. A conference with Food Administrator Hoover and a letter exchange with Secretary of Agriculture Houston assured him that the price was not the minimum but the absolute price.[32] In Gore's opinion, the laws of economics had been cast to the winds, but he resigned himself to working within the situation. Although opposing price fixing in principle, he advocated a higher absolute figure. In February, 1918, he introduced a resolution providing that the minimum price for the 1918 wheat crop be raised from $2.00 to $2.50 per bushel.

When this measure made no progress, Gore introduced an amendment to the agricultural appropriation bill proposing important changes in section 14 of the food control act. Not only designed to raise the guaranteed minimum wheat price to $2.50, this amendment would also substitute No. 2 northern wheat for No. 1 as the basic grade. Explicitly stating that the new price was to be the minimum and not the absolute price, it would also substitute the local elevator or the local railway market in the area where the wheat was grown for the principal interior primary markets as designated in the food control act.[33]

Because of agitation for a higher figure and unrest among the farmers, the President soon added twenty cents per bushel to the minimum price of wheat. The Wilson supporters insisted that $2.20 per bushel was adequate, but the farm representatives continued to labor for an even higher price. Responsible for steering the agricultural appropriation bill through the Senate, Gore took advantage of his position to include his amendment. The majority of the Agriculture Committee had favored his resolution, and it was no serious problem to obtain additional support for the wheat amendment. In March, 1918, by an overwhelming vote of 49 to 18 the Senate made the wheat amendment a part of the appropriation bill.[34]

Support for the Gore wheat amendment was not limited to the Senate. Gore received countless pieces of mail from all over the country favoring his position and explaining to him the conditions of the farmers in various sections of the wheat belt. Representatives of such farm organizations as the National Grange of the United States, the Farmers' Union of Oklahoma, the Wheat Growers' League, and the Nebraska Farmers' Union wrote the Senator attacking the existing price for wheat as unfair to the nation's wheat growers.

Gore believed these complaints to be just. He reasoned that the farmers were being discriminated against by being required to sell in a restricted market while having to buy in an unrestricted one. Analyzing the "Wheat Farmers' Dilemma," the Senator recognized four possible solutions. First, all restrictions whatever upon the price of wheat could be removed. If it were a commercial possibility to restore the wheat market overnight, he believed this reversal of the policy in effect would be the simplest solution to the problem. Second, the fixed price of wheat could be advanced to correspond with the general level of other advanced prices. When wheat could be sold for $3.75 per bushel if the market were open, Gore was attempting to apply this solution by raising the legal controlled price to $2.50. Third, the price of all other articles might be reduced to correspond with the reduced price of wheat. This Gore recognized as virtually impossible. As a fourth possibility he suggested that the price of wheat could be advanced and the prices of other articles reduced until they met on a common level.[35] But these suggestions were in reality academic. The Senator knew that the only practical approach to the problem was to raise the price of wheat as high as possible.

When the appropriation bill was considered in conference in April, 1918, all but one of the differences between the House and Senate versions were compromised with comparative ease; the conferees had trouble agreeing on the wheat amendment. With a big majority of the Senate behind them, the Senate conferees, led by Gore, refused to compromise on the $2.50 figure as the fair price for wheat. Several times the conferees reported to the Senate that they could not agree with the House leaders on a compromise on the wheat price, but each time at the recommendation of Gore they were instructed to insist on the $2.50 price. At last, on June 29 Gore showed the first sign of yielding when he agreed that a slightly lower figure might be acceptable. He suggested the reduction of ten cents per bushel.[36] The conferees then quickly agreed to a reduced price, and $2.40 was accepted as a uniform minimum price for No. 2 northern spring wheat at the principal interior primary markets and at any other such places the President might choose to designate. With this adjustment effected the appropriation bill was promptly accepted by both houses of Congress and sent to the White House for the presidential signature.

The President was not disposed to accept the wheat amendment. "Nothing more distinctly against the public interest has been put into a bill in many a month," he had written when the Senate had first accepted the amendment, "and I fail to see any need for it, from the point of view even of the farmer."[37] In a July veto message which the House subsequently refused to override, the President dissented from the amendment on principle as well as expediency. He believed that "such inelastic legislative price provisions are insusceptible of being administered in a way that will be advantageous either to the producer or to the consumer, establishing as they do arbitrary levels which are quite independent of the normal market conditions." He expressed his approval of the methods of regulation already in use, which he believed had resulted in a satisfactory manner "considering the complexity and variety of the subject matter dealt with."[38]

Gore was not happy with the President's action, although he admitted that he endorsed most of the veto message. He approved of the general principles relating to price-fixing laid down by the Chief Executive, but in this case he was willing to forego those principles. He believed, despite his convictions concerning price control, that the price of wheat should be raised in view of farmers' rising costs of production and operation. Gore had opposed many of the war measures because of his abstract principles, but when it came to the problem of wheat price fixing, his principles could be waived. Not overlooking the large number of wheat growers in western Oklahoma, the sightless Senator was not blind to the fact that he needed to repair his political fences. With the Oklahoma press generally hostile to him because of his opposition to the administration's war policies, Gore was making a desperate effort to appeal to the farm vote.

When national interest in food conservation was intensified

because of government propaganda and the long fight over the food control bill during the summer of 1917, this question persistently was raised: why were Americans urged to economize on food as a patriotic measure while the liquor industry was permitted to use valuable food materials in its products? A powerful movement was soon underway urging the adoption of wartime prohibition to prevent the waste of food materials in beverage alcohol.

Gore expressed constitutional doubts regarding prohibition in wartime, but he acknowledged that a bill might survive the test of constitutionality if it were based on the idea of conserving food because of emergency conditions.[39] Not long after the war had begun he gave encouragement to those advocating nationwide prohibition during the war when he introduced two measures, one of which would restrict or prohibit the use of food and feed materials in the manufacture of alcoholic beverages, the other granting the President power to commandeer distilled spirits in bond to be used for the manufacture of munitions and military hospital supplies.[40] Although believing that absolute prohibition in wartime would react adversely upon the country, Gore favored giving the President discretionary power to deal with the liquor situation.[41]

The fight to give the Chief Executive control over liquor stocks in wartime was won, and the food control bill included a provision to that effect. The Agriculture Committee chairman had appointed a predominantly "dry" subcommittee to deal with the question, but this subcommittee was inclined toward modified legislation; at its insistence a clause was inserted in the drastic anti-liquor House amendment leaving it to the discretion of the President to permit the limited use of foodstuffs in the manufacture of fermented liquors when in his judgment the public interest would thereby be served.[42] The final version of the bill disallowed the making of whiskey for the duration of the war, conferring on the President authority to take over all existing stocks of distilled spirits for use in the manufacture of explosives. Beer and wine were permitted to be made and sold if the President considered such activity not contrary to the public interest.[43]

With this as a starting point those who favored all-out nationwide prohibition during the war increased their agitation. The President, strenuously opposing its passage, believed wartime prohibition was unnecessary. To him it was not a food conservation measure but an attempt by the anti-saloon forces to use the war emergency to declare the country "dry" by congressional action.[44] But Wilson yielded to the pressure and in November, 1918, signed into law the wartime prohibition bill making it unlawful to sell distilled spirits for beverages from June 30, 1919, until the termination of the war and demobilization.[45]

This law did not end the agitation. Encouraged, the anti-liquor pressure groups increased their efforts to prohibit the sale of alcoholic beverages in peacetime. A proposed amendment to the Constitution providing for permanent prohibition had been introduced in the Senate in April, 1917, and had been passed on August 1.[46] Gore's affirmative vote had helped the resolution garner the two-thirds majority necessary for constitutional amendments. In December the House concurred in the Senate action, and by February 25, 1919, forty-five of the states had ratified the amendment, much to the amazement of the most ardent supporters of national prohibition. The Eighteenth Amendment became effective January 16, 1920.

As chairman of the Agriculture Committee Gore dealt with many peripheral problems relating to the war effort. Arguing that the nation's food supply could be substantially increased indirectly, he advocated larger appropriations to fight animal diseases, especially through the elimination of the southern cattle tick, and to exterminate prairie dogs and various predatory animals. He was quite perturbed when appropriation for the conservation of the meat supply by the eradication of animal diseases was reduced from $4,500,000 to $825,000. "Last week we appropriated $3,400,000,000 to exterminate human life. . . . Now we haggle about a modest appropriation to exterminate pestilence and disease and to multiply the means of maintaining human life," protested Gore.[47] Chiding the Senate for quibbling over an appropriation for the eradication of the cattle tick, he was quoted as saying, "I would rather have the honor of combating successfully the cattle tick, than of restoring a city in France."[48] He thought it was extremely short-sighted on the part of Congress for its members to sit and "pare cheese and nibble at cherries when the destiny of the Nation may be to a measurable extent affected by this [appropriation] measure."[49] Using the war as an excuse, Gore strove to increase portions of the agricultural allotment for certain areas in the South and West, sections containing his own state and constituents.

Nor did Gore overlook the powerful oil industry in Oklahoma while he was securing benefits for his constituency under the guise of war legislation. With the war machines consuming great quantities of oil, he realized the necessity of increased production in the oil industry, and he assisted it with indirect financial aid through legislation. Under the Sixteenth Amendment Congress was authorized to levy a tax on all income "from whatever source derived," although it was not allowed to tax capital. Congress found the taxing of oil complicated when the courts declared that oil in the ground constituted capital but that when the capital was brought to the surface it represented to some extent income if profits were derived from it. Undertaking to tax the income derived from the production of oil, Congress was faced with the difficult problem of exempting that part of the oil which represented capital. In the revenue act of 1916 the principle of cost depletion was adopted for the oil industry, but it was soon agreed that cost was not a fair measure of return upon capital in the hazardous oil business. This principle tended to hinder the development of the industry and was particularly vexatious in the face of the exceptional production requirements due to the war.

Senator Gore found a more satisfactory solution when he offered and secured the adoption of an amendment to the war revenue act of 1918. Known as the discovery depletion allowance, the fundamental provision of this amendment first inaugurated an acceptable principle for exempting from the income tax that portion of the proceeds of oil which represented capital by providing for the return of capital on the basis of fair market value rather than cost.[50] Although discovery depletion was abandoned in 1926 for percentage depletion, providing that in the case of oil and gas wells there should be a reasonable allowance for depletion based on percentages established by law, the basic principle was unchanged, and that general rule still remains in effect. Basically the depletion allowance is but an aspect of the depreciation allowance permitted in all businesses to provide for the return of capital untaxed. Other industries which gain income from extracting minerals from the ground have profited from this concept through the enactment of similar laws. Needless to say, the oil industry in Oklahoma was not unaware of Gore's prominent part in the passage of the original amendment and was not unappreciative of his activities during the war period.

At the close of the war the Senator introduced a resolution in which he suggested that farmers and farm laborers be mustered out of the army as soon as feasible so that they could make plans for producing a crop in 1919. This, he asserted, would add to an abundant harvest and help both the producers and consumers of this country and abroad.[51] But many legislators used "essential industry" as the reason for desiring to muster out constituents or their sons early, and Gore's resolution went unnoticed.

The Senator's plea to reduce waste did not end when the war was over. He opposed the sinking of the surrendered German fleet until an agreement had been made for the limitation or reduction of all existing naval establishments. "If those ships are sunk," he declared, "it will be conclusive proof that the foolkiller is not off on a furlough but that he is dead. Such folly is unimaginable."[52] To sink the enemy ships and then to spend millions of dollars for a navy in order to increase the demand for labor and to uphold the price of steel was not compatible with Gore's reasoning. He preferred that the German naval crafts either be apportioned to Great Britain, France, Italy, and the United States on the basis of the existing ratios or be sold to smaller countries, using the proceeds in the work of reconstruction and rehabilitation.[53]

Gore was in the forefront of those who wanted to "clean up the war legislation." After the Treaty of Versailles was defeated by the Senate, he introduced resolutions to repeal the food control act. Reminding his colleagues that it was a war measure, "and the excuse for its enactment has now passed," he desired to neutralize it as quickly as possible. He was convinced that its continuance was "fraught with danger to business, labor, and the farmers."[54] He also introduced legislation to repeal war daylight-saving time and to transfer the nation's communication systems from the government to their owners. Voting against a La Follette-sponsored substitute for the Esch-Cummins railroad bill, Gore expressed his opposition to a two-year extension of federal control over the nation's rails.[55] But the Esch-Cummins measure was more than a bill ending government control of the railroads; it also sought to encourage rather than discourage consolidation. Gore's distaste

108

for railroad monopolies through consolidation and the operators' real or imaginary exploitation of the farmers proved to be stronger than his opposition to federal control, and he voted against the Esch-Cummins bill too.

In retrospect, much of Gore's studied opposition to the President's recommended war legislation seems based on genuine convictions that some of it was unconstitutional or that the emergency did not demand the sweeping laws which were enacted. On the other hand, personal animosity to Wilson may have drawn a shade across his mental eyes. Gore continually insisted that his anti-administration stand was impersonal, and there is no direct evidence to the contrary; but the great mass of contemporary newspaper comment regarding his hostility to Wilson cannot be wholly discounted in view of his expressed attitudes toward many of the basic war measures. His apparent personal animus toward Wilson perhaps can best be explained in terms of Gore's own psychological and emotional needs. Many of his words and actions during the war seemed to be those of a man driven to keep himself in the public spotlight. A Senator who never rose to the first rank, he wanted desperately to feel "important," and one way to satisfy this need was through controversy with the Presidents. One senses that Gore reveled in the squabbles in which he participated. The fact that he was in the minority bothered him not one bit. Indeed, he seemed rather to prefer the role of the underdog, the opposer, the one in disagreement with the powers in control.

Gore's activities as a Populist against the dominant Democratic party in Mississippi and Texas tend to support this assumption, as does his voting record in his early years in the Senate when he went along with the progressive Republican minority. During the New Freedom days when progressive legislation which he favored was being passed, he apparently was out of his element. He made few positive contributions except in regard to agricultural appropriations. His career after World War I bears out these general assumptions. His stand on the League of Nations and his opposition to the New Deal were not out of character in view of the Senator's earlier years.

VIII. DEFEAT OF THE LEAGUE AND THE SENATOR

THE RATIFICATION of the Treaty of Versailles was the one important problem facing the Republican-dominated upper house of the Sixty-sixth Congress. The armistice had been proclaimed on November 11, 1918, and President Wilson had gone to Paris to help draft the treaty which had been signed at Versailles on June 28, 1919; it remained only for the Senate to put its stamp of approval upon the document. A special session of the Congress had opened on May 19 at the request of the President, and on July 10 the treaty was submitted to the Senate by the Chief Executive, who appealed for prompt ratification. In the meantime, many events had foreshadowed a stormy session and the ultimate defeat of the treaty. Wilson was confident that the American people so strongly favored the treaty that he could demand ratification and expect little resistance from the Senate. This feeling of assurance the President retained for many months even though the treaty progressed slowly in the hands of the Senate. Such confidence was ill-founded. Wilson had not reckoned on the strength or persistence of the rebellious Republicans and a few Democrats who refused to follow his leadership.

The American press had reported the treaty's progress at Versailles, and its terms were generally known to the reading public before the document was formally presented to the Senate. When thirty-seven Senators requested the President to separate from the treaty the covenant establishing the League of Nations, the President in a speech at the Metropolitan Opera House in New York City in March, 1919, vigorously defended the covenant and stated emphatically that the two documents were tied together with so many threads that it would be impossible to dissect the covenant from the treaty without destroying both.[1] On that same day, the last of the third session of the Sixty-fifth Congress, thirty-nine Republican Senators signed a round-robin resolution condemning the League of Nations as it then stood. This action indicated that enough Senators were opposed to the League to cause the defeat of the treaty unless the League provisions were altered considerably.

In his first public statement on the League question, Gore of Oklahoma indicated the stand he was to take throughout the League fight in the Senate. Favoring reservations, he believed that the Monroe Doctrine should not come under the jurisdiction of the proposed League. In an interview with the *Daily Oklahoman* the Senator mentioned the amendment which he later submitted for consideration as a provision in the League. This amendment, according to its author, would democratize war. With the proposed covenant providing that member nations refer their disputes to a "court of arbitration," the "executive council," or the body of "delegates," Gore's amendment would have added "THE PEOPLE." Gore believed that the "fathers and mothers whose sons are to fight these battles and die in distant lands" should have the privilege of expressing their advisory opinion before Congress declared war.

Gore also expressed his opposition to article 10 of the covenant. Unwilling to "bind the United States in advance to take part in every war that ever happens in every quarter of the globe, without reference to our rights, our interests, and our honor," he wanted the proposed League to state clearly that this nation would not be compelled to surrender its "independence or vacate the sovereignty of the United States." Concluding the interview he expressed a favorable attitude toward a permanent international legislative council which would meet annually to clarify, codify, and promulgate the rules and principles of international law and a permanent court of arbitration to decide justiciable questions.[2]

In March, 1919, Gore inserted in the *Congressional Record* a statement by William Jennings Bryan which probably expressed his own views. Bryan hailed the League as the greatest step toward peace in a thousand years but thought that the United States should have more votes in it, that it ought to be easier for nations to enter, that the right to reject a mandate should be plainly stated, that the Monroe Doctrine should be clearly preserved, and that full liberty of action in applying force or economic boycott should be reserved.[3] When the President laid the peace treaty before the Senate in July, the reservationists counted Gore among their ranks.

Upon receiving the treaty officially the Senate referred the bulky document to the Committee on Foreign Relations for study. A few days later the chairman of the committee, Henry Cabot Lodge of Massachusetts, announced that public hearings would be held on the subject. Beginning on July 31 and ending on September 12, the committee hearings were often held in both the morning and afternoon. Perhaps the most important part of the hearings was a conference which the committee had with the Chief Executive at the White House on August 19. At this meeting Wilson made it clear that he wanted no qualifications of the treaty in any way. To the suggestion that article 10 be altered Wilson stated that he felt this article constituted "the very backbone of the whole covenant. Without it the league would be hardly more than an influential debating society."[4]

The Republican-dominated Committee on Foreign Relations refused to heed Wilson's suggestion that no changes be made in the League. Reporting the treaty to the Senate on September 10, the committee in a majority report recommended forty-five amendments and four reservations. The amendments included the suggestion that the United States have as many votes in the general assembly as any other power (the British Commonwealth had been granted six to this country's one) and that China rather than Japan be given Germany's former possession Shantung. With the door left open for the addition of more, the four reservations provided that the United States retain the right to withdraw from the League, that it decline to assume any obligation under article 10 to preserve the territorial integrity or political independence of any other country or to interfere in controversies between other nations, that it reserve the right to decide what questions were within its domestic jurisdiction, and that it decline to submit for arbitration any questions which in the judgment of the United States depend upon or relate to the Monroe Doctrine. The report concluded that the League as it then stood "will breed wars instead of securing peace."[5]

The Democratic minority of the committee, led by Gilbert H. Hitchcock of Nebraska, reported that the Democrats on the committee opposed both the amendments and reservations to the treaty, offering the opinion that the reservations were designed to destroy the League and to defeat the treaty.[6] Porter J. McCumber of North Dakota returned an individual report in which he stated that the phraseology of the reservations was unnecessarily severe. Representing the views of the "mild reservationists," he recommended four substitute reservations in lieu of the ones proposed by the majority and added two others to replace the amendments proposed by the majority on the subject of Shantung and the voting power of self-governing dominions in the League.[7]

With the lines sharply drawn, the treaty of peace with Germany became the regular business before the Senate on September 15, consideration beginning section by section on the following day. Gore was ill when the debates on the treaty commenced and was not in his seat until September 30. He missed much of the discussion on amendments designed to eliminate American representatives from the commissions to establish the frontiers between several of the European nations and from the commissions to administer the Saar Basin and other areas. On October 2 these amendments were rejected. The six amendments designed to transfer Shantung to China rather than to Japan were brought to a vote on October 16 and were rejected. Gore voted against the "clouded title of Japan to the pilfered province of Shantung."

The reading of the treaty was completed on October 20, and two days later the Senate took up the two committee amendments which had been passed over in the reading. These amendments attempted to secure votes for the United States equal to those of the British Commonwealth in the general assembly and to prohibit a nation or its self-governing colonies from voting in a quarrel involving the disputant member. These amendments were rejected, Gore voting with Lodge on both of them.

After disposing of these committee amendments the Senate proceeded to discuss various amendments offered by individuals. Gore's amendment to democratize war was submitted, and on November 5 its author gave his first long speech on the treaty as a whole and his amendment in particular.[8] In this speech Gore expressed disagreement with those who had indicated that the ratification of the treaty and League would bring immediate industrial and economic peace. He also argued with those members who believed that textual amendments would delay the final adoption of the treaty. Since amendments did directly what reservations did indirectly, Gore believed that in discharging his highest constitutional function he should take direct rather than indirect steps. Thus, he "felt in duty bound in the interest of democracy and

113

peace to propose this amendment securing the people a right to an advisory vote."

The remainder of this speech was devoted to a defense of the "democratizing" amendment. Reminding his associates that the United States ostensibly went to war to make the world safe for democracy, Gore assumed that its purpose was thus to democratize the world. Expressing sympathy with this high ideal, the Senator dreamed of democratizing war. In a burst of oratory he announced that his amendment was in harmony with the spirit of the times, the great currents of human affairs, the genius of our free institutions, the principles of self-government, the theory that governments derive their just powers from the consent of the governed, "and the high resolve that Government of the people, by the people, and for the people shall not perish from the earth." Launching into a discussion of the League, Gore pointed out that it was not democratic in nature. Except for the plebiscite to be taken in Upper Silesia the League in his opinion was highly undemocratic. He used this exception to drive home the principle behind his amendment. "If the people of the Saar Valley . . . are to be permitted to decide by an advisory vote under what flag they will live, is it inconsistent to permit them to pass judgment upon the vital issues of peace and war?" he asked.

Stressing that his amendment would provide for an advisory vote which would not necessarily be binding, Gore reiterated that in the United States only the Congress had the power to declare war. But he believed that "an advisory vote would not be incompatible either with the letter or with the spirit of the Constitution." To the argument that the people were not qualified to pronounce judgment upon the issues of peace and war, Gore contended that the people were as qualified to declare war as kings, emperors, kaisers, and czars. "The voice of the people is the nearest approach to the voice of God," he proclaimed with finality.

Disappointed that the original League covenant did not embody the democratic principle of a referendum preceding an appeal to the sword, Gore ventured the opinion that if this principle were tendered by the United States it would be accepted by every nation which professed to love democracy. He then launched into a diatribe against war. His amendment, he insisted, was offered only in the interest of democracy and peace. It would be a calamity if nothing developed from the recent war to prevent or minimize the possibility of war, he announced. Explaining that his amendment was a step in that direction, he stated that all of his votes for amendments and reservations had and would continue to be for one object: to minimize the possibilities of war. He stated that his votes on the treaty had been and would continue to be cast in the interest of peace, to clarify the terms of the treaty, and to make the provisions of the treaty clear beyond any doubt.

Gore's unrealistic amendment received no substantial support. When the vote was taken on it on November 6, it lost 16 to 67, most of the favorable votes being cast by irreconcilables who voted for all amendments and reservations and then against the League on the final vote.[9]

After Gore's amendment was defeated, the Senate turned to the adoption of a new draft of reservations which had been reported on October 24 by Lodge on behalf of the Foreign Relations Committee. The voting on these reservations continued from November 7 through November 18. Gore supported every one of the fifteen Lodge reservations, fourteen of which passed the Senate by comfortable majorities. To reservation no. 2, which made the United States the sole judge as to whether it had fulfilled its international obligations when and if it wanted to withdraw from the League, Gore wanted to add that the President as well as the Congress would have the power to issue a notice of withdrawal from the League, but the amendment was defeated 18 to 68.[10]

The various substitutes offered by Hitchcock and others for the Lodge reservations were generally opposed by Gore. Two exceptions (both rejected) which Gore voted for included a substitute offered by Borah declaring that the United States would assume no legal or moral obligation under article 10 and one by Hitchcock which announced that the Monroe Doctrine would not in any way be impaired or affected by the covenant of the League and would not be subject to any decision, report, or inquiry by the council or assembly.[11] A substitute which was accepted and for which Gore voted was offered by McCumber, withholding the United States' assent to the section dealing with an international labor organization until Congress should later make specific provision for representation in that organization.[12] A resolution offered by Irvine Lenroot of

Wisconsin dealing with the voting power of self-governing dominions was also accepted, Gore's vote being cast in the affirmative.[13]

With a preamble (which in reality was a reservation) and fourteen reservations the Senate had by November 18 noticeably altered the League covenant and this nation's responsibility under it. On the next day Hitchcock read to the Senate a letter he had received from the President in which Wilson expressed the opinion that the resolution of reservations adopted by the Senate "does not provide for ratification, but, rather, for the nullification of the treaty." He added, "I sincerely hope that the friends and supporters of the treaty will vote against the Lodge resolution of ratification. I understand that the door will probably then be open for a genuine resolution of ratification."[14] With the reading of this letter the stage was set for the final vote on the Treaty of Versailles. The Senate promptly refused to ratify the document by a vote of 39 to 55.

Gore was one of four Democrats who refused to support Wilson's plea by voting for the treaty with reservations. Convinced that the treaty could not pass without reservations being attached, Gore had voted for many of them, and on the final vote he cast his ballot for the treaty with reservations. Those voting against the agreement were the irreconcilables who opposed the treaty in any form and the staunch Wilson supporters who voted in the negative hoping to be in a position to ratify the treaty without any reservations. Such was the dilemma before the Senate of the United States on November 19, 1919, when the Treaty of Versailles failed to be ratified.

After the rejection of the treaty, Atlee Pomerene of Ohio moved to present the treaty, resolution of ratification, and the reservations to a committee of conciliation. Composed of six Senators to be appointed by the presiding officer of the Senate, among whom were to be Majority Leader Lodge and Minority Leader Hitchcock, this committee was to be charged with the responsibility of trying to draw up a resolution of ratification with reservations which would meet the approval of not less than two-thirds of the Senate. La Follette's move to table this motion was accepted by a vote of 48 to 42, the closest important vote taken on the treaty, as Gore and others who favored the treaty with reservations but who were not trying to kill it with additional provisions voted against the tabling action.[15]

Newspapers hostile to Gore accused him of opposing the treaty in any form, and he was generally considered a member of the irreconcilable group. This propaganda was spread in Oklahoma to such an extent that the Senator accepted an invitation to speak before the Tulsa Kiwanis Club just after the defeat of the treaty for the avowed single purpose of explaining his position on the League. Stating that he favored a league of nations, he emphasized that he did not favor the proposed League. He wanted to see a "society of nations that would regulate international law, set up a code of justice and establish a court of conciliation," but he did not want an arrangement which would necessitate a vast army to enforce its decrees.[16] Advocacy of a watered-down version of the League did more to reveal Gore's basic isolationism than to convince his hearers that he favored an international organization.

After having adjourned *sine die* about midnight on November 19, the Senate convened in regular session on December 2, 1919. A little over a month later a bipartisan conference of nine Senators began meeting to try to reach some agreements on the treaty, but after two weeks the attempt was given up as futile, and the impending second defeat of the treaty loomed large. On January 31, 1920, the results of this strictly informal and unofficial conference were made public.[17] Lodge claimed that the conferees had reached a number of tentative agreements but had failed to agree to any changes in regard to the reservations dealing with the Monroe Doctrine and article 10. The President did not help the work of this conference when on January 26 he wrote to Hitchcock that any reservation or resolution stating that the United States would assume no obligation under article 10 would "chill our relationship with the nations with which we expect to be associated in the great enterprise of maintaining the world's peace."[18]

During the period between the defeat of the treaty in November and its reconsideration beginning in February, Gore continued to advocate his own brand of reservations. In January he circulated a compromise proposal on article 10 which exempted the United States from becoming involved in armed conflict not of its making and which reinsured Congress' power to declare war. But the foregoing proposal received little attention, since the more suitable McKellar-Kendrick proposal was being advanced in the interest of harmony at that time.[19] Gore had printed in the *Congressional Record* an article from the New York *Tribune* which stated that Switzerland, a neutral, had been accepted into the League notwithstanding that country's retaining more stringent reservations than the United States Senate was demanding. From his constituent mail Gore read a telegram into the *Record* stating that a house-to-house canvass in Miami, Oklahoma, showed 374 persons for the League, 1,173 against it. Such mail reinforced Gore's stand on the League issue.

On February 9, 1920, the Senate recommitted the treaty to the Foreign Relations Committee with instructions to report it back immediately, along with the resolution of ratification rejected in November plus the reservations previously adopted. The committee complied with these instructions on the following day. On February 11 Senator Lodge presented a number of proposed amendments to the reservations which had been discussed by the informal bipartisan committee in January, whereupon the Senate once again directed its attention almost exclusively to the treaty. Reservation no. 1 was readopted on February 21 and reservation no. 15 was accepted on March 18. Between those dates Gore had voted for all of the Lodge reservations as he had done in November of the previous year, although he often voted for substitutes and amendments (few of which passed) offered by Hitchcock and others softening the language of the reservations.

While the reservations were being considered Gore seldom spoke, although he was present for almost every roll call. He submitted a draft of a reservation to article 10 in which his "democratizing" clause was included, but it was never taken from the table. Another reservation reflecting his views pertaining to the political status of dependents whose people or their elected representatives had not been given a chance to vote on their status met a similar fate. A reservation to prohibit monopolies of the natural resources of various countries placed under mandatories by the League was introduced by Gore, but it was rejected.[20] Gore had previously expressed fears that Great Britain was trying to monopolize the world's oil supply and sources. His reservation concerning monopolies was designed solely to protect the United States from them.

With all the former Lodge reservations accepted plus an additional one offered by Peter Gerry of Rhode Island expressing sympathy for Ireland in her desire for independence, the Senate voted on March 19 to reject the resolution of ratification by a vote of 49 to 35.

Twenty-one administration Democrats who had voted against the treaty with reservations in November yielded to the strong forces at work for compromise, joining Gore and three other Democrats to vote for the treaty with reservations in March. But the votes were seven short of the necessary two-thirds majority. The treaty had failed a second and final time. The spring debates had been a rehearsal of old ideas covering familiar ground, and the reservations accepted in March were not significantly different from those of the past November. The treaty was returned to the President without the Senate's "advice and consent."

Throughout the treaty debates there had been three rather ill-defined but nevertheless definite groups into which the Senators formed: the administration Democrats led by Gilbert Hitchcock who wanted the treaty accepted with no reservations or amendments attached; the irreconcilables (ranging from 10 to 19 in number) led by William E. Borah, Hiram Johnson, Robert M. La Follette, and James A. Reed, who refused to vote for the treaty in any form; and the reservationists, of which there were several classes. Gore fell into the last group. He did not want to see the treaty defeated, but he was realist enough to understand party politics, and he knew that if the treaty were accepted it would be with reservations. Favoring the fundamental reservations which Lodge advanced, Gore manifested his growing isolationism by expressions of fear of entangling alliances and frequent wars.[21] Such fears Gore would have quelled had the Senate accepted the League with the basic Lodge reservations.[22]

As consideration of the treaty developed, the administration Democrats and the irreconcilables joined hands to defeat it. Its advocates generally voted against the reservations while the irreconcilables voted for them, both groups joining to vote against the treaty in its final form. The reservationists were a large group and do not lend themselves to easy generalizations, but they ordinarily voted for the reservations and then voted for the treaty in its completed form. Had the President released his followers and permitted them to vote for the treaty with reservations, the necessary votes would have been forthcoming and the treaty would have been accepted. Lodge had successfully maneuvered to place the ultimate responsibility of defeating the treaty on the friends of the President, thus eliminating responsibility from the Republicans, who were trying to pass the

119

treaty in a form which they considered would safeguard the future of the United States.[23]

Many factors entered into the defeat of the treaty. The non-entanglement tradition of past years, the jealousy of senatorial prerogative, personal enmity toward the President, resentment of the President's "dictatorial" methods, partisan politics, and Wilson's stubbornness, mistakes, and collapse all are basic in understanding the reason the Chief Executive and his supporters in the Senate were defeated in the contest over the Treaty of Versailles and the League of Nations.[24] Although not as influential as several colleagues, Gore played a part in that defeat.

When Gore was defeated for re-election in the Democratic primary of 1920, the New York *Times* attributed the reversal to the Senator's refusal to vote with his party on the League of Nations issue.[25] This explanation for Gore's defeat is far too simple. In view of his open opposition to many of the administration's emergency war policies, the Senator's political opponents had laid careful plans for his defeat. His stand on the League of Nations simply climaxed his differences with a popular President and with his own party in Oklahoma. When the majority of the Oklahoma electorate became aroused, mainly because of the Senator's stand on the draft and the food administration, political opponents took full advantage of the patriotic milieu and were able to keep the flames of opposition glowing if not burning brightly from 1917 to 1920. Gore assisted the opposition's cause by his indiscreet remarks and letters.

When the Oklahoma Democratic convention met in February, 1920, its prevalent mood was anger at Gore. "With the blush of shame and the lament of sorrow" the convention adopted a resolution deploring the action of its "other Senator."[26] Almost with one accord the delegates agreed to "get Gore." The politicians realized that having several candidates in the primary would split the vote, giving the incumbent a chance for renomination, and they set out to find one who was acceptable to all factions in the party. As early as August, 1917, Congressman Scott Ferris, for several years a Democratic wheel horse in the lower house, had been mentioned as a possible candidate to oppose the embattled Senator.[27] In the spring of 1919 the politicians brought pressure on Ferris to run against Gore, and he yielded to the party bosses' pleadings and expressed his interest in running. Although he was reluctant to enter the race after reflecting on the possibility of defeat at the hands of the wily Senator, he finally made the plunge and announced his intentions publicly in August, 1919, with the tacit understanding that no other Democratic candidates would file for the primary contest. When other aspirants, including Oklahoma City attorney E. G. McAdams and the state's attorney general, S. P. Freeling, expressed interest in or actually announced for the race, they were politely but firmly requested to withdraw in order to prevent the much-feared split vote. With only Gore and Ferris as contenders and the party organization placing its stamp of approval on the latter, who campaigned on the platform of supporting the President during the war, the Democratic primary became a contest between Gore's position and the administration's prestige.[28]

As soon as the treaty was dispensed with by the Senate in March, 1920, Gore began concentrating on the campaign for his political life. By April he had his organization well established, and by May it was in high gear. The "Gore Volunteers" worked unceasingly in carrying the Senator's case to the people of Oklahoma, and their campaign paper, the *Jeffersonian*, was widely distributed. But the Senator had to reckon with a strongly organized and united opposition. A few Democratic papers defended him, accepting articles written by him in which he explained his actions and votes during the war period.[29] But the papers friendly to Gore were of little influence in the face of the caustic *Daily Oklahoman*, the most influential, if not the bitterest, anti-Gore drum-beater in the state. The *Oklahoman* bombarded the state with propaganda calling Gore a rubber stamp of the Kaiser and intimating that he and the German leader would have voted the same way during the war.[30]

Many papers followed the *Oklahoman's* lead. One newspaper editor admitted in print that his only new year's supplication had been "Give us more strength to help beat Gore."[31] When the Ardmore *Ardmoreite* was mentioned as being the most bitter Gore opponent in southern Oklahoma, the Durant *News* challenged the statement. The *News* contended that it thought less of Gore than any other newspaper in the whole state.[32] At least twenty papers were so bitterly opposed to Gore that they refused to accept his paid advertisements, returning his uncashed checks.[33] Several Republican sheets came out for him, the most important of these being the Tulsa *Daily World*, but their influence meant little in the strongly Democratic state. Besides, it was generally conceded that they favored Gore be-

121

cause they felt that he would be the weaker of the two Democratic candidates in the general election in November.

The heated summer campaign was not limited to newspaper circles. Gore carried the campaign to the grass roots of the state, Ferris willingly following. Both candidates set gruelling paces for themselves. The Senator was a powerful stump speaker and adroitly used this mode of attack during the contest. But Ferris was a speaker of no small ability himself and he met and fought the blind orator on his own terms. Although both candidates were noted for their humorous speechmaking, the summer campaign lacked jocularity. Gore's apostasy became the only issue as the Oklahoma electorate grimly took sides. The height of the campaign saw the Congressman on the offensive attacking Gore's patriotism without qualification and stressing his own loyalty to the President; Gore vainly defended his record. In answer to the Congressman's statement that he had never failed to stand by the commander-in-chief, Wilson, Gore announced that his commander-in-chief was the people of Oklahoma. With a lefthanded thrust at Ferris, Gore remarked, "I shall not make the race upon the confession that I have worn a ring in my nose from the beginning nor upon the assurance that I will continue to wear a ring in my nose until the end. Why could not a Mexican parakeet make and keep that . . . promise quite as well as the congressman or myself?"[34]

Before the contest reached fever pitch, Gore had privately expressed confidence in his ability to win: "It looks like the soldiers and the farmers and the oil men will be pretty solid for me. These make a hard combination to beat in Oklahoma. If the farmers love me, the World is mine!"[35] Gore's assumption that he had the soldier vote in his pocket could not have been more wrong. An "Ex-servicemen's League Against Gore" proved to be one of the strongest agencies of propaganda against the Senator. Broadcasting many half-truths, quoting Gore's statements out of context, and in general severely damaging his campaign, this organization had the support of hundreds of war veterans, as well as important leaders in the American Legion.

An example of misquoting which seriously injured Gore's reputation was the charge that he had called American soldiers "summer soldiers and sunshine patriots," with the implication that the young men of this country were pampered and unpatriotic.[36] The rumor and misquotation resulted from a speech made by Gore on the Senate floor in June, 1916. To a bill designed to double the pay of the militia during the Mexican crisis, Gore objected. He felt that it would be a slam on a soldier's patriotism to offer to raise his pay under the circumstances. "It seems to me that this is rather an impeachment of the patriotism of these gallant heroes. It is a reflection upon their Americanism." He concluded: "Shall we treat these soldiers as milksops and mollycoddles? Shall we send these soldiers their valets, chiropodists, and manicurists to attend them? Shall we then by implication convey the idea that they are summer soldiers, that they are sunshine patriots, that they are knights of the drawingroom? I would prefer to treat them as real soldiers. Would they not prefer to be treated as real soldiers?"[37]

The truth was that Gore had not called the veterans unpatriotic but rather was appealing to their patriotism when he made these statements. But all of his efforts to correct the impression left by his opponents that he had called the national guardsmen unpatriotic were of no avail. Coupling this propaganda with his stand on the draft in 1917, which was also misinterpreted and misunderstood, the veterans' groups found it easy to work wholeheartedly for Ferris. The fact remains, however, that some of Gore's remarks were accurately quoted; the Senator often coined a phrase or emitted a quip when he would have been more discreet to remain silent.

One of the most interesting sidelights of the campaign occurred about five weeks before the primary election day. On June 26, 1920, the *Daily Oklahoman* printed an editorial entitled "Amende Honorable" in which it dramatically apologized for all the unkind remarks it had been broadcasting about Gore. Taking up point after point the editorial stated that the *Oklahoman* had been much too harsh on Gore's position, had judged his actions too severely, and had willfully misrepresented him. For this the paper publicly expressed regret, ending, "We make the amende honorable and trust to avoid like misrepresentations in the future."[38]

This reversal of editorial policy in the midst of a bitter campaign "created a sensation outranking anything that has occurred in Oklahome politics since statehood," a political news digest reported.[39] And no wonder. For over four years the *Oklahoman* had been Gore's most outspoken and influential critic, and this complete reversal was sensational to the point of being unbelievable. Therein lies the point of the episode: the editorial reversal could not be believed. Two days after the editorial had appeared, the *Oklahoman* blushingly admitted that the article had been clandestinely smuggled into the newspaper by a former employee who was out to embarrass the paper's staff. The paper claimed that the person who had accomplished this clever trick was a "disgruntled, discharged, and dishonorable former employe" and was a friend of some of Gore's campaign leaders. The *Oklahoman* ended the second sensational editorial with a counter-reversal: it had no apology to make for its attacks on Gore.

A full month later the paper printed a long explanation giving its final version of the incident. Oliver C. Patten had signed a written statement in which he said that Gore himself wrote the "Amende Honorable" column, and Patten confessed to having sneaked it into a copy basket in the editorial room. This affidavit supposedly settled the matter, which had been the talk of the state for weeks. Actually the truth may never be known. Gore had nothing to gain by such a trick, for it only served to divert attention from the campaigners. It was, indeed, a sly trick whatever the reason for its publication, but it probably helped neither side in the end. But if it did nothing else, it served to make an already exciting campaign even more interesting.

The returns of the primary revealed Oklahoma's opinion of those who refused to be loyal to Wilson. The stop-Gore movement proved effective, the Congressman leading the Senator 106,454 to 80,243.[40] No sectional cleavage appeared in the voting pattern, since both candidates came from Comanche County. Gore had a majority in thirteen counties on the Oklahoma Territory side and twelve in the east. As was expected, Ferris ran stronger in the cities, carrying Tulsa, Muskogee, Okmulgee, Shawnee, and Enid, winning by a three-to-one majority in the state's capital city. Although the defeat was decisive, it was not so overwhelming as to prevent speculation on the outcome had there been the usual number of six or eight or more candidates entered against the incumbent. If the leaders of the Democratic party in Oklahoma had not arranged for all candidates to withdraw except one behind which all factions could unite, they could conceivably have looked on as Gore continued at his senatorial post uninterrupted. Most certainly the vote in the primary would have been far closer.

The support which the Republican press in Oklahoma gave the Senator during the primary, coupled with his rejection by the Democratic party leaders, made some observers think that with defeat Gore might announce his support for the Republican national ticket. He did the opposite. Not only did he publicly state that he would support the nominations of James M. Cox and F. D. Roosevelt, he also offered his services (which were accepted) to the speakers' bureau of the Democratic National Committee to speak in behalf of the Democratic ticket.[41]

Ferris' was a Pyrrhic victory; he failed to win in the general election, and the cleavage of the bitter 1920 primary affected Democratic party politics for years. In the November election Oklahoma went for Harding and Coolidge by over 25,000 votes in the Republican landslide, and Republican Congressman John W. Harreld, who had won the G.O.P. primary over thirteen other opponents, led Gore's primary rival by over 30,000 votes to become the state's first Republican United State Senator. Despite Gore's public support of Cox and Roosevelt, he could not conceal his satisfaction with the results of the general election: "I heard a Democrat yesterday give his reasons why the [Democratic] ticket suffered such an overwhelming defeat in Oklahoma. He said that Harding, Harreld, Hayes, Harris, Herrick and h--- formed a combination that simply could not be beaten. . . . The country did not go Republican. It simply stayed American. . . . Senator Harding and I are warm personal friends."[42]

The words of two Oklahoma papers adequately summarized the attitudes of many of the journals of the state. The Bartlesville *Examiner* wrote, "The passing of Gore ends the political career of a unique figure in national life. The *Examiner* has not sympathized with the blind senator and has opposed his renomination, but it recognizes his ability and his independence and the perversion of his not mean talents, which brought about his political downfall."[43] The Tulsa *Daily World,* the most influential Republican paper supporting Gore in the primary, reflected the Senator's views of himself:

"Senator Gore has been defeated. . . . A precedent has been established which will deter for many years any man from acting or voting in the United States senate from a sense of duty, if he thereby gives offense to his party bosses.

"Gore dared to be his own man. That is his offense. Had he flexed the knee to autocracy, declared himself a rubber stamp statesman proud to do the chores of a party leader regardless of whether that party leader was right or wrong, he could have renewed his tenure of office without opposition."[44]

Gore viewed his defeat with little historical objectivity but with some satisfaction of his own inflated importance when he wrote, "I went down and took the count in the recent primary. Hannibal had his Zema [Zama], Pompey had his Pharsalia [Pharalus], Napoleon had his Waterloo, Lee had his Appotomax [Appomattox], and there are others."[45] More accurately, he simply said, "I ran a handicap race and lost."[46] After over thirteen years as a representative of Oklahoma in the nation's capital, the Senator was temporarily retired to private life.

A progressive in outlook during his early terms, Gore favored the passage of the New Freedom legislation. He leaned toward pacifism when World War I began, and throughout the war he followed his own uniquely independent path in waging that war. His isolationism manifested itself in the battle on the League of Nations in the Senate. By now a staunch economic conservative, the Senator retired to private law practice to lay plans for his eventual return to public life.

IX. LAW AND POLITICS DURING THE INTERIM

UPON RETIREMENT from the Senate in 1921 Thomas P. Gore opened a law office in Washington, D.C., specializing in tax matters. Having spent his mature years in the Senate, he had remained a comparatively poor man. By establishing his law practice in Washington, where he had many connections, he hoped to improve his financial condition as well as keep in touch with political activity in the nation's capital.

The most important single case in which Gore participated during the 1920's was a dispute over taxation between the Coronado Oil and Gas Company and the federal government. In January, 1914, the state of Oklahoma leased some of its public school lands to the Coronado Company for oil exploration. Renewals followed as the company successfully drilled for oil, turning over to the state treasury stipulated percentages of its gross proceeds from production of oil and gas. By the 1920's the lessee's entire income was being derived from the sale of its portion of output from the state-owned property. With the oil firm paying federal taxes on its earnings Gore saw an opportunity for making a handsome fee. Realizing that a federal instrumentality is exempt from state taxation as established by the famous *McCulloch* v. *Maryland* case[1] and that reciprocity was granted to the states in the same respect in *Collector* v. *Day*,[2] Gore concluded that reciprocal immunity from taxation of the instrumentalities of the federal government by state governments and vice versa should apply in the case of oil companies gaining profit from state-owned school lands. Explaining his theory to the Coronado Company and convincing its officials that he might be able to have reciprocal immunity from taxation applied to profits from state-owned oil lands, Gore received permission from the oil concern to advance the claim in its name.

Gore laid his theory before the United States Commissioner of Internal Revenue but was received with indifference. From time to time throughout the 1920's the attorney brought the question of reciprocal immunity to the front in various quarters, but each time he made no headway. He was overruled at every step in his fight with

127

the internal revenue bureau, ultimately losing before the board of tax appeals.

Late in the decade Gore resorted to the courts. After years of litigation and legal sparring, the case of *Burnet, Commissioner of Internal Revenue* v. *Coronado Oil and Gas Company*[3] reached the Supreme Court of the United States. Gore and his associates in the case, David A. Richardson, Samuel W. Hayes, and Eugene Jordan, contended that taxation by the federal government in this instance was illegal. They argued that a state and the federal government are both sovereigns, and that the federal Constitution prohibits one sovereign from taxing another; moreover, this bar to taxation extends to property and agencies of the sovereigns concerned. Since the Coronado Oil Company was engaged in the development of state-owned school land by prospecting for and recovering petroleum, it was thus acting as an agent of the state; therefore, the federal government could not constitutionally tax the company's income from such oil development. The state-owned school lands being exempt from federal taxation, the income of the company derived from school land development should not be taxed.

The brief for the respondent further argued that the governmental function of maintaining public schools involved not only establishing the schools but also raising the revenue to carry them on. Under the enabling act and the state constitution it was as much a governmental function of Oklahoma to obtain revenue for its public school fund from these public lands as it was to obtain it by taxation or by the issuance of bonds. With the leasing power of the state as much a right as its taxing power or its authority to issue bonds for school purposes, the leases themselves were thus governmental instrumentalities, Gore argued. He further contended that one of the aims of Congress and the state was to raise money for public school purposes, and the granting of school lands was intended to be a means to that end. The brief concluded by arguing that acts by individuals or private corporations should not be stamped as nongovernmental when carried out by the state government for a recognized governmental purpose.

Arguing the case before the Supreme Court in January, 1932, and again in March, Gore achieved success when the case was decided in his client's favor on April 11, 1932. The Court recognized that when Oklahoma undertook to lease its public lands for the benefit of the public schools, it exercised a function strictly governmental in character. The Court reasoned that since the states are essential parts of the plan adopted by the federal Constitution and since the Court accepts as settled doctrine that the United States cannot tax other governmental instrumentalities,—each government being supreme in its sphere—in order to preserve the dual system, the lease to the respondent was an instrumentality of the state for the purpose of carrying out its duty in respect to public schools. To impose an income tax on the lessee would amount to a tax upon the lease itself. Thus, in a five-to-four decision, the Court held that the income could not be taxed without interfering with a state instrumentality.

The Court upheld the Coronado Company's claim on the basis of *stare decisis*.[4] In *Gillespie* v. *State of Oklahoma*[5] the Court had ruled in 1922 that the income of a lessee from the sale of oil and gas taken from restricted Indian lands was not taxable by a state, because the lessee constituted in effect an agent used by the United States in fulfilling its duties to its wards. The Coronado decision of 1932 was the logical counterpart of this previous ruling.

The Coronado case is of particular interest because it represented the highest point of intergovernmental tax immunity reached by the Supreme Court up to that time. After the case was decided, the pendulum began to swing in the opposite direction, and by a series of rulings the principle upheld in the Coronado case was gradually weakened.[6] In March, 1938, in *Helvering, Commissioner of Internal Revenue* v. *Mountain Producers*[7] the Coronado and Gillespie cases were specifically overruled. Gore foresaw the end result when the Supreme Court began to veer away from the doctrine of reciprocal intergovernmental tax immunity and was not surprised when the doctrine which he had advanced was overruled.[8] This did not dull his satisfaction over the ruling of 1932, however, nor did the later reversal hinder the earlier decision from being financially profitable to him.

The oil taxation litigation consumed a large portion of Gore's time for the greater part of a decade. Although involved in several less important cases in his capacity as legal adviser during the period, in his own words he "took care of them on the side."

The most colorful of the minor cases in which Gore was involved was one dealing with the Red River boundary dispute.[9] When the fabulous Burkburnett oil boom began in Texas in 1918, the new field expanded rapidly northward to the Red River. By 1919 several companies were exploring along the low banks of the river, on the dry bed, and in some instances actually in the stream itself. Shortly after drilling in the area began, a dispute arose over the ownership of the river bed. Texas assumed it was land within her borders, but because of changes in the course of the stream, both Oklahoma and the United States government also claimed ownership of the bed.[10] Under these circumstances Texas and Oklahoma granted their citizens the right to explore for oil, several individuals taking out placer mining rights from the federal government.

Friction quickly developed as oil men rushed in to stake out claims and to sink wells in or near the river. To prevent unauthorized persons from boring in the river bed, twenty-eight Texas Rangers (members of the Texas militia "versed well in the gentle arts of six-shooting") were sent to the Big Bend region in 1920.[11] Owing to confusion over jurisdiction and law enforcement, serious armed conflict between the militia and rival aspirants for the oil and gas lands was imminent.[12] Under such conditions the controversy was taken into the courts, and the federal government as intervener joined Oklahoma, the plaintiff, against Texas, the defendant.

The Supreme Court of the United States hastily ordered a government receiver to supervise the disputed area until final decisions could be made.[13] When the receiver took charge in April, 1920, the Texas Rangers were withdrawn, and in their place a dozen armed guards were hired to police the area. These guards kept order in the receivership for over a year. The receiver drilled oil wells, operated the oil fields, and generally carried on the business of an oil-producing company.[14]

In the meantime, the Supreme Court was trying to settle one of the most complicated boundary controversies on record. The treaty signed by the United States and Spain in 1819 and ratified by the United States Senate in 1821 was ambiguous regarding the exact boundary line separating the territory of the two nations.[15] For years after Texas became a state it was generally assumed that the middle of the river was the exact dividing line between Oklahoma territory and Texas. But in the famous Greer County case of 1896 the Supreme Court ruled that the south bank of the main channel was the northern boundary of Texas.[16] Texas raised the boundary question again when the oil was discovered, but the Court refused to reverse its earlier decision.[17]

130

This did not mean that Oklahoma received the territory in dispute. Although Oklahoma established its ownership of the north half of the river by virtue of its riparian rights, the Court ruled that no part of the river between the two states was navigable; therefore, the title to the bed of the stream did not pass to Oklahoma on its admission to the Union.[18] The end result was that there existed a narrow band of United States public domain over five hundred miles long and from one-fourth to two miles wide lying within the state of Oklahoma. The oil-producing land consisted of a 43-mile strip of this area.

With every square foot of this area potentially valuable oil land, $12,000,000 in royalties being paid out of it by 1924, much attention was given to marking the precise location of the shifting "cut" of the south bank. This was no easy job when it was often difficult to distinguish the flat, sandy river bottom from the surrounding but equally low, sandy lands. After many years of work, however, the task was completed and the final decree of the Court was made in 1930.[19]

When the Court decided against Oklahoma's claim to the southern half of the river bed, it also ruled that this land had never been subject to location or acquisition under the mining and land laws of the nation. This decision resulted in the cancellation of the claims of many individuals who had explored the oil lands, since these persons had relied upon placer mining laws as they developed the area.[20]

Many of the original placer miners had spent considerable sums of money in order to extract the oil from the ground, and when these individuals suffered losses as a result of the Court's invalidation of the private claims, some of them petitioned the government for reimbursements. One of the most successful of these persons was Oklahoma State Senator Tom Testerman, who hired Gore as his legal counsel. Testerman asserted that he was the first explorer to go into the area, staking out a claim in December, 1918. Declaring that he brought oil to the surface in August, 1919, Testerman argued that he was the first to prove the existence of oil there.[21] He claimed that he had spent a total of $120,000 obtaining leases, buying equipment, and exploring for oil.[22] Gore requested the government to reimburse the losses of Testerman from funds inuring to the Bass Petroleum Company because of his prior claims to certain property allowed that company by the government receiver.[23]

With the Court ruling against Testerman, Gore turned to legislative channels to retrieve the losses.[24] Gore persuaded his friends and former colleagues in Congress to pass legislation authorizing the Secretary of the Interior to adjust and determine the equitable claims of citizens who had explored in the south half of the Red River before February 25, 1920.[25] At Gore's urging the Department of the Interior ruled that Testerman came within the terms of this legislation, and Testerman received over $101,000 for royalty losses.[26] Winning reimbursements despite the Supreme Court's ruling, Gore was not displeased regarding the outcome of this litigation.[27]

The Comanche-Kiowa-Apache Indian tribes of southwestern Oklahoma had also joined in the boundary controversy soon after the discovery of oil. At a council including all of the older members of the tribes, the Indians drew up a statement in which they claimed that the section containing the oil lands was within their reservation boundaries.[28]

In 1865 the United States and the Comanche and Kiowa Indians signed a treaty which confined the two tribes to a large reservation embracing the present panhandles of Oklahoma and Texas as well as a large part of southwestern Oklahoma.[29] Included within these boundaries was a considerable portion of the upper part of the Red River. It was soon realized that the commissioners who signed this treaty had erred when they set aside land for the Indians within the borders of Texas, because the federal government owned no public lands in Texas. Another agreement was reached in 1867 at Medicine Lodge, Kansas, and this treaty set the boundaries of the Indian reservation within the present limits of the state of Oklahoma.[30]

The 1865 treaty had provided for the eastern section of the tribal lands to extend to the northern boundary of Texas. The 1867 treaty, drawn by Indians and commissioners who assumed that the Texas boundary was the middle of the Red River, contained the phrase "middle of the main channel" of the river as a definition for the southern boundary of the Indian territory. The Indians laid claim to the land south of the mid-channel of the river on the grounds that those who drew up the second treaty could not have known that the Texas boundary did not extend to the medial line of the stream. Had it been known that the south bank was to be ruled as the Texas boundary, the Indians contended, the treaty would have used the phrase "south bank" or "Texas boundary" instead of "middle of the main channel" of the river. By this reasoning and on the basis of other boundary delimitations agreed upon in 1867, the Indians asserted ownership of the land between the mouth of the north fork of the river to the ninety-eighth meridian. The oil-producing land lay between these two points.

The Indians' claim proved to be more acceptable than those of Oklahoma or Texas. The Court ruled that the wording of the treaty was explicit, despite the probable intent of those who drew up the 1867 agreement. With such clear language in the document, the Court declared, the problem of Indian claims could not be settled by judicial means.[31] When the Indian lands were opened to white settlement soon after the turn of the twentieth century, this narrow strip of river bottom was not claimed by homesteaders. Since it had not been granted to Oklahoma, it thus remained unallotted and unappropriated public domain of the United States lying within the limits of Oklahoma.

Representatives for the Indians did not give up when the Court denied the Indians' claim to the south half of the stream. In view of the Court's strictly legal ruling concerning the phrasing of the Medicine Lodge Treaty, Oklahoma's U.S. Congressman, Elmer Thomas, approached the question from another angle. The treaty wording was an honest mistake, Thomas contended, and the federal government should rectify the error by giving the profits from the oil lands to its wards. Thus, in December, 1923, Thomas introduced a bill to have the oil royalties from this public land go to the Kiowa, Comanche, and Apache tribes of southwestern Oklahoma.[32]

The House Committee on the Public Lands held hearings on the bill in April, 1924, and January, 1925, and various persons, including former Senator Gore, appeared before the committee to argue the Indians' case. Reporting upon the poor shelter and clothing of the Indians, Gore testified that the tribes' treasury was virtually depleted and that the government would soon be required to appropriate money to care for these wards. He suggested that by allowing the Indians to have the oil profits, inevitable appropriations from the United States Treasury could be deferred for a time.[33]

As a result of the pleas of Gore, Thomas, and others, Congress enacted a statute which authorized a trust fund to be set up for the Kiowa-Comanche-Apache Indians by which these tribes would receive all the royalties from the oil produced in the south half of the Red River, except certain sums of money awarded to a few successful claimants. The Indians were required to pay 37½ per cent of these royalties to Oklahoma in lieu of state and local taxes.[34] Once again Gore had assisted in a successful venture for Oklahomans.

A former Senator with over thirteen years service but still only in his fifties, Gore was a comparatively young elder statesman during the decade of the 1920's. Throughout this period he appeared before civic groups and other organizations, including the American Legion of New York County and the Academy of Political Science in the City of New York, speaking on subjects ranging from rural credits to post-war depression and recovery.[35] Shortly after his retirement in 1921 he delivered a Commencement address at Cumberland University, Lebanon, Tennessee, being awarded an honorary Doctor of Laws degree by his alma mater. Further recognition to the ex-Senator came for a brief period when he was made special lecturer on the history of law at National University in Washington, D.C.[36]

But Gore's activities in the 1920's were not limited to his law practice and speaking engagements. Political aspirations were ever present in his thoughts, and politics consumed a great part of his time and effort. Although living in the nation's capital during the 1920's, former Senator Gore retained his legal residence in Oklahoma, and he was never out of touch with the political situation in his home state. Hardly had he been relieved of his official duties in 1921 when friends began suggesting him for governor of Oklahoma. Gore was reminded that a four-year term in the governorship would put him in line for a United States Senate seat at the next election,[37] but he refused to show interest in the gubernatorial post. He preferred the national scene, and all his political activity during the twenties pointed directly or indirectly to his return to the Senate. Since friends kept him informed of political conditions in Oklahoma, he was constantly prepared to leap into its rowdy politics when he felt the time was right.[38]

Not long after the Senator's defeat in the Democratic primary election of 1920, political leaders in Oklahoma proposed a plan to reorganize the Democratic party. They suggested that a preferential convention be introduced at which the party would officially approve certain candidates to run in the direct primary election. It was also recommended that the county unit rule be negated for nominations to district offices and be replaced by a two-thirds majority of the convention necessary for a nomination. The proposals were violently opposed and were dropped but not before Gore expressed his opinion of them. Recalling that the section of the state constitution providing for direct primary elections had been reinforced by an act of the state legislature, he publicly disapproved of this proposal, contending that the party had no right to invalidate the primary election law by nominating candidates for offices in preferential convention.[39] The ticket of those in control of the convention would "STALK through the democratic primary," he wrote. To the Oklahoma chairman of the National Democratic Committee he expressed his opposition. "The proposition to empower the State convention to reject the unanimous choice of a district must be looked upon either as a piece of humor or as a piece of madness. I hardly know whether I am more distressed or astonished by this extraordinary proposition. It is big with disaster."[40]

Holding a convention prior to the direct primary election for the nomination of party-supported candidates to run in the primary was definitely a step backward, according to Gore. He saw the proposal as a means by which the party hierarchy could gain almost absolute control of the primary contests, with the power to dictate election results in a perennially Democratic state. The independent politician who had recently been harshly treated by his opponents high in the state's party was repelled by this possibility. He knew his own future comeback depended not on the wishes of the party leaders but upon his appeal to the farmers.

Robert L. Owen, who had entered the Senate with Gore in 1907, announced near the end of his third term that because of poor health he would not run for re-election. Owen lived on for many years, but his decision to retire at this particular time foreshadowed an exciting chapter of Oklahoma politics. John C. Walton had been elected to the governorship in 1922, and within a few weeks after taking office he was accused of unnecessarily enlarging the public payroll. The fiery Governor deliberately alienated all but his few closest friends with his belligerent attitude toward the charge, and impeachment proceedings were soon widely and openly discussed. Such talk did not deter Walton. When proceedings actually were instituted, the Governor suspended the right of habeas corpus, placed the state under martial law, and had machine guns pointed toward the members of a grand jury when they attempted to assemble in Oklahoma City to investigate the charges against him. But the fighting Governor was waging a losing battle. In November, 1923, the state senate found Walton guilty on eleven of sixteen counts, and Lieutenant Governor M. E. Trapp filled out the deposed Governor's term.[41]

While the impeachment charges were being drawn up, Walton frantically searched for an issue which would divert public attention from his official record and place him in a more favorable light with the Oklahoma electorate. He settled on the issue of the Ku Klux Klan. The Klan had become rather strong in Oklahoma politics during the early twenties, but many people were suspicious of it. Walton played upon these suspicions. Although his fight against the Klan did not prevent the Governor from being ousted in 1923, it became the prelude to the United States Senate race the following year. Using the Klan as his whipping boy, Walton announced his candidacy and began a vigorous campaign to capture the Democratic nomination for the seat being vacated by Senator Owen.

Gore had supported Walton's candidacy in 1922, but on the opening day of the impeachment trial he delivered a speech before a joint session of the state legislature strongly criticizing the state administration.[42] This stand against the unpopular Governor won applause over the state; it was becoming increasingly evident that hostility to Gore was diminishing. The former Senator insisted that his speech against Walton was not political and that he was not running for Owen's seat, but an editorial writer for an Oklahoma City newspaper pondered, "Gore looms as a senatorial possibility. Can it be that his star is rising at the moment when the star of Walton is disappearing?"[43] As the months passed, it was apparent to political observers that no strong contender had appeared to oppose the candidacy of the anti-Klan Walton, and pressure was placed on Gore to make the race. In March, 1924, when Gore's candidacy in the forthcoming Democratic primary was still a matter of conjecture, the Okmulgee *Democrat* expressed the tacit thoughts of many in this statement: "We did not agree with Senator Gore in many of the votes he cast during the last two years he was a member of the United States Senate, but we were always conscious that he was voting as he thought right. We cannot help but admire the man who has the stamina to stand for the things he regards as right regardless of popular clamour. Senator Gore is honest, very able, thoroughly loyal to his state, a progressive Democrat, who would probably be able to unite the various factions in the state.

"Why not Thomas P. Gore for senator?"[44]

As early as April, 1924, most observers assumed that Gore was running for the vacated post, but he declined to make a public announcement of his candidacy. His lengthy answer in late March to a telegram sent to him from the managing editor of the Tulsa *Tribune* indicated that the former Senator was laying definite plans to enter the race. In view of the possibility of Gore's candidacy, the *Tribune* editor requested Gore to explain his stand on the tariff on oil and his relationship with Edward L. Doheny, then being criticized for his part in the sensational Teapot Dome scandal. Gore admitted that he was not a protectionist and had opposed the tariff on Mexican crude oil, but he tried to soften his answer by reminding the editor that a Republican House, Senate, and President also favored that tariff. In the same paragraph he pointed out that he twice assisted in the defeat of a federal tax on gasoline. Nor did he fail to mention the depletion clause which he helped make into law, saving Oklahoma oil interests millions of dollars.

Of the scandals relating to the naval leases Gore pleaded ignorance, his first knowledge of the affair having been derived from the public press. Stating that Doheny was one of the first persons to employ his legal services after he left the Senate in 1921, Gore admitted having given professional advice relating to Mexico's mining laws to the oil-splattered Doheny. But he reminded the inquirer that the oil hearings had revealed that William G. McAdoo had served Doheny in a similar capacity, and McAdoo had not been tainted. Gore felt that he himself should not be charged with guilt by association. He emphasized that he could not ask the support of anyone who thought that such a professional tie would influence his official conduct. Using the *Tribune* as a sounding board, Gore closed this letter requesting that the people of Oklahoma write him frankly expressing their choice for Senator.[45] Spending most of the spring of 1924 in Oklahoma feeling out the sentiment of the state, Gore spoke before numerous civic organizations. He continued to stress that he would run only if a sufficient number of his friends urged him to enter the contest,[46] but by June it was an open secret that he was definitely in the race.

Failing to heed a suggestion that he wait until the 1926 campaign,[47] Gore filed for the Democratic nomination to the Senate post on the last day the lists were open. Less than a week later he was sorry that he had joined the scramble for the seat. The primary race developed into a struggle over one issue only: the Klan. The impeached former Governor's single-plank platform against the Klan and his persistent attacks on the Invisible Empire played up the issue until no other was of importance. Former state auditor E. B. Howard of Tulsa received the endorsement of the Grand Dragon of the Klan, who called upon all members to support the Tulsan, while C. J. Wrightsman, a Tulsa oil millionaire only mildly sympathetic toward Klansmen, was backed by the *Fiery Cross,* the official publication of the state's secret society. Former state attorney general S. P. Freeling jumped into the race as an avowed opponent of Waltonism, while Gore tried to remain neutral on the Klan issue at a time when neutrality was forgotten in a race typified by extremism. Gore welcomed the votes of both the anti-Klaners and the Klansmen, but he refused to take a stand for either. When candidates were being compelled to "stand up and be counted" on the burning issue of the day, Gore was unwilling to embroil himself, expressing disappointment that the Klan issue overshadowed all others.[48] The *Fiery Cross* attacked Gore as a candidate of the big oil interests, linking his name with the Doheny-Sinclair combination, but the electorate refused to show undue interest in the oil scandals.

As the campaign progressed it was apparent that Walton's anti-Klan stand was winning him votes. Freeling, whose campaign was obviously lagging far behind, proposed on the eve of the election that all candidates entered against Walton withdraw except one selected by the Democratic central committee,[49] but the suggestion was rejected because the other candidates were unwilling to make the sacrifice. The results of the August 5 balloting clearly indicated the disastrous outcome of an election in which one candidate was opposed by a multiple field. The ex-Governor headed the list with 91,510 votes, while the Klan-endorsed Howard candidacy received 83,922. Gore ran a poor third (56,249), with Wrightsman close behind (51,291) and Freeling bringing up the rear with 15,384.[50]

In his second primary loss within four years Gore had been attacked on three grounds: his war record, his betrayal of the Democratic party, and his connection with Doheny as an attorney.[51] He attributed his defeat to the results of a *Daily Oklahoman* straw vote showing his candidacy faltering, followed immediately by the Klan's endorsement of Howard. In his opinion this combination

138

revolutionized the whole situation in thirty-six hours. He believed that the counties where he had the strongest support of those voters opposed to Walton about-faced and voted for Howard, who had no substantial strength in those areas previously.[52] Actually the poor showing was due to Gore's refusal to take a stand on the dominant issue of the day, along with the fact that he was anathema to Democrats who respected the memory of Woodrow Wilson.

The general election in November was an anticlimax to the heated Democratic primary. W. B. Pine, who had captured the Republican nomination in a field of six, his strongest opponent being Eugene Lorton, publisher of the Tulsa *World*, was not a Klan candidate. Walton's great publicity campaign against the Klan fizzled when he had no opponent to attack as pro-Klan. Pine won over Walton with comparative ease, as many Democrats, including the editor of the *Daily Oklahoman*, refused to support Walton as the party's nominee. Normally Democratic Oklahoma sent its second Republican Senator to Washington, and from 1924 to 1926 only Republicans represented the state in the Senate.

As soon as the primary ended, Gore returned to Washington to his law practice. Office work prevented his oratorical participation in the general election, although he backed the Democratic candidates on the national level. After John W. Davis was selected as the Democratic presidential nominee, Gore telegraphed: "You were my first choice from the first. Congratulations. Command me."[53]

The fact that Gore resided in Washington did not keep his name out of Oklahoma political conversations. Throughout 1925 Gore and United States Congressman Elmer Thomas were often mentioned in Democratic circles as possible candidates for Republican John W. Harreld's Senate seat in 1926. Gore exhibited his characteristic humor in the fall of 1925 when friends suggested his name for three offices, Governor, Senator, and Congressman for the sixth district. He enjoyed quipping that it would be much better for three-thirds of his friends to favor him for one office than for one-third to favor him for each of three offices.[54]

When Elmer Thomas definitely entered the Senate race, leaving the sixth district contest wide open, Gore filed for the vacated office. But after a trip to western Oklahoma to ascertain sentiment, he found that many of his former supporters had already pledged themselves to other candidates; therefore, he withdrew from the race only a few days after filing for it. Some of his backers were puzzled by this reversal because the field of candidates was large and the Senator's chances for a comeback appeared good.[55] Jed Johnson, a member of the state senate, won Thomas' old seat, and it may have been his strong candidacy that convinced Gore that he should not run for Congress. Whatever the reason, Gore finally decided to continue as a private citizen before making another bid for a coveted Senate post. Thomas, winning easily in the primary against the declining Walton, his closest opponent, and defeating the incumbent Harreld, was destined to represent Oklahoma in the Senate for twenty-four years.

When the Oklahoma Democrats began laying plans for the 1928 national convention, old animosities were overlooked, and national committeeman Scott Ferris chose Gore to be one of the "big eight" of the sixteen delegates from Oklahoma.[56] Gore's first choice for the presidential nomination was James A. Reed of Missouri, and during his seconding speech for Reed, Gore threw the Houston convention delegates into gales of laughter by his sardonic ridicule of Herbert Hoover. His pointed barbs of wit directed at the G. O. P. and its candidates brought shouts of glee and howls of approval from the vast Democratic throng.[57] In a left-handed thrust at Republican President Calvin Coolidge, Gore seconded the nomination of a man "who has never kept silent when silence was sin."[58] To his Democratic listeners he urged a united party for the coming campaign: "Let's all kiss and make up, no matter who we have to kiss."[59]

After four caucus ballots the Oklahoma delegation agreed under the unit rule to cast its eight votes for Reed,[60] but Alfred E. Smith of New York was nominated by the convention on the first ballot. Following his own advice for party unity, Gore campaigned for Governor Smith after withdrawing as a candidate for Congressman from Oklahoma's sixth district for the second time in two years.[61] Spending the greater part of September and October campaigning for the national ticket, he toured twenty states, most of his time being spent in Illinois, Nebraska, and Oklahoma. Over station WGN (Chicago) Gore assailed all Republican Presidents since Grant. Of Coolidge he said that the man who would make a "sphinx seem like a chatterbox" was the "greatest novelist that ever sat in the White House, for he writes fictitious speeches and messages concerning fictitious prosperity and fictitious economy." He resurrected his fight with Hoover during the war days by reminding his listeners that Hoover was responsible for prices being fixed below the market price during the war.[62] He appealed to the isolationism of the voters of the Midwest when he accused the G. O. P. candidate of being pro-British. But the Republicans had the better of the race in 1928, when the "solid" South was penetrated by the dual issues of prohibition and religion.

Gore was living in Washington when the stock market crash of 1929 occurred, but he kept a careful watch on economic conditions and political developments in Oklahoma as the Great Depression got underway. As the elections of 1930 approached, industrial activity in Oklahoma lessened noticeably. Coal, zinc, and lead mines in the eastern part of Oklahoma shut down. Thousands of laborers were put out of work. The bottom dropped out of the oil market, and Oklahoma's largest industry suffered devastating losses. Oklahoma farmers, knowing little prosperity since the days of World War I, were plagued by mortgages, surpluses, and falling prices. In addition, they were experiencing the first of a series of drought years which struck rural families by the hundreds of thousands in the thirties.

Although never having captured control of the state government, the Oklahoma Republicans had enjoyed their most successful era during the 1920's, electing two United States Senators and a host of lesser officials. But stigmatized as the party of the depression they were a minor factor in the state's political activity of 1930. Attention was riveted on the Democratic primaries, where the choices of public officials would in all likelihood be made.

In the early spring of 1930 Gore went to Oklahoma to survey the political situation and to deliver speeches at dinners held by the League of Young Democrats. Mail began pouring into his offices at the Huckins Hotel in Oklahoma City, and increasing numbers of people dropped in to visit the former Senator. After much hesitation for fear of a third straight primary defeat, Gore announced that he desired to run for the Senate and plunged into the campaign with vigor. A thorough organization was established, the central headquarters keeping in contact with nearly every precinct leader in the state who was working for the former Senator. As he had done in his first national race, Gore himself took to the stump, making his appeal to the marginal farmers in Oklahoma by attacking the trusts, bankers, warlords, and diplomats.[63] His plain, straightforward comments in the rural areas on the economic conditions of the nation had their effect.[64] When farmers asked Gore to explain why a $100 steer sold for less than $50, Gore was able to get straight to the point, discussing the origin of the trouble in simple terms and suggesting the way to a possible cure of the undesirable situation.[65] This method of dealing with economic conditions won him many votes.

Gore's primary opponents included three former Oklahoma governors—J. B. A. Robertson, Lee Cruce, and Henry Johnston—and a millionaire oil man, Charles J. Wrightsman.[66] These contestants attacked Gore's candidacy by resurrecting all the old arguments of the 1920 campaign, with a few additional ones thrown in for good measure. Gore's voting record during World War I, his opposition to Wilson, and his speeches concerning American soldiers were publicized anew. An issue unique to this campaign was raised, one recalling the first Oklahoma senatorial election. Gore had won a seat in 1907 because he was the leading western candidate after polling third place behind two easterners. The tacit agreement among the politicians to have a Senator from each side of the state had not been a problem in subsequent elections, and the east-west issue had all but been forgotten. The opposition press raised the sectional issue in 1930, since Gore's legal residence in Lawton was only a few miles from Medicine Park, home of the state's popular Senator Elmer Thomas. Attacking Gore for ignoring the old geographical arrangement, the press made much of the fact that Gore had originally won a seat because the gentlemen's agreement prevailed.[67] With the newspapers beating the sectional drums, Gore took no chances, promising to move to the east side if he won, although the other candidates gave little attention to the sectional aspect of the contest.[68]

The voting pattern in the primary showed every county on the west side going for Gore, scrapping the old geographical arrangement permanently. The three ex-governors were "also-rans"; Gore and Wrightsman were chosen for the run-off primary, the former Senator leading the oil man by only 179 votes. Gore's victory was the most unexpected outcome of the first primary. Few observers thought the old politician would reveal so much strength in his single-handed comeback.

The run-off contest found the two leading newspapers of the state making surprise reversals in policy in their coverage of the Gore candidacy. The perennially antagonistic *Daily Oklahoman* created a mild sensation when in a front-page editorial it sided with Gore as "the best available candidate." The Tulsa *Daily World*, the only major paper in the state which had favored Gore in the 1920 primary, cast its lot with Wrightsman, reasoning that Oklahoma needed a wealthy man in the Senate during a time of economic crisis.[69] The switch was not as unusual as it appeared on the surface. Located in the oil center of Oklahoma, the *World* could hardly be expected not to support one from its own fold, and the *Oklahoman*, with more interest in the governor's race than the senatorial contest, was making a desperate but futile bid for the rural vote for well-to-do Frank Buttram over "Alfalfa Bill" Murray, the two run-off candidates in the governor's race.

The gubernatorial campaign had moved to the center ring of the Oklahoma political circus, overshadowing the Senate contest. The penniless Murray, who appealed to the rural element of Oklahoma as no one else could, had run far ahead of the field in the first primary. Gore was not unaware of the fact that the impecunious "Tribune of Tishomingo" was a sure-fire vote-getter. During the second campaign, Gore pictured himself to the voters as the man with the hole in his pocket running against a "multimillionaire," making political capital of his own moderate (though far from poverty-stricken) circumstances. Gore intensified his attacks on the "moneyed interests," and he relentlessly repeated that a rich man could not enter the United States Senate. With poverty and blindness associated in the minds of the poorer classes, Murray and Gore came to be thought of together. This was inevitable. A pair of impoverished but unbowed advocates of the people were linked in their fight against Buttram and Wrightsman, two bright symbols of special privilege.[70] With Murray and Gore each crying, "You can't sell a millionaire to a pauper people,"[71] the down-but-not-out boys won handily over their opponents. Contrary to tradition, more Oklahoma voters turned out for the second than for the first primary.

Wrightsman had unwittingly alienated the masses by declaring that he was above political graft because he had plenty of money.

Since most of his listeners had empty pockets, his attack on corruption backfired. Looking down his nose at the annual salary of Senators, he hinted that a "gentleman" could scarcely live on $10,000 a year. Nor did he win the sympathy of the laboring classes when he stressed that he was a *friend* of the poor man and the laborer, with the implication that he certainly was not one of them. Inadvertent references to his mansion and butler may have lost more votes than they gained.[72] The oil candidate would have been better off had he made no speeches during the run-off.

The two Democratic nominees continued their pauper approach against their Republican opponents. Tying his campaign more firmly than ever to the Murray bandwagon, Gore spoke often of the friendship he and Murray had when they were both poor, struggling lawyers in Corsicana, Texas.[73] "Murray and Gore" car stickers emphasized the association of the political war horses for the November election, as did their advocates who spoke often of "Tom and Bill" in the same breath.[74]

In the face of Gore's growing strength the old "Ex-Service Men's League Against Gore" was revived, with its headquarters in Oklahoma City's largest hotel. The veterans' group distributed countless pieces of propaganda against the former Senator, containing half-truths and fallacious statements as it lifted out of Gore's speeches and from their context such terms as "conscripted slackers," "sunshine patriots," "Mollycoddles," and "feather-legged cowards." A letter written by one of the organization's leaders and distributed to hundreds of veterans recalled that Gore had been denounced in the 1920 race by Scott Ferris, present Democratic National Committeeman, and by Judge Sam Hayes, present Democratic State Chairman, for being "disloyal and unpatriotic to his country, and unworthy of democratic support."[75] The letter failed to point out that Ferris was Gore's rival in the memorable contest ten years earlier and that Hayes had been soundly beaten by the Senator in 1914. The Ku Klux Klan was also active against Gore,[76] but it was no longer the potent political force which it had been earlier in the decade.

Gore's Republican opponent was the incumbent W. B. Pine, who was backed by wealthy oil interests in the state. A pamphlet published by the Democratic state headquarters had the dubious title of "God vs. Gold, Man vs. Mammon, Gore vs. Pine," but the implication was clear. Playing on his opponent's name, Gore delightfully paraphrased the Bible when he punned countless times that "a tree, even a pine, should be judged by its fruit."[77] Bringing chuckles from his sympathetic audiences, the Democrat enjoyed referring to Lew Wentz, wealthy Republican party boss in Oklahoma, and Pine as the "Gold Dust Twins." But all was not fun and frolic during the campaign. When economic conditions took a turn for the worse, the challenger gained votes with the keynote of all his speeches centering on the crisis. He grimly remarked, "If the people are satisfied with things as . . . they are, they should vote the Republican ticket."[78] When Gore heard a rumor that the postmasters of the state were active in behalf of Pine, he shot a letter to the Postmaster General of the United States bluntly stating, "If consistent with your policy to notify them of the rules and regulations of your Department regarding pernicious political activity I would greatly appreciate it."[79]

The incumbent campaigned in dead seriousness. Except for an occasional reference to "Goresque sarcasm" he seldom mentioned his wisecracking opponent. Refusing to involve himself in a face-to-face debate with Gore, Pine instead exploited the possibilities of the radio, which had become a valuable means of mass communication by the closing days of the campaign.[80] Personable, competent, and with remarkably organized publicity, Pine did everything he could to appeal to the Democratic majorities of the state. Divorcing himself from the Republican administration, thus counteracting much of Gore's hostile criticism of Hoover, Pine vainly struggled to keep the voters from identifying him with the depression.[81] His campaign paper, the *Oklahoma Record*, revealed Pine's efforts to be independent of the Republican party by appearing "in the interests of the campaign of Senator W. B. Pine for re-election to the United States Senate on the republican ticket, *but as a representative of Oklahoma and its people.*"[82]

Pine's methods were almost successful. With the entire state landsliding to the Democratic side and many of the candidates receiving pluralities of upwards of 100,000, Gore's victory by 24,000 votes seemed narrow by comparison. His past record, the oil interests' support of his opponent, his somewhat ambiguous stand on prohibition and labor, together with Pine's personal popularity and independence from the Republican party, almost combined to beat the returning Senator. But Gore's campaign benefited from the popularity of the colorful Murray, the frog-throated "Sage of Tishomingo" who shouted to his listeners to vote Democratic, all the while wiping his perspiring brow with a red bandanna handkerchief. Gore probably would not have won had he not linked himself with Murray, who overwhelmed Republican Ira Hill by nearly 100,000 votes for the largest plurality any Oklahoma gubernatorial candidate had ever received.[83]

Besides Murray's role in Gore's victory, two other major factors contributed to it. One was worsening economic conditions in Oklahoma in 1930, which Gore appeared to understand as he talked about them with voters, and the other was the mood of isolationism which had dominated the American and Oklahoma scene in the 1920's. Criticism of Gore's isolationist and pacifist tendencies, which played a large part in the Senator's defeat in 1920, did not influence Oklahoma voters to any extent in 1930. After his defeat in 1920, Gore had expressed confidence that a reaction would come and that he would be able to re-enter public life. Having privately predicted that he would return to the Senate in 1933, he missed the exact date but not the main fact that Oklahoma voters would one day find their views not wholly out of accord with his.[84] Gore often recalled Will Rogers' statements that the Senator had been ten years ahead of his time and that the people would send him back to the Senate when they caught up with him. Memories of the bitter primary of 1920 dimmed considerably after a ten-year span, and in the pacifist reaction of postwar disillusionment the humorist's prophecy came true.

X. BATTLING A DEPRESSION INDEPENDENTLY

ALTHOUGH SENATOR GORE was re-elected to office in November, 1930, the Congress of which he was a member did not convene until over a year later. In the meantime the worldwide depression deepened as President Hoover's remedies had little effect on chaotic economic conditions. In the early summer of 1931 a number of leaders of the hard-hit European countries appealed to the United States to help them avert financial catastrophe. Since Congress was not in session, the President telephoned various leaders of both parties in Congress, securing the support of enough to assure him that his proposed action to offset Europe's possible financial collapse would be approved when Congress met. After consulting with American financial experts, Hoover suggested a one-year moratorium on all intergovernmental debts and reparations payments.[1]

When the new Congress convened, the first item of business was to give a vote of confidence to Hoover's moratorium plan. Even though it was a foregone conclusion that the Senate would approve the extralegal action, Gore refused to accept the plan and expressed his disapproval publicly. He believed that the proposal would serve as a "mere opiate" rather than as an antidote to the economic problems. "It deals with symptoms and not causes," he announced. "It does not lay the ax at the root of the tree of evil." Ever the defender of the federal Treasury, Gore predicted, correctly in most cases, that the nations would never pay the uncanceled remnants of their debts. He expressed his lack of faith on the Senate floor: "If some curious antiquarian of the future should do us the honor to ransack the record of this day, I wish him to note that there was one doubting Thomas, one realist, who did not share this illusion."[2] He suggested that before the moratorium be allowed, the foreign nations should pledge themselves to a reduction of armaments. There could be no real prosperity in this country or abroad, he felt, as long as the taxpayer was heavily burdened with the costs of military establishments.[3]

147

The House added an amendment to the joint resolution legalizing the Hoover moratorium in which it declared the policy of the United States to be to grant no further extensions or moratoriums. Gore, believing that such a policy could never be followed if a single moratorium were granted, facetiously declared that the Senate should add a proviso to this part of the resolution reading, "Provided, That this is no joke."[4] When a colleague read an article to the Senate which stated that "President Hoover electrified the world with his moratorium plan," Gore retorted, "I should like to add that he electrocuted the American taxpayer."[5] Despite Gore's opposition the moratorium received overwhelming endorsement by Congress, and it was hoped that perhaps this was the beginning of bipartisan cooperation in attempts to fight the economic depression.

This optimism was increased when the Congress passed legislation providing for the creation of the Reconstruction Finance Corporation. The passage of this important piece of legislation indicated that the majority of the members of the legislative branch of the government were willing to work with the executive in fighting the depression at home as well as abroad without regard to politics. But Gore did not favor the establishment of the RFC, and although he did not vote on the measure in its final form, he voted for several amendments which attempted to cut down the expenditures of the agency and against provisions to extend its lending powers.[6]

Legislation on the moratorium and the Reconstruction Finance Corporation was passed despite Gore's protests, but he and others were able to convince a majority of their colleagues that the La Follette-Costigan bill, providing for a federal appropriation of $750,000,000 to be used in cooperation with the states in relieving suffering caused by unemployment, should not be passed. Gore believed that if this bill passed, the dole in America would have commenced. As one of the outspoken critics of the bill, he tried to amend it so as to make it as palatable as possible in case it passed. He offered an amendment to require a certain proportion of the money to be applied to the payment of wages for services rendered, but his suggestion was rejected.[7] Prompted by a letter telling of a man who had paid a speeding fine with his welfare check, Gore tried to amend the bill to require social workers to give food, fuel, and clothing instead of money to financially insecure families. This too was rejected. The major talking point against the bill was that it provided for no additional revenue to cover the proposed expenditure. Relentlessly reminding the Senate that the total deficit of the federal Treasury was over two billion dollars, the opponents were able to defeat the bill.

The defeat of the La Follette-Costigan "give-away" plan was only a minor victory for the opponents of such legislation. As the depression deepened, more ambitious plans for temporarily remedying the financial conditions of the country were conceived and passed. Gore was unequivocally opposed to all such measures. Advocating a strict separation of the federal and state governments, he opposed the dole of federal relief favored by the administration and passed by Congress. When the federal government gave carloads of flour to the Red Cross for free distribution, Gore said, "If any of our governments must bestow gifts, gratuities, alms, doles, it ought to be done either by the State governments or the city governments, where they have immediate contact and can superintend the dispensation of charity."[8]

Gore was appalled by stories of people on relief who were being given free flour but who refused to help unload the food from the trains in which it was shipped to the distressed communities.[9] He incessantly preached that people on relief should work for the relief commodities rather than receiving them free. "The day on which we began to make these loans by the Federal Government to States, counties, and cities was a more evil day in the history of this Republic than the day on which the Confederacy fired upon Fort Sumter," he declared.[10]

Gore repeatedly stated that the policies of the Hoover administration to relieve the distress caused by the depression had not been well conceived. As he put it, "They have not been based upon sound principles. They do not promise results. I think they will aggravate our grief instead of relieving it. I do not believe that depression or distress can be ended by gifts, gratuities, doles, and alms handed out by the Federal Treasury, and extorted from taxpayers that are bleeding at every pore."[11] He tenaciously clung to the principle that for every dollar leaving the Treasury there should be compensation in return. He could not fathom deficit spending.

Gore was in complete accord with bills and amendments to cut expenditures. Various measures to reduce appropriations for the Treasury, the Post Office, the Bureau of Foreign and Domestic Commerce, the War Department, the Ocean Mail Service, and the like always received his support.[12] He voted consistently for amendments providing for reductions and against amendments providing for exemptions from those reductions. Confessing his distaste for cutting the salaries of government employees, he nevertheless favored this policy out of necessity. He preferred to have cuts all along the line rather than outright dismissal of many employees while others were retained at their usual salaries.[13] He even voted nay on an amendment providing that employees whose salaries did not exceed $2,000 a year were not to be affected by a proposed reduction. He reasoned that the cuts should be accepted by everyone in a time of crisis. He recorded himself in favor of reducing Senators' salaries as an example for other government workers. Desiring stringent retrenchment in financing, Gore was obsessed with trying to balance the budget.

But the Senator's compulsion to retard deficit spending did not mean that he favored overburdening the taxpayer to build up the depleted reserves of the Treasury. On the contrary, he went so far in his opposition to heavy taxation that he voted against the revenue bill for 1932. He did not believe that the government could tax itself out of the distress any more than it could borrow or spend itself out of adversity. With this idea dominant in his mind, he usually opposed the tax plans presented in the Senate. Advocating that taxes be based on wealth alone, he succeeded in having two amendments accepted which were designed to insure payment of income taxes by those receiving high salaries and executive bonuses. One of these provided that on salaries above $75,000 paid by a corporation, the excess could not be charged as a regular operating expense of the business. The other one allowed for a taxable rate of 80 per cent on any bonus of more than $75,000 paid to a single individual.[14]

The Senator could never be made to accept the theory of federal control even during so drastic an emergency. "If we need government enterprise in hard times, may it not be an improvement in good times over private enterprise?" he queried.[15] With this attitude Gore opposed a bill which provided for the purchase and sale of cotton under the supervision of the Secretary of Agriculture. He expressed his interest in the relief of the cotton farmer, but he felt that this approach would prove to be "an illusion and a cheat" to the farmer. Similar reasoning explained his opposition to the Federal Farm Board, which distributed government-owned wheat and cotton to the Red Cross and other organizations that in turn distributed it free. He felt that this was completely destroying American agriculture and that this country's agricultural economy would never be the same as a result of the Farm Board's policies.[16] He saw the Farm Board's efforts as sinister means by which it could "bootleg" its surplus cotton and wheat into the markets of this country.

Gore favored an emergency measure designed to amend the Federal Farm Loan Act, providing for additional capital for the federal land banks, but at the same time he did not want to sacrifice the land-bank system or the American taxpayer while saving the deserving borrower. Thus, when an amendment setting aside $25,000,000 for extensions was introduced, he could not refrain from speaking against it. "It is not a pleasant task to be hanging out red signals morning, noon, and night," he commented apologetically, "but I am afraid that some Senators and some borrowers perhaps have not been bearing down quite hard enough on that part of their devotions, 'Lead us not into temptation.' I think we are venturing into quicksands, and we may go beyond our depth and . . . capacity to retrace our steps."[17]

The Senator did not favor government appropriations to state-owned agricultural colleges. "When once we start this policy we can never stop it," he predicted. "When the lips of a State institution are once attached to the udder of the General Government they cannot be riven loose."[18] The policy of matching dollars by the central government and the state governments represented a dangerous trend to Gore. He believed extravagance was bred under these circumstances. By this time Gore had come to hold that if a state could handle a problem alone, the federal government should keep hands off. Only when curbing insect plagues and animal diseases which did not respect state lines should the federal government lend assistance to the states.

When the legislature explored ways to prevent another economic disaster ignited by a panic on the stock exchange, Gore freely expressed his theories in regard to a solution. He recognized the necessity for investors and the rights of legitimate speculators who dealt in stocks, but he would prevent the gamblers from playing the market if he had the power. The janitors, the waitresses, the cab drivers, and others who were buying on margin without reference to intrinsic value or earning power of the companies in whose stocks they dealt were the individuals Gore desired to curb. Knowing virtually nothing about economic conditions, these people, out to make money easily, never thought of assets or earnings of a given company. Continuing to buy certain stocks simply because they rose in the past, these gamblers were, in Gore's estimation, the fundamental cause of the stock market crash. To the people who had only a few dollars to invest yet invaded the stock market without real knowledge of its practices, Gore attached the label "lambs." He expressed a desire to find a way to prohibit the "lambs" from playing the market, keeping them out of the way of the "bears" and the "bulls." He reasoned that they not only hurt themselves but also the entire stock market and the economy of the country. In his words, he was searching for a way "to guard the fool against his folly."[19]

Gore believed that easy credit was also a primary cause of the stock market crash. "The use, the misuse, the overuse, and the abuse of credit" was a major if not the controlling cause of the money panic.[20] He blamed the Federal Reserve Board for inviting disaster when in 1927 it lowered the discount rate to $3\frac{1}{2}$ per cent, making easy credit available to thousands of gullible people. He believed that the crash and the resultant depression were due to a lack of confidence, but his solution for restoring that confidence was negative in nature. Doubting the value of legislative or administrative efforts, he felt that as the depression continued prices would finally hit bottom and stay there long enough for people to be convinced that they were going no lower. When this time arrived, he theorized, the depression would slowly come to an end as people gained confidence that prices would go no lower.[21] He did not predict how long this period would last, but he gave little encouragement that it would be a brief time.

The only positive suggestion for curing the depression which the Senator from Oklahoma made during the Republican administration was his advocacy of the revival of international trade. Since protectionism triumphed during the Republican supremacy of the twenties, Gore was sure that the tariff barriers aided depression. He was convinced that these walls would have to be lowered if not removed for trade and prosperity to return. When the country embarked on a "buy American" spree, Gore declared that it would lead to "good-by

America" in the markets of the world. The Senator was convinced that the philosophy of buying only American goods was harmful to the United States and also believed that it would hinder worldwide recovery. Such a policy was to him both shortsighted and unwise.

When a member of the Senate introduced an amendment suggesting that to help solve the labor shortage only American crews be employed on United States ocean mail liners, Gore ridiculed the suggestion. The logical conclusion of such an act would be to provide the American crews with American oxygen so that their pulmonary apparatus would not be damaged by the salted seas. Continuing his satire, he requested that the Senate devise an amendment requiring American ships, "when they go down to the sea, to follow the waters emptied into the ocean by the Hudson, the Mississippi and the Columbia, and ply only those waters which originate in America." In a roar of noes and laughter, the Senate caught Gore's point and voted down the proposed amendment.[22] Nor did Gore agree that a protective tariff assisted American labor. He insisted that if trade were freely carried on, in the long run the American laborer would profit.

Gore's role during the Republican administration was primarily one of critic and opponent. Thinking that all of the efforts of the administration were in vain, Gore was a stalwart advocate of laissez faire in the midst of one of the world's worst economic crises. On one occasion he dourly remarked that a depression could no more be relieved by laws than disease could be prevented by the passage of a resolution. He concluded, "This is an economic disease. You might just as well try to prevent the human race from having a disease as to prevent economic grief of this sort."[23] He knew that economic laws were far more powerful than the enactments of the United States Congress, and except for his comments that trade should be stimulated, he advanced no concrete suggestion for solving the problems of the depression.

If Gore offered no solutions for such problems, he at least helped the morale of his colleagues by not taking current concerns too seriously. His wit and humor kept his fellow members in a gayer mood as darker days closed upon them. Punning on the President's name, he spoke of the Treasury being cleaned out with a Hoover vacuum.[24] When the President insisted that prosperity was hovering just around the corner, Gore changed the verb to "Hoovering" and chuckled at his own cleverness. He facetiously suggested placing a tax on red ink, for by so doing the government would gain large sums of revenue and could meet the deficit in the Treasury. In the midst of increasing regulation to which he was unalterably opposed, Gore reflected his own economic philosophy when he observed, "I do not believe in the fairies."

Long before the 1932 presidential campaign, Democratic politicians made extensive plans for returning to power. When Franklin D. Roosevelt wrote a number of letters to political observers all over the country in 1928 after Al Smith's defeat, Gore was included. Roosevelt asked for the Oklahoman's opinion on political conditions in his section of the country. The New Yorker's professed reason for writing these letters was to keep the Democratic party's national organization functioning between election years. "This is no time to discuss candidates," he wrote, "but it seems to me that it is the time for putting into effect a permanent working organization."[25] In answer Gore included a copy of a letter he had written to the chairman of the National Democratic Committee in which he had given his analysis of the Democrats' 1928 defeat and his suggestions for victory in 1932. Stressing that they should take advantage of the "breaks" during Hoover's administration, he suggested that the party schedule a big rally not later than Jefferson's birthday in 1930. He also favored keeping the Democratic organization intact at all times rather than allowing it to deteriorate between elections.[26]

Gore was one of the speakers at the annual Jefferson Day dinner in New York City, sponsored by the National Democratic Clubs in April, 1931, when he urged the party to unite for victory. He suggested that the Democratic approach during the campaign revolve around Hoover, hunger, and hard times. He recommended that the next Democratic platform be condensed into six words: less taxes, more trade, no trusts.[27] This approach had been successful for his own candidacy during the trust-busting prewar era, and in 1932 it seemed to him a valid approach on a national scale.

When the Democrats met in convention at Chicago in the summer of 1932, Gore was present as a delegate-at-large from Oklahoma. The backers of several candidates, including Roosevelt, Al Smith, John N. Garner, and Albert Ritchie, hoped for Oklahoma's twenty-two votes, but on the first ballot the Oklahomans lined up for favorite son Governor William H. Murray.[28] At 4 A.M. on the morning of June 30, during the course of the second ballot, Murray startled the convention by placing in nomination the name of Oklahoma's famous humorist, Will Rogers. The convention took the nomination for what it was, a gesture of appreciation, and Rogers received only the votes of his Sooner friends.[29] This move by the Oklahoma delegation may have been no more than a tribute of respect for the state's most popular native son, but Rogers and Gore thought very much alike on political questions, and the gesture may have been a genuine effort on the part of the Gore-led Oklahomans to stampede the convention for the humorist.

On the third ballot Oklahoma split its vote evenly between Garner and James A. Reed. When the convention adjourned after the completion of the third ballot, Roosevelt had a commanding lead, needing only eighty-five votes for the necessary two-thirds majority. July 1 was spent by the leaders of the convention in behind-the-scenes bargaining as they made plans for the Roosevelt victory and the election of a vice-presidential nominee. That evening F.D.R. won on the fourth ballot without difficulty, Oklahoma jumping on the band-wagon with her twenty-two votes. After "Cactus Jack" Garner was nominated for the Vice-Presidency, the convention adjourned, its delegates confident that their Messiah, who had broken precedent and appeared at the convention to accept the nomination in person, would deliver them and the country from economic chaos within a few months.

Gore was happy with the selections. A few weeks after the convention ended, he wrote a long letter to Roosevelt in which he stressed the need for party organization. He recalled at length the well-developed political machinery (for which he was responsible) used by the party in the presidential election of 1912. Although attempting to convince Roosevelt that a smoothly functioning organization was important to a successful campaign, he emphasized in his letter that "there is no substitute for personal touch or contact with the individual voter."[30] This statement Gore may have made because of his fear that Roosevelt, with a physical handicap, might prefer to carry on the campaign without stumping the country. Certainly Gore's activities in the summer of 1932 gave added evidence of the Senator's strong belief in personal contact. He officially opened the Democratic campaign for the national ticket in various Oklahoma counties, being the principal speaker at an October Saturday night rally in Oklahoma City. Dwelling on the hard-times theme, he asserted, "The man who wants more Hoover prosperity is the one who should heed Mr. Coolidge's advice not to change engineers during a wreck—dead or alive. If anyone wants any more of this Hoover prosperity, he is just a glutton for hard times. He has a tapeworm for trouble."[31]

True to tradition, Gore did not limit his campaigning to his own state. Continuing to speak on the economic theme, he made puns that reached the ears of the farmers of other depression-ridden areas. His itinerary included many Midwestern states, climaxed with a week of speeches in California.[32] Having campaigned in Hoover's home county of Santa Clara, Gore was credited with carrying that county for the Democrats.[33] The old politician's appeal throughout the campaign had been to both Democrats and Republicans. After having a resolution adopted at the Chicago convention which invited the support of Senator George W. Norris and other progressive Republicans to assist in the election of a Democratic ticket,[34] Gore asked the voters to go to the polls without regard to previous political affiliation.

Following a conference with Roosevelt soon after the convention, Gore had sent a mimeographed letter to thousands of voters in Oklahoma, including this sentence: "I went up to Albany a few days ago and saw the present Governor of New York, who as I hope, will be the next President of the United States. I promised him Oklahoma by 100,000 and I placed your name on the surety bond."[35] Many of the recipients of this letter believed that Gore's estimate was too low, and some predicted Oklahoma would go for Roosevelt by a 200,000 majority. The prognosticators were far below the correct total. When the final tabulation was made, Roosevelt's majority was well over 300,000 in the economically hard-hit state of Oklahoma. The vote was almost equally one-sided throughout the nation. Roosevelt coasted to a victory in the electoral college by 472 to 59. Primarily on the issue of the economic condition of the country, the Democratic party had been swept back into power for its first administration since the days of Woodrow Wilson.

The Democratic platform for the 1932 campaign included a plank recommending the repeal of the Eighteenth Amendment. Pending repeal, the delegates went on record favoring immediate modification of the Volstead Act. This action by the convention placed Gore in a delicate dilemma. In his comeback race two years earlier he had pledged his support of the Democratic platform of Oklahoma, which endorsed the Volstead Act. During the last months of Hoover's administration, he refused to support any move to change the strictly worded prohibition law. Keeping his pledge to the state platform, he even voted against a Senate resolution favoring action by the governors of the various states to obtain a referendum on the liquor question.[36]

Having been admonished by Oklahoma observers to soft-pedal the prohibition issue in 1932, Gore wisely followed their advice most of the time. But when the Republicans adopted a plank in their national platform in which they stated that they desired to modify but not repeal the Eighteenth Amendment, Gore made fun of the move by saying that it was a "wet-dry" plank written by an "ambidextrous amphibian." Hoover received his share of criticism for double-talking on the prohibition issue, but one defender of Hoover said that the President should not be attacked on the liquor issue since he was already "carrying water on both shoulders" because of the economic crisis. To this Gore laughingly replied, "The President is not carrying water on both shoulders. He is now doing a cake walk with Rebecca's pitcher on one shoulder and the little brown jug on the other shoulder, under the guise of 'a noble experiment.' "[37]

Since the national election was being interpreted as a mandate on the prohibition issue, Gore found himself faced with a ticklish problem which he handled with finesse. When the new Democratic administration passed a revenue-gaining amendment to the Volstead Act, Gore asked to be excused from voting, explaining his reason for this request. Quoting the 1930 Democratic platform of Oklahoma which he had endorsed as a candidate that year, stating that all United States senatorial and congressional candidates were to "oppose the repeal of the eighteenth amendment or any effort to weaken the Volstead law, unless and until the people themselves, by their expressed will, shall have otherwise directed," Gore announced that since the people had not expressed themselves he felt he could not vote for the amendment. Reading from the national platform of 1932, Gore pointed out his dilemma and was excused from voting on these grounds. Thus, the Senator diplomatically side-stepped the explosive prohibition problem until the necessary states voted to repeal the Eighteenth Amendment. Gore could have alienated many of his followers in the strongly dry state of Oklahoma had he gone against his pledge to the state platform. As it happened he was able to avoid an embarrassing vote.

At the time he drew favorable publicity for refusing to go against campaign pledges.

But prohibition had not been the major issue in the 1932 campaign. Economic issues were paramount, and the Democrats played upon them masterfully. The new President-elect, looked upon by many as a deliverer, had won the election and was preparing to take over the reins of the government to inaugurate a program destined to change to a considerable degree American society.

XI. "IS THE CONSTITUTION A MERE SOUVENIR?"[1]

ALTHOUGH SENATOR GORE had been a strong supporter of Franklin D. Roosevelt's candidacy for the presidency in 1932, he was disappointed soon after Roosevelt took office. Gore hoped that the new President would be able to solve the pressing economic problems of the nation with a minimum of radical changes; instead, Roosevelt inaugurated a revolutionary program generally unacceptable to the Senator. Gore's distaste for government regulation dated from the days of the First World War, and when the New Deal went far beyond the dreams of the most recent Republican President, whose mild policies Gore had opposed, the Senator openly revolted.[2]

Gore voted for the banking holiday bill, but he had misgivings about the unlimited plenary power granted under it. In the face of the haste used in preparing the emergency measure, he suggested that its provisions be valid only during the first session of the Seventy-third Congress. Concerned over the effects this act might have on state banks, Gore offered an amendment to permit such banks to become temporary members of the Federal Reserve System without being required to subscribe to the capital stock of the Federal Reserve Banks. This, he thought, would help restore a sound banking system in the country. But the Senate rejected all amendments, accepting the legislation as originally written.

A few days after the passage of the emergency banking law, Gore submitted a resolution proposing an amendment to the Constitution giving Congress complete control over all banking. Requiring all state banks to receive consent from Congress before being chartered and subjecting all state banking laws to the control of Congress, this amendment would have given the national legislature power to make all laws necessary to provide for a more uniform system of banking throughout the nation.[3]

Along with the subject of banking was the ever-present problem of the currency. In April, 1933, the President officially forbade the hoarding of gold and gold certificates, and two weeks later the nation formally abandoned the gold standard. In the meantime, many groups throughout the country were clamoring for an inflated currency. In May Congress authorized the Chief Executive to inflate the currency by the addition of $3,000,000,000 in new treasury notes or to reduce the gold content of the dollar up to 50 per cent. Currency manipulation did not appreciably increase commodity prices, and in the following January the President was given permission to devalue the dollar, to impound all gold in the Treasury and the Federal Reserve Banks, and to create from the accruing profit a stabilization fund of $2,000,000,000. With the value of the dollar at 59.06 cents the nation returned to a modified gold standard.

The problem of the currency was a vexing one to Senators. Both Gore and his Oklahoma colleague, Elmer Thomas, spent many hours wrestling with the question. In the tradition of William Jennings Bryan and the silverites, Thomas was an out-and-out inflationist. By January, 1933, Thomas would have backed any scheme for inflating the currency. Proclaiming his friendship for his farm constituency, he believed that only through inflation could the farmers receive a fair return for their arduous labor. He believed that if more currency were circulated, farm prices could be tripled. With the farmers' purchasing power restored through inflation, the group would then receive fair prices for its products, he illogically reasoned, and the farmers would no longer be an unequal element in American society. So convinced was Thomas that inflation of the currency would solve the money problem that he even suggested wooden scrip as a medium for legal tender.[4]

Thomas outspokenly blamed the Federal Reserve System for the deflation of the currency and the depression. Accusing the authors of the Federal Reserve Act of favoritism toward the banking classes, the "Sage of Medicine Park" was quoted as saying, "The Federal Reserve Board has its hands in the pockets of every man who lives on the face of the earth."[5] During the 1930's Thomas introduced no less than twenty-five bills and resolutions embodying monetary proposals, offering in addition nearly twenty amendments of a similar nature to measures sponsored by other legislators. In all of these Thomas was working toward one goal: inflation of the currency. Blasting the ears of his colleagues with long speeches on the subject, he angrily threatened to take all the bank deposits away from the depositors and give them to those who had no money in the banks. Writing letters, making public speeches, delivering radio addresses, giving interviews, filling the *Congressional Record* with extended remarks, and circulating letters among his fellow Senators, Thomas pleaded for cheaper money and the wider circulation of silver.[6] With high-sounding half-true statements and oversimplified solutions, Thomas' arguments seemed plausible chiefly to the uninitiated.

Thomas' colleague from Oklahoma was on the other side of the money fence. While Thomas was shouting triumphantly that his inflation bill "will take $200,000,000,000 from the hands of those who have it, including the bank depositors, and give it to the debtors," Gore was blithely remarking, "If we must inflate the currency, why don't we license all the counterfeiters? That would get the money into the hands of the people."[7] While Thomas was angrily ranting on the subject, Gore was quiet and witty. When Thomas hailed the nationalization of silver as an important step that eventually would lead to an international monetary conference and perhaps to the establishment of a world bank in New York City to handle international settlements, his colleague expressed doubt that the expansion of the currency through nationalization would be beneficial. "I have more faith in turnip patches and gardens," Gore declared. "They at least provide feed for animals and food for people."[8]

Gore did not favor the coinage of silver, but if the step had to be taken, he desired to make the silver coin worth as much in specie as in bullion. This he felt was indispensable to a sound system of money. "It seems to me this effort to return to silver and to make it money is the same as would be an effort to abandon the freight train and the trucks and return to the oxcart and the mule team and the stage coach."[9] He voted against a bill which authorized the Secretary of the Treasury to purchase silver and issue silver certificates. Nor did he favor bimetallism, which he considered a "financial and monetary impossibility." When it was pointed out that a bimetallist measure put the country half on and half off the gold standard, Gore was reminded of the story of an old farmer who when asked what he thought of a mermaid replied, "Too much woman to fry, too much fish to hug."[10]

Gore's distrust of silver and bimetallism did not necessarily indicate that he held the gold standard to be inherently good per se. Believing that the gold standard demanded certain economic conditions before it would function adequately, he noted that such conditions had been destroyed for the time being and that a return to the gold standard was not the solution to the depression. If he did not favor inflated greenbacks, gold, silver, or bimetallism, what was the Senator's solution to the problem? The nearest he came to answering that question was when he expressed accord with the "re-establishment of an international standard of value and payment of some sort" which he deemed necessary for the revival of world trade and prosperity.[11] The Oklahoman's thinking on the subject of money was hazy, and he advanced no significant suggestions or solutions.

Along with the problems of banking and currency went the regulation of the stock exchanges. The Democrats had included in their national platform a promise for thoroughgoing reform of the whole security and investment business. When two important laws were passed, providing for the regulation of the stock exchanges, Gore expressed disapproval of the measures. He did not oppose regulation of stock exchanges, but he believed that these particular laws were too "extreme, radical, and revolutionary."[12] When it was remarked in his presence that one of the bills needed "teeth," Gore responded, "I do not want so many teeth in it that it will frighten everybody out of business."[13]

As a member of the Senate Banking and Currency Committee, Gore was prominent in the hearings on the abuses in the stock market. Not antagonistic toward the stock exchange itself or the system of trading in stocks and bonds, he indicated a genuine interest in trying to eliminate abuses. He particularly desired to control syndicates which "rigged" the market for their own benefit. He warned that those who used such methods could ultimately stop the market completely, "and that is a good deal like abolishing a red-light district, which would make it worse instead of better."[14] He himself introduced legislation to regulate the stock exchange based on a report from and with the approval of the Assistant Secretary of the Department of the Interior, but this bill did not have enough "teeth" to suit the administration leaders.

Gore made only one long speech in the Senate in regard to the regulation of stock exchange abuses, and an observer, who thought Gore "intelligent, independent, and fearless," called it "one of the soundest and sanest addresses . . . delivered in this chamber for many a day."[15] Agreeing with the general aims of the National Securities Exchange Act, Gore praised the Senate for amending the original draft which, in his opinion, had been drawn up on the assumption that the "guillotine is the surest cure for a bleeding at the nose."[16] But even with the amendments the bill remained unacceptable to him. He not only felt it had too many teeth in it, but also believed that it was analogous to a dragon with gnashing teeth which would close its jaws on the capital market and kill it. Convinced that little constructive action could be taken to improve the economic situation, he pointed out that much could be done to hurt it; this bill he placed in the latter category. As a result of this legislation private enterprise would not be able to finance itself from its own sources, he theorized, and would be compelled to call upon the government in order to survive. To his thinking this was a fundamental step in the direction of socialism.[17]

The Hoover administration had been unsuccessful in its efforts to alleviate farm distress, and 1932 marked the nadir of the agricultural depression. Farm relief was high on the Democrats' plan to improve the economic situation, and Roosevelt and his assistants boldly prepared to alleviate depressed agricultural conditions. The primary objective of the Agricultural Adjustment Act of 1933 was to establish farm prices at a level commensurate with the price farmers had to pay for other articles. It sought crop and acreage restrictions mainly by means of government contracts which provided attractive benefit payments or commodity loans to cooperating farmers. At first including only the basic products—wheat, cotton, corn, hogs, rice, milk, and tobacco—the list of restricted commodities was steadily expanded. When it was suggested that flax be included in the list of crops to receive government subsidy under the bill, Gore announced, "I merely want to give notice that Oklahoma is the leading broom-corn-producing state. . . . I can resist the temptation now, but, if flax goes into this bill, I might insist on broomcorn treading on its heels, because I, as well as others, am about to lose my virtue."[18] The Senator's threat prevented flax from being inserted at that moment, but over his protest it was included later, along with peanuts, rye, barley, grain sorghums, sugar beets, and sugar cane.

Gore did not give nearly as much attention to this bill as one would expect of a public servant who held his seat because of the good graces of the rural voters of his state. His main interest in the measure seems to have been in the reduction of the appropriations for the various officials who were to administer the program. He showed more interest in his pet project to slow down the depletion of the Treasury than in the more fundamental aspects of the bill. When the final version of the bill was accepted, Gore was "necessarily detained from the Senate on official business."[19] Whether he would have voted for it is a moot question.

The Senator disapproved of many of the activities of the "Triple A" program. He voiced opposition to the government's regulating the choice and quantity of crops to be planted by the farmers. He scoffed at crop reduction as a way to decrease surpluses and increase demands for food products, and he questioned the policy of "murdering" pigs under the program.[20] He recognized that values could be enhanced by destroying wealth, but he saw the situation in a strikingly different light when he remarked, "We cannot feed the hungry with a decimal point or clothe the naked with dollar marks."[21]

Gore's opposition to the recovery policies of the administration had become quite noticeable by the spring of 1934. The Bankhead Cotton Control Act, which limited the cotton crop to about ten million bales, granted liberal benefit payments to planters and guaranteed a price of ten cents a pound. Before its passage in April, 1934, the bill provoked Gore's outspoken opposition. Trying to neutralize a reaction from his farm constituency in the cotton areas of Oklahoma which favored the bill, he announced that it was "a duty and a privilege to carry out the ascertained wishes of the farmers of my State when I can do so without violating my official oath to support and defend the Constitution of the United States," but he stated that he could not conscientiously cast his vote for the measure.[22] His objections to the bill were both economic and constitutional. Economically, he believed that the farmers were "winding a boa constrictor about themselves that one day may break every bone in their bodies." On the question of constitutionality he declared that individual liberty was being infringed upon. He reasoned that the measure took property without due process of law and without just compensation.

Gore's disapproval of the New Deal's farm policies was not limited to his opposing the constitutionality of the legislation. When the administration announced plans to abolish the tenantry system in the rural areas and to rehabilitate the marginal farmers, Gore expressed doubt about the advisability of such an undertaking. Speaking from the standpoint of an economic conservatism now thoroughly ingrained, he remarked, "The tenantry system, while it may have many evils, is a system that does exist, and whatever does exist has reason for existence. It is the result of the play of economic forces. It is easy to tear down an existing system; it is not so easy to set up another system in its place. . . ."[23] Gore was aware of the abuses of the tenantry system, especially in the South, and he was sympathetic with the aims of the proposed legislation, but he was sure that the solution should be evolutionary. An artificial system established overnight in a given community would hardly be successful, he thought, since the tenantry bill did not take local conditions into consideration. He insisted that his opposition to the measure rested on the fact that it did not help the "honest-to-God small tenants" who most needed assistance. To prevent abuse and scandal he suggested that the land to be bought by the government and to be distributed to tenants be allotted in no larger than 160-acre tracts for each tenant.[24]

Gore also opposed the government's making loans to agricultural corporations. Such corporations he called "Frankenstein monsters to destroy farmers." The proposed system of loans he compared with the camel in the famous fable—once the nose is in the tent the entire animal is soon there. He favored adjusting farm mortgages in order to make payments easier for the hard-pressed farmers by reducing the principal of the mortgage indebtedness, by cutting the rate of interest, or by converting short-time loans into long-time ones. He voted against the administration's bankruptcy act for farmers, although he gave no explanation of his vote. The administration's important rural electrification bill received absolutely no attention from the Senator. On the basis of the Senator's votes on other farm measures, it may be assumed Gore did not support this bill.

Although expressing his opposition to government competition with private enterprise by voting against the measure establishing the Tennessee Valley Authority, Gore, viewing the program of conservation as indispensable for the future of the country, was one of the prime movers for soil conservation. The damaging dust storms of the early thirties, with the loss of valuable topsoil by wind and soil erosion, forced Gore to favor government intervention in this area. The conditions resulting in the "dust bowl," contributing to the migration of the army of "Okies" from the Sooner State to the Pacific Coast in the 1930's, weighed heavily on the Senator's mind. Generally opposed to federal regulation, he acknowledged erosion control as a proper function of the central government, since it entailed problems which the individual farmer or state could not handle alone.

To solve the dual problems of flood and erosion, Gore advocated a network of dams and reservoirs on the Mississippi River's tributaries, as well as terraces and other conservation measures on individual farms. With this in mind Gore introduced a bill to protect the land of the Mississippi watershed against soil erosion. A similar House bill was ultimately accepted, but Gore deserves recognition for his strong advocacy of this conservation measure. Gore also introduced a bill to establish within the Department of Agriculture a soil conservation service to deal with flood waters affecting the navigability of streams. Again his bill was not the one which finally became law, but the phrase "soil conservation service," suggested by Gore, was substituted for "soil erosion control service," the name originally applied to the new agency within the Department of Agriculture.[25]

Gore could not resist voting for a Senate bill providing for farm relief through conservation and utilization of the soil resources of the nation, even though he had serious objections to the measure on economic grounds ("It substitutes artificial forces for natural forces") and for administrative reasons ("It places more power in one man than [it] should"). He preferred a measure with more definite terms, standards, and limitations, but he confessed he had no other such measure available. Since he had a special interest in the subject of conservation, he laid aside his doubts and supported the administration's rural relief measure. In his opinion the conserving of the nation's soil was the most important constructive work done by the federal government during the depression years.

Excluding general legislation regarding soil conservation, Gore did not give an overabundance of effort to the needs of his farm constituency during the 1930's. He was usually out of step with the New Deal legislation attempting to meet rural needs, and he played the role of opposer more often than that of advocate. The Senator's interest in farm assistance was no longer as intense as it had been during his earlier period in the Senate.

The moving of his legal voting residence from Lawton to Oklahoma City was symbolic of Gore's shifted emphasis in regard to his constituents. In his earlier terms in public office Gore had been the defender of progressive measures, the farmers, and the poor, but during the 1930's—even though he insisted he was still a voice for the

166

farmers—it was apparent that his interest no longer lay primarily with his first love. His economic conservatism became more appealing to the wealthier industrial class, especially the oil interests. For example, Gore's opposition to the federal gasoline tax, although he harped on the expense added to gasoline for farmers' tractors, was due to the large oil constituency in Oklahoma City and Tulsa. Voting against the gasoline tax was a part of his general plan to cut taxes, but the fact that Oklahoma was a large gasoline-producing state was the primary reason for this stand. He felt that states—but not the federal government—should have the power to tax gasoline. Predicting that once a temporary federal gasoline tax was inaugurated it would never be discontinued, he commented, "If you can arrange to live until this Federal gas tax is lifted, you will put Methuselah on a nursing bottle."[26] He declared that the added tax would make the price of gasoline prohibitive for the average buyer and would irreparably damage the oil business. But all of his efforts were in vain. Both state and federal governments levy more taxes on gasoline today than Gore ever dreamed they would, and the oil industry still exists.

Gore's assistance to the prominent oil interests in his state did not end with his opposition to the gasoline tax. He often figuratively shed public tears for the overtaxed oil industry. During the Wilson era Gore had been instrumental in effecting a depletion allowance which greatly benefited the oil producers. During his last term in the Senate he attempted, although unsuccessfully, to obtain a greater allowance for oil depletions.[27] But many Senators believed Gore's amendment would infringe upon federal control over interstate commerce, and it was rejected.[28]

The problem was temporarily settled with the passage of the National Industrial Recovery Act, section 9 (c) granting the President power to prohibit the interstate shipment of oil produced in defiance of the laws of the separate states.[29] The question was raised anew in January, 1935, when the Supreme Court ruled that the "hot" oil provisions of the act constituted an unconstitutional delegation of quasi-legislative authority to the executive.[30] Gore, rushing to the aid of the small producers who stood to be hurt by large companies' taking advantage of the ruling, immediately introduced two resolutions to meet the contingency created by the Court's decision. When these resolutions made no progress in committee, he and Tom Connally of Texas pushed through a bill on the subject which became law within six weeks after the adverse decision. This act gave the federal government power to prohibit the shipment in interstate commerce of contraband oil.

The most obvious example of Gore's metamorphosis in regard to his constituency and convictions can be seen in his action on the tariff in the 1930's. His long-time stand against the protective tariff principle, dating from his earliest days in the Senate and expressed freely during the Republican supremacy of the twenties, was reversed when the subject of a tariff on oil was raised during the depression. Although opposed to monopoly in general, Gore was compelled to align himself with the high tariff group during the depression when protective tariffs were placed on certain American products. He circumvented his previous antiprotectionist stand by saying that the hard times demanded a tariff on oil (even though he had long stood for free trade during economic depressions), and he soothed his conscience by announcing that he preferred an embargo on a monthly basis rather than a tariff law.[31]

Gore opposed the spectacular New Deal experiments to rehabilitate and regiment industry for purposes of recovery and reform, especially the National Industrial Recovery Act. Contending that the N.I.R.A. was unconstitutional, Gore voted against its passage. When the Supreme Court vindicated the Senator's position in May, 1935, by declaring in a unanimous decision that the act was out of accord with the Constitution, Gore could hardly restrain himself. He wrote an open letter to the press of Oklahoma in which he gave himself verbal pats on the back by reminding his readers that he had predicted this outcome, hinting that his stand upholding the Constitution in the face of popular disapproval should be remembered when re-election time appeared the following year. He also wrote a letter to Chief Justice Charles Evans Hughes the day after the decision, praising the Court's action and recalling his defense of the Constitution during the debates on the bill. On second thought, he decided that such a letter from a legislator to a member of the judiciary might constitute a breach of propriety and did not mail it.[32]

Gore had labored for the Democratic presidential candidate in 1932, but he soon realized that his own conservative ideas were out of step with the radical solutions advanced by Roosevelt and his administration. The aging Senator's laissez faire economic principles directly clashed with government regulation and control.

XII. "THE DOLE SPOILS THE SOUL"

NOT LONG AFTER THE INAUGURATION of the revolutionary program of the New Deal, it was apparent that Senator Gore was out of step with the times. Along with his constitutional and economic opposition to governmental control of industry went his philosophy regarding federal relief, a prominent aspect of the Rooseveltian program. Gore insisted throughout his last term in office that relief should be administered at state and local levels rather than by the federal government. But his opinions carried little weight as the administration set out to provide relief on a gigantic scale for the depression-ridden nation.[1]

Because of his attitude toward the "give-away" programs and his constant wish to protect the taxpayer, Gore could be nothing but a perennial opponent of the New Deal relief measures. Every measure of this kind invariably lifted more money from the taxpayer's pocket, and the Senator took it upon himself to plead the cause of those who ultimately financed the measures. His emphatic and frequent remarks in behalf of the overburdened taxpayer incurred the charge that he was giving too much attention to those paying the bills. Gore had a ready answer to this charge: "To destroy the taxpayer would be like cutting down the fruit tree to get the fruit. It would be like destroying the hive to get the honey. If I may say so, it is like cutting off the udder of the cow to get the milk. It destroys the source alike of revenue and of relief."[2] So powerful was the Senator's feeling on the subject of taxation that he voted against all of the large tax measures passed by the Congress during his last years in the Senate. He could not bring himself to vote to place heavier loads upon the taxpayers.

Gore's efforts to reduce spending in order to assist the taxpayer appeared most noticeably when the large federal relief measures were introduced. When Congress debated the bill appropriating the enormous amount of $4,880,000,000 for relief, much of it to be used by the Works Progress Administration, Gore freely expressed his dissent. As a result of his disapproval, several thousand unemployed people in southeastern Oklahoma assembled in a mass meeting and drew up a resolution demanding that he support the measure and stating that if he refused to vote for it, he should avoid Pittsburg County during the next senatorial race. A telegram signed by the mayors of the small Oklahoma towns of Hartshorne and Haileyville, who headed the "committee on unemployed" in that area, announced those sentiments to the Senator. Gore apparently welcomed this impudent challenge as an opportunity to express his resentment of political intimidation in general. He replied with the following telegram, which has become well known in senatorial circles regarding attempts of pressure groups to influence legislators' voting habits: "This will acknowledge your exceedingly diplomatic and hospitable telegram. It shows how the dole spoils the soul. Your telegram intimates that your votes are for sale. Much as I value votes I am not in the market. I cannot consent to buy votes with the people's money. I owe a debt to the taxpayer as well as to the unemployed. I shall discharge both. None but the bully resorts to threats and none but the coward yields to them."[3] Soon after this telegraphic exchange the Senator defiantly voted in the negative on the relief bill.

Gore not only opposed emergency relief measures but also refused to support public welfare legislation. While the National Housing Act was being considered, he expressed his opposition on the grounds that the federal government was entering a field entirely out of its jurisdiction. He predicted that if all the proposed social measures of the New Deal were passed, the government would eventually finance everything and drive private financing completely out.[4] In a blanket attack on pensions for the aged, the Senator held that even assistance for persons over sixty-five should be opposed on the principle that it would tend to make the recipients cease to have initiative.[5] He expressed disapproval of the administration's efforts to institute old-age benefits and social security both as relief measures and public welfare legislation. On occasion he also expressed fears of socialism advancing under the guise of the New Deal.[6]

Although generally opposed to pensions because he believed they tended to make people dependent on government aid, Gore did favor compensation to veterans whose earning capacity had been impaired in the war.[7] For these debts he was more than willing to take revenue from the taxpayer. When he was accused of opposing legislation for disabled veterans, Gore made it clear that he had deep understanding and sympathy for "those who run life's race with a handicap."[8] This

170

is not to say that the handicapped Senator favored giving aid to all disabled veterans indiscriminately. He held that pensions should be awarded according to the extent of injuries and the extent of the need. Well-to-do veterans who received $30 per month and then applied the pension to their income tax received no kind words from Gore.

Various measures to grant bonuses to veterans were introduced in Congress from time to time during the depression, but none of them made significant progress. The difficulty to surmount in most of this legislation was the method of raising money to pay the bonuses. Providing for currency inflation in order to meet the additional expenditures, many of the proposals would have created a larger economic problem. So closely related had the bonus and inflation become by 1935 that it was almost impossible to separate the two politically. The inflationists were unwilling to vote for a bonus without fiat money, while the bonus supporters desired to raise cash for the payment by attaching a revenue-raising provision. Gore stood with the group which demanded that the money be supplied by some means other than that of inflating the currency. He was not averse to the bills which provided legitimate means to raise the money, but to inflation he was unalterably opposed. On one occasion Gore seriously suggested that the bonus money be appropriated out of the nearly five billion dollars available for relief under the W.P.A. At another time he advanced the idea that the bonuses be paid with debts collected from foreign countries.[9]

After many failures Congress in January, 1936, passed the Adjusted Compensation Payment Act. A simple bonus bill devoid of either inflationary or taxing features, this measure, finally eliminating the bonus question from American politics, was a political compromise. Without inflating the currency and without levying a heavy tax to meet the additional $1,500,000,000 payable immediately, the measure was supported by all the various factions. After plaguing the legislators for years, the bonus tangle was finally acceptably solved. Not consistent with his stand on the previous bonus bills, Gore voted for this measure both when it was first before the Senate and when it was passed over the President's veto.[10] Having said absolutely nothing about this measure on the Senate floor, he gave no hint of his reversal. Gore's change of attitude can only be interpreted in the light of the forthcoming Oklahoma Democratic primary in which he was to run for re-election.

171

The debates on the bonus question brought back memories of World War I to the elder members of the Senate. They were further reminded of an earlier day when President Roosevelt in January, 1935, suggested that the United States adhere to the World Court. Had the administration been able to bring the issue to a vote in the Senate before the opposition became relatively well organized, it might have won. But Hiram Johnson, William E. Borah, George W. Norris, and Thomas P. Gore, old-line progressives who had expressed their fears in debates on the League of Nations and on the Court during the twenties, were aroused when the World Court question was reintroduced in the thirties.

Gore's part in the opposition centered around his appeal to American citizens as contrasted with world citizens. In a long speech entitled "I Am a Mere American," delivered on the day of the final vote, Gore expressed his love for America. He referred to his antagonists as "those intellectuals, those emotional, those international eunuchs whose souls are so dead they never to themselves have said: 'This is my own, my native land.' "[11] He did not want this country to go counter to its isolationist traditions and become embroiled in European affairs.

Making capital out of the fact that several members of the World Court had defaulted in their war debts to this country, Gore magnanimously asserted that he favored joining the Court if arrangement could be made to guarantee payment from those members. Offering a reservation which provided that the United States' adherence would not become or remain effective as long as any member indebted to this nation was in arrears for a period of more than six months, Gore revealed his antagonism toward the defaulting nations and his concern for the national Treasury. He generously stated that he would be willing for the United States to endow the World Court with a billion dollars if the Court would secure for this country the money owed it by the European debtors.

Gore did not fail to make an appeal to the mothers of the country. Declaring that he would "never vote to draft American boys and ship them across the sea to fight and bleed and die in anybody's battles but our own," he called attention to his stand—by that time not so deplorable—during World War I.[12] With fervent emotion he appealed to his colleagues not to cast votes which would tend to involve this country in wars. "I would not sacrifice the life of one American boy,

I would not break the heart of one American mother, to guard the boundaries or to maintain the territory of all the faith-breaking and debt-defaulting nations on this globe," he said, reiterating a sentiment he had expressed in 1919 during the League fight.[13]

Because of the wide anti-Court publicity of the newspaper and radio, especially the isolationist editorials of William Randolph Hearst and the emotional broadcasts of radio priest Charles E. Coughlin, the public at large became aroused.[14] Soon telegrams and letters were pouring into Washington urging Senators to vote against membership in the Court. When the final vote was taken in January, 1935, the Court resolution was rejected, lacking seven votes of the necessary two-thirds majority.[15] The vote not only reflected the violent opposition of men like Johnson, Borah, Norris, and Gore, but it also emphasized the failure of the Court's friends to make a vigorous and organized appeal for its ratification. The Senators leading the fight against the Court have been criticized for voting their "fears and prejudices,"[16] and perhaps the indictment is deserved, but the vote on the Court reflected the revulsion many Americans felt for the gathering storms across the Atlantic.[17]

When the Democrats became the majority party in the Senate in 1933, Gore was elevated to the chairmanship of the Interoceanic Canals Committee. In this relatively minor position he spent a great deal of time working with legislation relating to the Panama Canal. Because of his interest in legislation affecting the Panama Canal, Gore and his wife combined a winter vacation cruise with an inspection tour of the Canal Zone in December, 1934. Sailing from Los Angeles, the couple spent four days in the canal area, returning to Washington via a Caribbean route.[18]

The Senator's major work as chairman of the Interoceanic Canals Committee related to legislation correcting the undesirable dual system for collecting tolls at the Panama Canal. Before the completion of the canal and its opening to commercial traffic, a special set of rules based upon the cargo-carrying (i.e., earning) capacity of the ships traveling through the channel was drafted and adopted for the use of the waterway. These regulations, a part of the Panama Canal Act passed and approved in 1912, set the maximum toll at $1.25 per net registered ton under the terms of the Panama Canal rules of measurement.[19] In 1913 President Wilson proclaimed the fixed rate of $1.20 per net registered ton as ascertained under those regulations. Hardly had the rules been promulgated when West Coast lumber interests claimed that additional tonnage on a ship's deck should legally be considered as a part of the tonnage of the vessel. The shippers held that the application of the $1.20 rate produced an amount in excess of $1.25 per net registered ton, the maximum charge permissible under law. When the question was submitted to the Attorney General in November, 1914, he ruled that the phrase "net registered ton" referred to the United States registry rules of measurement rather than the Panama Canal rules.[20]

A dual system of toll collection was an inevitable outgrowth of the Attorney General's ruling. It developed that as ships passed through the canal they paid the cheaper toll, whether this was at the Panama rate or at the United States registry rate. Every President from Wilson to Roosevelt had recommended a clarification of the dual system, as had every Secretary of War and every governor of the Canal Zone.[21] No less than twenty-five bills to correct the situation were introduced before 1935, eleven of them necessitating hearings. Gore was determined to pass the corrective legislation. Involving much of his effort during the first session of the Seventy-fourth Congress and commanding most of his time in the second session, legislation regarding this subject overshadowed all other to which he gave his attention during his last years in the Senate.

Hearings were held in April, 1935, to assist the Congress in arriving at legislation to dispel the confusion and to place the toll charges on the basis of the earning capacity of the ships, with a common standard to be applied to all vessels. But powerful pressure lobbies for the American shipping concerns which profited by the dual system encouraged opposition among the legislators on the question of the toll rules. This opposition made Gore more determined to alter the rules to make them less discriminatory. Carrying the fight for the new legislation almost singlehandedly during his last months in the Senate, he related over and over again the history of the dual system of rules, the defects of the simultaneous operation of different rules, and the purpose of the proposed legislation. Each time he tried to pass his bill, amendments were added which had the effect of emasculating it. Although opposing a measure providing for another investigation of the subject, he finally conceded defeat of his original proposal, and an altered bill passed the Senate and became law in April, 1936.

As a result of the passage of the investigatory measure, President

Roosevelt appointed a committee to look into the problem of Panama tolls regulation, which recommended a single system of measurement based on the Panama Canal rules. A measure passed in August, 1937, provided that tolls based on actual earning capacity determined in accordance with the Panama Canal rules be levied on merchant vessels, army and navy transports, colliers, hospital ships, supply ships, and yachts.[22]

Gore's involuntary retirement from public office in the summer of 1936 prohibited his having a direct hand in the final outcome of the tolls squabble. Although the problem was finally solved, the Senator had failed in his last attempt to pass one of the few constructive, albeit minor, pieces of New Deal legislation advocated by him. So often had he been a member of the opposition and so seldom an advovate of constructive legislation that his failure in regard to the rules controversy appeared ironic indeed.

With the New Deal reaching its highwater mark by 1936, the policies of Franklin D. Roosevelt became the significant issues in Oklahoma's Democratic primary campaign of that year. Under these conditions Thomas P. Gore—white-haired, portly, blind, and sixty-five—unsuccessfully battled three New Dealers in the summer race. Oklahoma's Governor E. W. Marland, breaking precedent by seeking the Senate post while in office, advocated the New Deal program, although he believed that the federal old-age pension law required an amendment to the Oklahoma constitution before being valid in that state. Congressman Josh Lee, completely identifying himself with the administration by his votes and speeches during the previous two years in the House of Representatives, also joined the fray. The third important candidate seeking the coveted seat was Gomer Smith, vice-president of the national Townsend old-age pension movement.

Marland had a powerful political machine and appeared to be the strongest contender for Gore's position. Gore himself indicated this when he directed most of his campaign tactics against the Governor. He laughed at Marland's insistence that an amendment to Oklahoma's constitution was required in order for federal old-age pensions to be awarded in Oklahoma. A simple law passed by the state legislature would be sufficient, Gore declared.[23] Having campaigned for Marland in the 1934 gubernatorial contest, Gore summarized his attack on his opponent's candidacy when he persistently told the voters that they should "keep a good governor."[24]

Not to be discounted was the suave, golden-throated, friendly Congressman from the fifth district. Josh Lee, forty-four years old, Director of Public Speaking at the University of Oklahoma, and versatile entertainer on the stump, had a well-functioning voluntary campaign organization. Known all over the state and appealing to the rural element with the slogan "a farm for every farmer," the "boy orator" conducted a lively campaign. Gore had only ridicule for Lee's candidacy. He often stated during the campaign that if the Congressman could deliver on his promise of a farm for every farmer, he (the Senator) would withdraw from the race.[25] The incumbent dismissed Lee with quips about the "noisiest freshman" not being worthy of a degree granted by the people of Oklahoma until he had accumulated more hours of credit.[26] Gore later recalled that he knew Lee was his strongest opponent, but he was trying to slow down the professor's campaign by minimizing it publicly.

The Gomer Smith candidacy was the most radical one of the campaign. Attacking entrenched wealth and advocating the well-publicized Townsend scheme to give $200 per month to all old-age pensioners, Smith converted many of the older voters to his cause.

As the primary battle lines were drawn, it was the conservative Gore against the field. A surprisingly clean campaign, it was virtually devoid of the name-calling commonly stimulated by stump-speakers during primary campaigns. Lee and Marland, running on the same basic program, had little to say about each other's candidacy. They both assumed that one of them would meet Gore in the run-off, and neither wanted to antagonize the anti-Gore supporters of the other. But the Governor and the Congressman pulled no punches in their attacks on the incumbent's record. Required to defend his votes against New Deal legislation, Gore fought with his back against the wall from the beginning.[27] Vainly trying to take the offensive, he pitched his campaign on a note of isolationism.[28] Stating that he would refuse *again* to vote to send American boys overseas, he sought to appeal not only to the pacifists but also to women voters.[29]

Gore had more support from influential backers in this race than during any of his previous contests. Since the three largest newspapers in the state battled in his behalf (the Tulsa *Daily World* became his personal apologist), he had more favorable publicity than ever before. He also had more money at his disposal and a better organization than previously. Despite these apparently favorable conditions, Gore's campaign in 1936 was not equal to his former ones. The oppressive heat of that Oklahoma July slowed down the veteran campaigner, and being on the defensive he was not so effective at the hustings as he had been in the past. His battle cry of "Gore Once More" was not contagious, and his worn platform of fewer taxes, more trade, no trusts, and no war had little attraction since the basic issues centered around the New Deal.

When the final vote was tabulated, the forecasters were shown to have completely misjudged the contest. It had been considered a *fait accompli* that the old warhorse would be in the run-off, and in the end most of the prophets agreed that the popular young Congressman would meet the incumbent in the second race. Lee's dynamic appeal upset the political applecart, and he and Marland were placed in the run-off with 168,030 and 121,433 votes respectively. Gomer Smith ran a close third with 119,585, while Gore was far behind with 91,581.[30] Lee went on to win the run-off and the general election by sizable margins. In the second primary Smith had endorsed Marland, while Gore's headquarters had worked for Lee, although the retiring Senator himself remained noncommittal. Nor did Gore find it expedient to campaign for the national Democratic ticket in the November election, this being the first time since reaching maturity that he failed to do so.

When the prognosticators analyzed the election results, they came to realize what a powerful impact the New Deal had made on the Oklahoma populace. Gore's assertion of independence in the face of the national administration was seen as the important element in his defeat. Another factor was the prejudice aroused among the lower classes by the support given him by business and metropolitan newspapers. During the campaign it was apparent that he was not appealing sufficiently to the rural voters. The wealthy and conservative urban vote was cast for the Senator, but he lost much of his former strength in the country.[31] His affinity with oil interests in his old age caused the loss of his appeal to the marginal farmers, and this loss was an important determinant in his last campaign.

For the second time in his career Gore had been defeated for a Senate seat primarily because of his opposition to a popular program. His stand against Wilson and the war measures was only a portent of his final retirement in 1936, when, in the high tide of the New Deal, the settled conservative was washed ashore. He realized that his political career was over with this defeat and at times he showed a tinge of bitterness, but on the whole he kept his humor, philosophically remarking, "The people giveth and the people taketh away."[32] The end had at last come to the public career of a colorful and controversial personality on the national political stage.

From the *Daily Oklahoman,* February 16, 1936.

XIII. THE RETIREMENT YEARS

ALTHOUGH T. P. GORE had retained his legal residence in Oklahoma since 1901, at the time of his political retirement in 1936 he had lived in his adopted state less than seven years—from the time he moved to the Indian lands until he was officially sent to Washington when Oklahoma was admitted to the Union. The ten-year interim of the 1920's found him practicing law in the District of Columbia, and when he retired, Gore remained in the urban center which had been home for many years. Establishing a law office in the Union Trust Building in downtown Washington, the elderly Senator admitted that he felt a "good deal like a law student just out of law school venturing . . . upon the GREAT ADVENTURE."[1]

As an attorney, Gore specialized in Indian affairs and tax matters, fields to which he had given much attention during his public career. A representative for the Osage Indians, he handled a considerable portion of the tribe's litigation with the federal government in these last years. He was one of two attorneys selected by the Kiowa, Comanche, and Apache Indians at a general council held at Anadarko, Oklahoma, in December, 1946, to represent these tribes before the Indian Claims Commission.[2] Gore was also an economic adviser to the Chase National Bank of New York City, keeping that firm informed of the activities of the national legislature on bills dealing with banking and currency. In this position he gave legal opinions on many topics, writing briefs on such subjects as "Tax-exempt securities under our dual system of Government," "Constitutionality of Title I of the Banking Act of 1935," and "The Commerce Clause of the Constitution."[3] He also represented various oil companies in their legal tangles with the federal government over taxation.[4]

Gore was certain that the tide of public opinion which swept him out of office in 1936 would never reverse itself during his lifetime, and upon his defeat he entertained no thoughts of staging a comeback. Despite the handwriting on the wall, the veteran politician could not refrain from listening when scores of his friends continually suggested that he enter various contests. Hardly had he removed his files from the Senate office building when he began receiving letters suggesting that he enter an Oklahoma race. Within six months after the adjournment of the last Congress of which he was a member, he began feeling out political sentiment in Oklahoma,[5] and in less than a year he admitted, "My sword is getting restless in its scabbard and I may insist upon serving as a high private in the rear ranks."[6]

The aging campaigner volunteered to speak in Oklahoma during the summer of 1937 in a campaign against a planned deficit, and observers correctly interpreted his move as the release of a trial balloon to test political winds. The former Senator's mail increased, but reaction was varied, his supporters being divided over whether he should run for Senator, Congressman-at-large, or Governor. The Chickasha *Star* had initiated speculation about the last-named possibility when on the last day of 1936 it ran an editorial entitled, "Why not Gore for Governor?" The Senator had no interest in the governorship and did not seriously consider it, but he chuckled when he wrote, "I am now engaged in a three-cornered race with myself. . . . The race is a close one. It looks like that if I ever dream of thinking of re-entering politics that I will be obliged to have a run-off primary with myself."[7]

When the state's fifth district Congressman, Robert P. Hill, died unexpectedly in October, 1937, Gore was boomed to fill the vacated position. The special election was set for December, and Gore announced early in November that he was a candidate for the unfilled post. Returning to Oklahoma to discuss the race with his friends, he discovered that many of them had already pledged themselves to support another candidate. Under the circumstances he decided to withdraw from the race, for he realized that the elements supporting his candidacy in the contest would be most uncertain. Besides, Gomer Smith, ultimate winner of the race, had the support of several militant organizations, and the Senator's prospects were not bright.[8]

The fact that Gore placed his hat on the rack instead of in the ring in this instance was not to be interpreted to mean that he had no further political ambitions. He knew that there would be more time to prepare for a major campaign the following spring, and he preferred to wait until that time. The possibilities of his being a candidate in the summer elections were foreseen when he released a statement to the press in March, 1938, in which he attacked the national administration's policies and made a plea for a reduction rather than an increase of states' taxes. Using his customary techniques preliminary to a campaign, he was testing the anti-Roosevelt sentiment in the state as the 1938 elections drew nearer.

The post which Gore most desired in 1938 was the Senate seat of his former colleague, Elmer Thomas. He received many letters from writers who were dissatisfied with Thomas' voting record and his rubber stamping of Roosevelt's program, encouraging him to run against Thomas, but Gore knew that the letters written only to him did not tell the whole story. Although not a strong Senator, Thomas had the presidential blessing, and his wild inflationary schemes, no matter how fanciful, often caught the imagination of the uninitiated voter in Oklahoma. Gore finally concluded that the incumbent could not be beaten at that time (which proved to be true), and he turned his attention to the race of his second choice.

The contest over the congressional seat for the fifth district, which had been temporarily filled only a few months before, was given deliberate consideration by the former Senator. After much indecision Gore joined in the closing hours of the filing period the group desiring Gomer Smith's post. The former Senator's strategy for victory was based on the fact that there were seventeen other entrants. He hoped to capture all the conservative anti-New Deal votes, while his opponents neutralized each other's strength by splitting the liberal ballots. Considerable surprise was evoked in Oklahoma when Gore announced his candidacy, but there was no rush of predictions that the retired Senator could stage a successful comeback. In fact, so uninterested were his former supporters that Gore immediately began to have misgivings about a conservative's chances even with a large field; within a few weeks after filing he withdrew from the race. He explained his withdrawal as due to poor health. In February, 1938, Gore and his wife had been knocked unconscious when the automobile in which they were riding was completely demolished after smashing broadside into a garbage truck in Washington. The couple had been hospitalized for ten days, and Gore had spent an additional month in bed at home. Since the effects of the accident continued to plague him and since his doubts about the race were increasing, Gore finally withdrew, clinching a decision he had been pondering for several weeks.

This was the aging Senator's last withdrawal. He entered no other contests, but as the 1942 senatorial election drew near, he wrote, "I am 'sorta' like an old fire horse that when the bell rings likes to rush with the crowd to the conflagration!"[9] Actually he knew that his political career was past, and only a few months before he had pessimistically stated that he could not carry a single precinct in Oklahoma because he was so out of joint with the times.[10] Although an exaggeration, this statement was basically sound. There was no place on the Oklahoma political scene for one who voiced loud suspicions of President Roosevelt's leadership.

The burial of Gore's hope for a future campaign did not mean that he lost all interest in politics. On the contrary, he spent many hours of his last years of semi-retirement in the Capitol at Washington, listening to debates on the floor of the Senate, attending hearings, and giving his views on current events and trends. In 1940 he attended the Republican National Convention at Philadelphia as an observer. But he did not limit his political activity to watching from the sidelines. He assisted office seekers in their Oklahoma campaigns, wrote his old senatorial comrades to use their influence in order to get federal appointments for his friends, and penned letters of encouragement and congratulations to politicians on the national level.[11]

When Josh Lee, who had defeated Gore in 1936, was running for re-election in 1942, the Republicans nominated ex-Senator W. B. Pine, whom Gore had ousted in 1930. After Pine's sudden death the Republicans substituted seventy-one-year-old Ed H. Moore, a wealthy, conservative oilman and a long-time friend of Gore. To the surprise of both Lee and Moore and contrary to nearly all predictions, the Republican challenger defeated the Democratic incumbent. Gore was elated that his old friend had won over his former rival. Not only did he congratulate Oklahoma's third Republican Senator but he also gave him advice and encouragement, as well as suggesting to his friends in the Senate that they help Moore get desirable committee assignments.[12]

Besides writing letters to political friends, issuing press releases (in one of which he opposed a $35,000,000 road bond proposal in Oklahoma), pondering the possibility of running for office again, and continuing his private law practice, Gore had time to correspond with friends and relatives over the country, expressing his opinions on the Roosevelt regime. Writing of the "Infantile Deal gibberish," punning on a Democratic slogan with "Don't swap horses in the middle of a

Dream," and mocking those in power with "To be a New Dealer you don't have to be crazy but it helps," Gore continually criticized the Roosevelt administration.[13] He often laughingly remarked that a man could not be honest and intelligent and a New Dealer at the same time; one could have two of these traits in combination but not all three of them at once!

Using such *noms de plume* as "Junius Americus" and "Cato the Censor," the old gentleman amused himself by writing letters to editors giving his views on the Roosevelt rule, the political scene in America, and the world situation in general. The third-term issue received an unusual amount of opposition from the retired Senator, although he was cognizant that the President continued to be popular and could be elected again. He expressed his opinion this way: "I have always thought that F. Don Quixote Roosevelt is invincible and I am still pessimistic on that point."[14] Except for writing his private opinions to his friends and relatives, Gore remained in the background during the national election of 1940, although he did send the following slogan to a leader of the Willkie for President Clubs: "Better have a man in the White House who has several public utilities than one who has no public utility."[15] Confined to his bed because of illness on the day of the election, Gore expressed no sorrow for being unable to exercise the right of suffrage, since in his opinion the two candidates, Roosevelt and Willkie, were "identical twins."[16]

The threat of war was uppermost in many Americans' minds when they voted in the 1940 presidential campaign, and their trusted leader in both domestic and foreign affairs shattered the no-third-term tradition by being elected again. With a virtual mandate from the people, the President advanced his lend-lease proposal a few months after the election. Gore had long been suspicious of the Chief Executive's domestic legislation and more recently of his actions in foreign affairs. The lend-lease bill made him more dubious than ever before. He had come to believe that Roosevelt was deliberately maneuvering to get the United States into war in order to overcome the nation's economic doldrums, and he saw the lend-lease proposal as another step in that direction. When the President's suggestion was enacted, Gore expressed the opinion that the "dictator . . . having won all the triumphs and trophies of peace . . . now desires to add martial splendor to his accumulated glories. Selah."[17] Not only did Gore think the President was determined to maneuver this nation into war, but he also believed that Roosevelt desired to create "some world wide organization of which he is to be the head and front."[18] Despite these sentiments, Gore offered his services to the Chief Executive three days after the infamous attack on Pearl Harbor: "I wish to observe my seventy-first birthday by placing my services at the disposal of the government. If it should happen at any time that I could render any service of any kind toward winning the war it is yours to command, mine to obey."[19] But as the war progressed, Gore receded farther from the public eye, having virtually nothing to say about world affairs, although he did express his opposition to the bank and funds established as a consequence of the Bretton Woods Conference.

Refusing to vote for either Thomas Dewey or Harry Truman in 1948, Gore referred to himself as a Dixiecrat during that campaign.[20] With antipathy toward the federal government growing through the years, he had come to be a defender of states' rights, and he disliked Truman's civil rights program.[21]

The aging blind man, a mild diabetic in his later years, did not ever fully recover from the automobile accident of 1938, and his weakened physical condition was agitated further by insomnia and a circulatory ailment.[22] In September, 1947, a vacation tour of the Southwest ended suddenly when Gore's automobile overturned on loose gravel in New Mexico, the Senator again being hospitalized, this time with minor though persistent injuries. Flown from Roswell, New Mexico, to Oklahoma City in an army transport plane after the accident, he spent the next three months in the hospital and the greater part of the last year and a half of his life in a wheel chair. This semi-immobile state hampered the old Senator considerably. In his adult years he had been accustomed to walking for exercise, clutching the arm of his male secretary and striding vigorously down Washington's streets in the early morning hours. These enjoyable daily constitutionals were regretfully omitted during the last months of his life. Stricken with a cerebral hemorrhage in February, 1949, Gore had a partial paralysis of hands and tongue before his death three weeks later. After being unconscious most of the last three days of his life, the seventy-eight-year-old ex-Senator died in his Washington apartment at 9 A.M. on March 16, 1949. Funeral services were held two days later after the body lay in state in the rotunda of the capitol in Oklahoma City.

Three years before his death, the retired Senator had remarked that he would like to be buried atop Mt. Scott, the highest peak of the Wichita Mountains, a small, rocky range rising starkly above the surrounding flat prairie lands of western Oklahoma near his original Oklahoma home in Lawton. But this request was not carried out, and his body was interred in the Rose Hill Cemetery in Oklahoma City. Shortly after the Senator's death, the two houses of the Oklahoma legislature adopted resolutions of respect to the Honorable Thomas Pryor Gore, commemorating his "great ability, fidelity and loyalty to his convictions."[23] When a copy of each of these resolutions was sent to the Senator's widow a few days later,[24] the last official act concerning Oklahoma's blind Senator had been accomplished, and men still living turned their minds back to their daily tasks.

The public career of Thomas P. Gore cannot be accurately understood without attention to his political concepts. Reared in the rough-and-tumble political milieu of post-Reconstruction Mississippi, he grew up while the farmers of that state were beginning to make noticeable headway in political circles. As a result of this background he had become a rabid Populist before having serious political aspirations. Elected to the Senate from Oklahoma as a Democrat, he was immediately stamped as a progressive. He generally followed better-known progressive leaders in his early years in the Senate, advocating low tariffs, trust-busting, and regulation of monopolies, especially the railroads which were taking advantage of his Oklahoma farm constituency. He also favored the progressive legislation of the New Freedom era after having played a part in the nomination and election of Woodrow Wilson.

Gore revealed his pacifist sentiments prior to World War I. In the progressive-pacifist tradition he opposed the United States' entry into war and voted against this nation's joining the League of Nations. This isolationism was further developed during the twenties, and he helped prevent the United States from joining the World Court in 1935.[25]

During the thirties the Senator generally voted against the New Deal legislation. Even though he was a staunch conservative in his old age, he claimed to be a "true" progressive. Reminded of his opposition to the New Deal as an illustration of his conservatism, Gore used an analogy of a cannon ball fired at night which appeared to be standing still if a flash of lightning came while the ball was in the air. Said he, "I am going as fast as the cannon ball but I am not going as fast as lightning."[26] To him the New Deal was "going too far too fast." Claiming to be in the Jeffersonian tradition in his later years, Gore believed in the philosophy that the government which governs least governs best. He was not in accord with the trend toward government regulation and centralization apparent during the New Deal. Control of industry and regulation of the economy had no place in his philosophy of government. This philosophy caused him to object to most of the social measures inaugurated under the New Deal impetus. Rising above his own blindness without significant help from others, the Senator believed that federal relief hindered initiative and encouraged laziness. He did not like paternalism in government, because he believed that it would destroy the self-reliance and self-respect of the individual. He preferred that people in need be made to help themselves rather than be given charity.

When Gore retired from the Senate in 1936, he stated that through his career he had tried to steer his course by the "fixed star of principle" and not by the "shooting stars of expediency."[27] Yet there is a marked difference between his early progressive career and his later conservative one. He cannot be charged often with voting on grounds of expediency, but obviously his outlook on government regulation and federal domestic supports changed with the years. But if some of his general principles underwent metamorphoses, this is not to say that Gore was unprincipled. He clung tenaciously to his beliefs and altered them only after much thought. The words "independence" and "conviction" best characterize the Senator's public career. Although a strong party man, he demanded that there be room within the framework of the Democratic party to allow him his convictions. Many times he voted as his conscience dictated in the face of overwhelming pressures, sometimes to the extent that it looked as if he had a martyr complex. Independent to the point of being ineffective, Gore was throughout his political life a loner, a maverick.

The psychological and mental make-up of the Senator inclined him to oppose rather than to advocate, and much of Gore's time in the Senate was spent in opposition to policies and bills suggested by others. This was true, for example, during the struggle over American neutral rights prior to the United States' entry into World War I, when the Gore Resolution was the focus for his and certain other Senators' opposing President Wilson's foreign policies. Gore's attitudes and votes on the League of Nations may also best be explained

186

by this tendency to oppose. His almost total disagreement with the New Deal during his last term in the Senate is a further illustration of this personality trait. Generally, Gore did not get along well with any of the five Presidents who occupied the White House while he sat in the Senate. On the one hand, he criticized the first Roosevelt's and Hoover's handling of domestic problems (specifically the panic of 1907 and the depression of the early 1930's), while on the other hand he was dissatisfied with Wilson's foreign policies. He expressed distaste for Taft's conservatism while he was a progressive, but he did not like the second Roosevelt's progressivism when he was a conservative.

Gore's most tangible legislative contributions related to agriculture, Indians, and oil. As chairman of the Senate Agriculture and Forestry Committee during the Wilson administrations, he had much to do with agricultural appropriations and other proposals relating to rural areas. Throughout his career, he was a persistent advocate of soil conservation. Although not as helpful generally to the Oklahoma Indian tribes as was his first colleague, Robert L. Owen, Gore gave significant aid to the Indians, especially during his early years in the Senate. Interested in the welfare of the oil industry so prominent in the state which he represented, he was the author of an amendment to the Revenue Act of 1918 exempting oil companies from the income tax on a stipulated portion of the proceeds from oil that was considered to be capital. Known as the discovery-depletion allowance, this concept was later revised, but the basic principle has been retained. Later expanded to include scores of other mineral industries, it has been a boon to industrial production.

Gore's political and senatorial career cannot be accurately interpreted without particular attention to his blindness, its effect on his work and habits, and its influence on his interests and attitudes throughout his life. Although he minimized it to the extent that many people often thought of him as a physically normal individual, his blindness was a political asset in a state where many farmers lived in near-poverty and could sympathize with the hardships of others. Gore did not use his blindness to play upon the voters' sympathies, but he was admired for overcoming his handicap, and this admiration was undoubtedly expressed at times with votes due to sympathy. Because of his blindness, Gore could not develop the ability to associate names and faces, normally an important trait in any successful politician, but his substitute was perhaps more effective: he learned to associate

187

names and voices with amazing accuracy. Developing a keen sense of hearing, Gore transformed a handicap into a positive asset, particularly when he was campaigning, because he was able to recognize scores of people by their voices.[28]

Although Gore was totally blind by the time he was twenty years old, at a later age he allowed several attempts to be made to restore the sight of his left eye. In 1908 he underwent treatment for the eye with the hope of restoring partial sight, and a few years later he indicated interest in the methods of a faith healer who claimed divine powers.[29] The Senator submitted himself to a relaxation method of treatment in 1921, but all efforts to restore his vision were in vain.

Mrs. Gore, a constant companion to her husband except during his campaign tours, was often pictured as the "eyes" of the blind man. When the Wright brothers were experimenting with air travel at Kitty Hawk, North Carolina, in the summer of 1909, Senator and Mrs. Gore were among the observers, the Senator witnessing the flights through the expert explanation of events by his wife. A devoted couple, they traveled together a great deal during his career, Mrs. Gore driving their automobile on numerous pleasure and business excursions. In 1929 the Gores took a seventy-two-day cruise of the Mediterranean. Touring North Africa, the Near East, and parts of Europe, Gore with the aid of his wife's word pictures and his own imagination "saw" the giant pyramids of North Egypt, the Holy Land, Greece, Constantinople, and other tourist sights in the Mediterranean area.[30] The couple enjoyed the sights of Paris and London on their return trip home. With Mrs. Gore present the Senator often watched football and baseball games and other sports events in Washington and Oklahoma. At county fairs he touched the various animals being exhibited and judged them by this method.

Gore's opinion was often sought by parents who wanted the Senator to recommend ways of handling their sightless children. Writing countless letters of encouragement to such parents, Gore freely related his philosophy on the care of the blind. He believed that handicapped children should not be isolated from physically normal ones nor placed in an institution surrounded by other blind children. Knowing that blind children would be in competition with those who had sight when they grew up, Gore believed that they should be made aware of that competition early in life. He advised that the handicapped child be treated like the other children in the family as far as was practicable, with as little distinction as possible because of the deficiency. He further advised that such a child should not be permitted to develop self-pity.[31]

He recommended that blind children begin studying braille not later than the age of seven, although he himself seldom had occasion to use the braille he had learned as a youth. Since he preferred to read up-to-date news rather than the classics or the Bible—the traditional books in braille—the Senator soon lost his ability to read braille. He recognized the value of phonograph records in education of the blind, and when the radio came into prominence, he was quick to realize its educational possibilities for them.

Because he did not want to segregate the blind, the Senator recommended that institutions for them be placed in urban rather than in rural areas.[32] When Oklahoma entered the Union, he desired to have the state's institute for the blind located not far from a university so that the blind would have the benefit of the university's lectures, classes, and library facilities, as well as increased contacts with normal people. He was not happy when the state's leaders placed the institute in an isolated area.[33] Gore never used seeing-eye dogs and did not recommend them for other blind persons; he felt that the blind tended to become too dependent on the animals.[34] Summing up his philosophy, Gore wrote, "The greatest service which the sighted can render the sightless is to help them to help themselves; this is better than charity."[35]

The successful blind politician never withheld his support when he was asked to aid the cause of the blind. Among those he advised was a young sightless attorney who ran for office and who requested a statement from Gore to help him refute those persons who charged that a blind man should not hold public office.[36]

After his rise to national prominence, Senator Gore lent his assistance and prestige to many organizations established to aid the blind. From 1912 to 1914 he served on the advisory board of the New York Association for the Blind. When the National Library for the Blind was established in 1911 to make available embossed books and music and to employ blind persons for the copying of books into raised print for the library, Gore was appointed its first vice-president. During World War I, he offered the services of this library to the government to prepare printed matter for blinded soldiers if the need arose.[37] The Senator became president of the organization in 1936, retaining that position until 1946, when the independent library was merged with the Library of Congress, Division for the Blind.

Perhaps the most lasting contribution of the sightless Oklahoma Senator was his inspiration to the blind. Refusing to allow his physical handicap to hinder his ambition in life, he reached his most coveted goal—the United States Senate.

NOTES

I

1. Albert D. Kirwan, *Revolt of the Rednecks; Mississippi Politics: 1876-1925* (Lexington, Kentucky, 1951), 3-5.

2. There were four Gore children—in order of birth Mary, Thomas, Ellis, and Dick.

3. Old Choctaw County was a part of the original home and lands of the Choctaw Indians. A few years after Gore's birth the part in which he was born was renamed Sumner County and in 1881 the name was again changed, this time to Webster.

4. After Thomas P. became a Senator he showed interest in his ancestry and wrote numerous letters on the subject. The information on the Gore ancestry has been compiled from these letters in the Thomas P. Gore Papers (University of Oklahoma Library).

5. Thomas P. Gore to Mrs. C. E. Castle, July 17, 1945, *ibid.*

6. Gore to Robert Gandy, February 23, 1947, *ibid.*

7. Walthall (Mississippi) *Warden,* March 3, 1882. In his mature years Gore had a glass eye which matched his other eye so closely that few people were aware that one of them was not his own.

8. Personal letter from E. E. Gore, March 2, 1955.

9. Pittman later recalled that Gore "liked Math, disliked Latin, loved the natural sciences, and was especially fond of the social sciences." C. H. Pittman, "Oklahoma's Blind U.S. Senator," *Sturm's Oklahoma Magazine,* V (November, 1907), 42-43.

10. Walthall *Warden,* November 25, 1887; March 16 and October 17, 1888.

11. *Ibid.,* April 10 and 17, 1889.

12. *Ibid.,* July 27 and November 16, 1888; November 13, 1889.

13. *Ibid.,* July 27, 1888; Gore to Dawes Gore, May 29, 1947, in Gore Papers.

14. Walthall *Warden,* July 27, 1888.

15. *Ibid.,* May 25 and December 19, 1888; Gore to Mrs. Addie Doolittle, November 14, 1946, and Gore to Mrs. Kathleen Bankston, March 29, 1947, in Gore Papers.

16. Walthall *Warden,* August 20, 1889; Robert C. Latham, "The Dirt Farmer in Politics: A Study of Webster County, Mississippi, During the Rise of Democratic Factionalism, 1880-1910" (M.S. thesis, Mississippi State College, 1951), 16.

17. Walthall *Warden,* July 22, 1891; September 9, 1891.

18. *Ibid.,* June 10, July 22, and August 12, 1892; James Creelman, "The Blind Senator from Oklahoma," clipping from an unidentified newspaper, n. d., in Gore Papers.

19. Grenada (Mississippi) *Sentinel,* October 8, 1892, quoted in William B. Gregg, "The Agrarian Movement in Grenada County" (M.S. thesis, Mississippi State College, 1953), 72-73.

20. Walthall *Warden,* October 21, 1892.

21. Cumberland *Mississippi Populist,* April 26, 1894.

22. Gore to William J. Cummings, June 12, 1947, in Gore Papers.

23. Robert C. Cotner, *James Stephen Hogg: A Biography* (Austin, 1949), 396.

24. *Winston County Journal,* November 2 and 9, 1894.

25. Personal letter from E. E. Gore, March 2, 1955. The two Gores were licensed to practice in March, 1895. See *Clerk's File Docket and Civil Fee Book, no. 4, Navarro County, Texas, February 11, 1895 to June 16, 1896,* 238-39.

26. Personal letter from E. E. Gore, March 11, 1955. Ellis served as deputy from March until October, 1895. See *Attorney's Order Book, Civil, no. 2, Navarro County, Texas, August 7, 1889 to November 28, 1898,* 253-304.

27. Asa H. Langston to O. A. Luckett, Jr., October 25, 1895, in A. J. McLaurin Papers (Mississippi State Department of Archives and History).

28. Quoted in William David McCain, "The Populist Party in Mississippi" (M.A. thesis, University of Mississippi, 1931), 62.

29. J. H. Caldwell to A. J. McLaurin, October 1, 1895, in McLaurin Papers.

30. Eupora *Sun,* May 23, 1895.

31. *Ibid.,* July 13, 1895.

32. *Ibid.,* March 14, June 22 and 29, July 20, and October 11, 1895.

33. *Ibid.,* June 7 and July 13, 1895.

34. *Ibid.,* July 13, 1895.

35. *Ibid.,* July 13 and 20, 1895.

36. James Sharbrough Ferguson, "Agrarianism in Mississippi, 1871-1900: A Study in Nonconformity" (Ph.D. dissertation, University of North Carolina, 1952), 550-51.

37. Jackson *Clarion-Ledger,* quoted in Eupora *Sun,* August 10, 1895.

38. Kosciusko *Star,* November 8, 1895.

39. Carl Allen Ray, "The Political Career of Thomas Pryor Gore" (M.S. thesis, Mississippi State College, 1955), 44.

40. The two Gores were granted their second licenses to practice law in Texas on April 8, 1896. *Civil Docket, District Court, Navarro County, Texas, April, 1894, 1895, 1896,* 168-69.

41. *Tax Rolls, Navarro County, Texas, 1898,* no. 2765. Gore to E. A. Walker, January 22, 1945, in Gore Papers.

42. *Criminal Minutes, District Court, Navarro County, Texas, no. 4, October 7, 1895 to December 18, 1902,* 233.

43. *Ibid.,* 258, 291, 317-18.

44. See pamphlet entitled "The Bond-Gore Case," in C. B. Ames Papers (University of Oklahoma Library); personal interviews with Pierce Colquitt and Marion Martin, August 15, 1958.

45. *Who's Who in America, 1946-47* (Chicago, 1947), 899-900; Luther B. Hill, *A History of the State of Oklahoma* (Chicago, 1908), II, 116.

46. Campaign literature, 1936, in Gore Papers.

47. Personal interview with Mrs. Thomas P. Gore, May 23, 1953.

48. Gore to F. G. Eisehen, June 16, 1942, in Gore Papers.

49. Personal interview with Mrs. Thomas P. Gore, November 17, 1954.

50. Unidentified newspaper clipping, in Fred S. Barde Papers (Oklahoma Historical Society).

51. November 6, 1902.

52. Bird S. McGuire, Republican from Pawnee, beat Cross by less than 400

votes in a race in which almost 95,000 votes were polled. *Congressional Directory* (2nd ed.), 58 Cong., 2 Sess., 134.

53. *Journal of the Council Proceedings of the Seventh Legislative Assembly of the Territory of Oklahoma* (Guthrie, 1903), 25-26.

54. *Ibid.*, 35, 114, 285.

55. Oklahoma City *Daily Oklahoman*, March 1, 1903; *Council Journal, Seventh Legislature, O.T.*, 99.

56. *Ibid.*, 203.

57. *Daily Oklahoman*, November 26, 1903.

58. May 8, 1903.

II

1. *Congressional Record*, 52 Cong., 1 Sess., 522.

2. Roy Gittinger, *The Formation of the State of Oklahoma* (Berkeley, 1917), 198-99.

3. *Daily Oklahoman*, December 5, 1905.

4. *Cong. Record*, 58 Cong., 2 Sess., 5153.

5. Guthrie *Daily Leader*, July 12, 1905.

6. *Sturm's Statehood Magazine*, I (September, 1905), 15-16.

7. An undated carbon copy is in the Gore Papers.

8. Lewis E. Solomon, "The Personnel of the Oklahoma Constitutional Convention of 1906-1907" (M.A. thesis, University of Oklahoma, 1924), 9.

9. Gore had written to Murray just before the convention opened, "We have in mind a suitable man for President. I think you should be given the chairmanship on public lands." William H. Murray, "The Constitutional Convention," *Chronicles of Oklahoma*, IX (June, 1932), 135; Gordon Hines, *Alfalfa Bill: An Intimate Biography* (Oklahoma City, 1932), 189.

10. W. F. Kerr, "Thomas Pryor Gore," *Sturm's*, IX (January, 1910), 61; William H. Murray, *Memoirs of Governor Murray and True History of Oklahoma* (Boston, 1945), II, 84.

11. *Daily Oklahoman*, December 3, 1905.

12. James Ralph Scales, "Political History of Oklahoma, 1907-1949" (Ph.D. dissertation, University of Oklahoma, 1949), 57, 71-72.

13. Gore to Irving Hurst, October 15, 1938; Hurst to Gore, September 7, 1938, in Gore Papers.

14. *Daily Oklahoman*, March 21, 1906; Shawnee *Weekly Herald*, July 5, 1906; *Sturm's*, IV (March-April, 1907), 16p-q.

15. June 6, 1907.

16. Scales, "Political History of Oklahoma," 73.

17. *Daily Oklahoman*, September 6, 1907.

18. Gore's interest in the matter was revealed when he wrote, "Don't you think it is a good idea for you to arrange and have from five to fifteen telegrams to go in to the President within the next day or two from your city requesting his signature to the proclamation?" Gore to Lee Cruce, October 26, 1907, in Lee Cruce Papers (University of Oklahoma Library).

19. See *Cong. Record*, 60 Cong., 1 Sess., 4001, 4016, 4018.

20. *Ibid.*, 3566-68.

21. *Ibid.*, 7247-50.

22. Gore to Franklin L. Burdette, August 18, 1939, in Gore Papers.

23. Franklin L. Burdette, *Filibustering in the Senate* (Princeton, 1940), 90.

24. *Daily Oklahoman,* December 29, 1907.

25. Victor Murdock, "Dennis T. Flynn," *Chronicles of Oklahoma,* XVIII (June, 1940), 112.

26. *Official Report of the Proceedings of the Democratic National Convention . . . 1908* (Chicago, 1908), 41.

27. Gore was one of more than a dozen who seconded Bryan's nomination, but this longer speech was unexciting and roused little enthusiasm. The decision for Bryan had been reached on July 8, though it was not official until the early morning hours of July 11. *Ibid.,* 237-41.

28. Gore to R. L. Williams, September 15, 1908; Williams to Gore, September 26, 1908, in R. L. Williams Papers (Oklahoma Historical Society).

29. John E. Lamb to Williams, October 2, 1908; Norman E. Mack to Williams, October 3, 1908, *ibid.*

30. Williams to Gore, September 26, 1908; Williams to Mack, October 5, 1908, *ibid.*

31. Oklahoma City *Times,* January 20, 1909; Blackwell *Times-Record,* January 21, 1909.

32. For further information on this subject, see Ralph Arden Wasson, "A Study of the Speaking Career and Speeches of Thomas Pryor Gore" (M.A. thesis, University of Oklahoma, 1941).

33. Typed statement signed by Maurice F. Lyons, in Maurice F. Lyons Papers (Division of Manuscripts, Library of Congress).

III

1. George E. Mowry, *Theodore Roosevelt and the Progressive Movement* (Madison, 1946), 53; George E. Mowry, *The Era of Theodore Roosevelt, 1900-1912* (New York, 1958), 244-46; John A. Garraty, *Henry Cabot Lodge: A Biography* (New York, 1953), 266.

2. *Cong. Record,* 61 Cong., 1 Sess., 3078.

3. *American Review of Reviews,* XL (July, 1909), 9.

4. *Cong. Record,* 61 Cong., 1 Sess., 2651-52; New York *Times,* June 3, 1909; Thomas R. Marshall, *Recollections of Thomas R. Marshall* (Indianapolis, 1925), 319.

5. *Cong. Record,* 61 Cong., 1 Sess., 2493, 3134, 3467, 4299, 4314.

6. *Ibid.,* 4299.

7. *Ibid.,* 2052-53, 2140, 3958.

8. George M. Fisk, "The Payne-Aldrich Tariff," *Political Science Quarterly,* XXV (March, 1910), 42.

9. Mowry, *Roosevelt and Progressive Movement,* 58; *Cong. Record,* 61 Cong., 1 Sess., 3344.

10. Mowry, *Roosevelt and Progressive Movement,* 95-96.

11. *Ibid.,* 97; *Cong. Record,* 61 Cong., 1 Sess., 5578.

12. *Cong. Record,* 61 Cong., 1 Sess., 7366.

13. "Brief Review of Official Record of T. P. Gore in the United States Senate 1907 to 1914," 4, pamphlet in Gore Papers.

14. Mowry, *Roosevelt and Progressive Movement,* 103-104.

15. *Cong. Record,* 61 Cong., 2 Sess., 2772.

16. *Ibid.,* 62 Cong., 1 Sess., 1965, 3164.

17. *Ibid.,* 3165.

18. *Ibid.,* 3165, 3358, 3433-34.

19. *Ibid.,* 2442-43, 3165.

20. *Ibid.,* 61 Cong., 3 Sess., 3639.

21. *Senate Documents,* No. 484 (ser. no. 6155), 62 Cong., 2 Sess., 431-36.

22. *Cong. Record,* 61 Cong., 3 Sess., 3760; 62 Cong., 2 Sess., 8987.

23. "Brief Review of Official Record of T. P. Gore," 4, in Gore Papers.

24. Gore to Lee Cruce, November 2, 1907, in Cruce Papers. Gore also favored removing restrictions from minors' lands so that they could be improved and be of value before the minors became adults. Gore to J. G. Ralls, February 8, 1908, in J. G. Ralls Papers (University of Oklahoma Library).

25. The opening of the Indian rolls was a delicate operation. Many who had the legal right to enrollment were often left off the rolls when they were opened, while some were enrolled who had no right to Indian money. By 1910 Gore felt that there should be no further legislation upon this subject. As a practical measure to keep peace in Oklahoma, he felt that the rolls should not be opened again. "It would only entail more delay, annoyance, hardship, and inconvenience to the general public if the rolls were reopened," he wrote, and, besides, "If the rolls should remain open for a thousand years there would still be those contending that they had been unjustly omitted from the list." Gore to W. N. Redwine, April 7, 1910, in W. N. Redwine Papers (University of Oklahoma Library).

26. Gore to the Attorney General of the United States, May 10, 1910, quoted in *Cong. Record,* 61 Cong., 2 Sess., 9064.

27. *Cong. Record,* 61 Cong., 2 Sess., 8793.

28. *Ibid.,* 8880.

29. *Ibid.,* 9063.

30. *Daily Oklahoman,* August 4, 1910.

31. *Hearings before the Select Committee of the House of Representatives appointed under authority of H. Res. 847,* 61 Cong., 2 Sess. (Washington, 1910), I, vi.

32. *House Reports,* No. 2273 (ser. nos. 5853-54), 61 Cong., 3 Sess., quoted in *Cong. Record,* 61 Cong., 3 Sess., 3714.

33. *Ibid.,* 3713.

34. *Sturm's,* XII (March, 1911), 14.

35. "Brief Review of Official Record of T. P. Gore," 12, in Gore Papers.

36. *Cong. Record,* 65 Cong., 3 Sess., 4593; Gore to Miss Julia Ann Park, March 5, 1945, in Gore Papers.

37. *Cong. Record,* 63 Cong., 3 Sess., 5156; 63 Cong., 2 Sess., 10717, 11017 ff.

38. T. P. Howell to Gore, November 24, 1915, in Gore Papers.

IV

1. Gore in conversation with Link, August 15, 1942, quoted in Arthur S. Link, "The South and the Democratic Campaign of 1912" (Ph.D. dissertation, University of North Carolina, 1945), 71.

2. Gore to Henry S. Breckenridge, May 25, 1911, quoted in Vinita *Weekly Chieftain,* June 2, 1911.

3. Louis Brownlow, *A Passion for Politics: The Autobiography of Louis Brownlow, First Half* (Chicago, 1955), 572.

4. Maurice F. Lyons, *William F. McCombs: The President Maker* (Cincinnati, 1922), 41.

5. William F. McCombs, *Making Woodrow Wilson President* (New York, 1921), 80, 106.

6. *Daily Oklahoman*, January 16, 1912.

7. New York *Evening Post*, January 19, 1912. This statement was for press consumption. Actually Wilson's managers thought the affair to be not only a billow, "but a cyclone and hurricane all rolled into one." When Harvey's statement was published, Gore, McCombs, and Pence spent three days in Washington "trying to steady the boat." Gore in conversation with Link, August 15, 1942, quoted in Arthur S. Link, *Wilson: The Road to the White House* (Princeton, 1947), I, 373.

8. Lyons, *McCombs*, 52-53.

9. McAlester *News-Capital*, January 27, 1912.

10. *Daily Oklahoman*, January 14 and February 4, 1912.

11. *Ibid.*, September 3, 1911.

12. *Ibid.*, February 10, 1912.

13. Muskogee *Daily Phoenix*, February 21, 1912.

14. *Daily Oklahoman*, February 22, 1912.

15. Muskogee *Daily Phoenix*, February 23 and 24, 1912.

16. *Official Report of the Proceedings of the Democratic National Convention ... 1912* (Chicago, 1912), 50.

17. Charles W. Bryan in New York *Times*, March 6, 1921.

18. *Official Report of 1912 Convention*, 137-38.

19. *Ibid.*, 183-85.

20. McAdoo recalled in his autobiography that Gore was "skillful and active" as one of the floor leaders and praised him for his "great work." *Crowded Years* (Boston, 1931), 152. McCombs' secretary, Maurice F. Lyons, called Gore "a power on the floor." See Lyons Papers. The New York *Times*, August 12, 1912, said, "Senator Gore was referred to by Gov. Wilson just before the deciding ballot was cast at Baltimore as a field general so capable that it would be mere impertinence on his own part to intervene in the situation instead of trusting all to the Senator."

21. *Official Report of 1912 Convention*, 220; Link, *Wilson*, I, 449.

22. Link, *Wilson*, I, 450.

23. *Official Report of 1912 Convention*, 232, 301-302, 338.

24. Josephus Daniels, *The Wilson Era: Years of Peace—1910-1917* (Chapel Hill, 1944), 68.

25. Ray Stannard Baker, *Woodrow Wilson, Life and Letters* (Garden City, New York, 1931), III, 371.

26. Gore to John J. Raskob, December 15, 1928, in Gore Papers.

27. Gore to Franklin D. Roosevelt, July 25, 1932, in Franklin D. Roosevelt Papers (Franklin D. Roosevelt Library).

28. Gore to "My dear Democratic Friend" (mimeographed), October 3, 1912, in Josephus Daniels Papers (Division of Manuscripts, Library of Congress).

29. W. D. Jamieson to T. P. Gregory, November 7, 1912, copy in Edward M. House Papers (Yale University Library), quoted in Link, *Wilson*, I, 482.

30. M. L. Davies to W. F. McCombs (telegram), July 26, 1912, in Daniels Papers; Louisville *Times,* September 13, 1912.

31. House to Wilson, November 28, 1912, quoted in Charles Seymour (ed.), *The Intimate Papers of Colonel House* (Boston, 1926), I, 94-95.

32. New York *Times,* January 9, 1913.

33. Hollis *Post-Herald,* November 7, 1912; Mangum *Weekly Star,* November 28, 1912. The Phoenix *Arizona Gazette,* December 9, 1912, suggested Gore for Secretary of the Interior.

34. *Cong. Record,* 63 Cong., 1 Sess., 4564-67.

35. Arthur S. Link, *Wilson: The New Freedom* (Princeton, 1956), II, 213.

36. *Cong. Record,* 63 Cong., 2 Sess., 1218-20.

37. New York *Times,* March 12, 1914.

38. Wilson to McAdoo, June 27, 1913; McAdoo to Wilson, July 1 and 18, 1913, in Woodrow Wilson Papers (Division of Manuscripts, Library of Congress).

39. Williams to McAdoo, March 25, 1913, *ibid.*

40. Vardaman to William H. Murray, August 18, 1913, quoted in campaign circular of 1914 election, in Gore Papers.

41. John Melton for McAdoo to Wilson, August 2, 1913; Parker to Wilson, October 16, 1913, in Wilson Papers.

42. New York *Times,* August 30, 1914.

43. *Cong. Record,* 63 Cong., 2 Sess., 5108.

44. *Ibid.,* 65 Cong., 2 Sess., 10987; 65 Cong., 3 Sess., 3026; 66 Cong., 1 Sess., 229, 232.

45. C. S. Jackson to J. P. Tumulty, February 7, 1914; Wilson to Tumulty, February 19, 1914; Wilson to Franklin K. Lane, February 25, 1914, in Wilson Papers.

46. Wilson to Tumulty, February 19, 1914, *ibid.*

47. New York *Times,* April 14 and May 18, 1914.

48. *Cong. Record,* 63 Cong., 2 Sess., 10069, 10071-73.

49. *Ibid.,* 10074.

50. D. F. Houston to Gore, December 9, 1913, quoted in *Senate Reports,* No. 831 (ser. no. 6762), 63 Cong., 3 Sess.

51. *Ibid.,* No. 987 (ser. no. 6762), 63 Cong., 3 Sess.

52. D. F. Houston to Gore, December 21, 1914, and June 29, 1915, in Department of Agriculture Papers (National Archives).

53. *Cong. Record,* 63 Cong., 2 Sess., 7557. Another bill dealing with the same subject later passed the lower house, and Gore's committee recommended its passage in the Senate, but other matters were more pressing and this bill also died.

54. *Ibid.,* 16814.

55. *Ibid.,* 8896-97.

56. George E. Putnam, "The Federal Farm Loan Act," *American Economic Review,* VI (December, 1916), 771.

57. *Senate Documents,* No. 214 (ser. no. 6519), 63 Cong., 1 Sess.

58. Wilson to Gore, March 21, 1913, in Wilson Papers. The other members were Congressman Ralph H. Moss of Indiana, Harvie Jordan (a planter from Atlanta, Georgia), Kenyon L. Butterfield (president of the Massachusetts Agricultural College, Amherst), and Clarence J. Owens (director of the Southern Commercial Congress).

59. Wilson to Glass, May 12, 1914, *ibid.*

60. Wilson to Morris Sheppard, December 22, 1913, *ibid.*

61. Gore in address before the New York Credit Men's Association of New York City, January 25, 1916, *Senate Documents,* No. 386 (ser. no. 6952), 64 Cong., 1 Sess., 7.

62. Wilson to Fletcher, May 23, 1916, in Wilson Papers.

63. Herbert Myrick to Tumulty, July 14, 1916, *ibid.*

V

1. Oklahoma newspapers which risked editorial comment on the story immediately defended the Senator. Typical was the attitude of the Tulsa *Democrat,* April 5, 1913: "Suspend judgment on that story from Washington. There have been frame-ups of this sort, and Oklahoma has some frame-up artists who are not dead."

2. New York *Times,* February 13 and 17, 1914.

3. *Harlow's Weekly,* V (February 21, 1914), 3. For a fuller account of the trial, sympathetic to Gore, see the autobiography of one of the defendant's lawyers, Monan Pruiett, *Criminal Lawyer* (Oklahoma City, 1914), 305-35. A bitter attack against Gore can be read in a highly prejudiced pamphlet entitled "The Bond-Gore Case," in C. B. Ames Papers. This anti-Gore brochure was so malicious that it was barred from the mails by federal postal officials. Kingfisher *Weekly Free Press,* July 20, 1914.

4. February 20, 1914.

5. Kingfisher *Weekly Free Press,* July 30, 1914.

6. Boise City *Cimarron News,* July 23, 1914.

7. Gore to constituents (mimeographed), July 1, 1914, in Gore Papers. A campaign circular reprinted a letter from Wilson to Eugene M. Kerr, April 24, 1914, in which the President expressed the "warmest admiration for" and the "greatest confidence in" Gore. *Ibid.*

8. Wilson to Gore, October 30, 1914, *ibid.*

9. The official vote gave Gore 119,443 and Burford 73,292. Gore's total might well have been much more had many people not voted for the Socialist candidate Pat Nagle, who polled almost as many votes (52,229) as the Republican candidate. *Harlow's Weekly,* VII (December 19, 1914), 190.

10. Thomas P. Gore, "The True Basis for America's World Influence," *Annals of American Academy [of Political and Social Science],* LXVI (July, 1916), 135.

11. *Cong. Record,* 64 Cong., 1 Sess., 1136-37.

12. The only indication I have found that the Senator did not favor the President's Mexican policies after January, 1916, is a proposed amendment to the Constitution offered by him in the Senate on February 2, 1916. Gore suggested that Congress also have power to call forth the militia *"to carry on war"* [my italics], as well as to execute the laws of the Union, suppress insurrections, and repel invasions. It must be pointed out, however, that this proposed amendment was offered at a time when Gore was beginning to suspect the President of trying to maneuver this country into war, and he may have made this move mindful of the European situation rather than the Mexican crisis. *Supra,* 70-77.

13. Arthur S. Link, *Woodrow Wilson and the Progressive Era, 1910-1917* (New York, 1954), 180. For penetrating comments about these progressive-pacifists, many of whom, like Gore, had come from Populist backgrounds, see Richard Hofstadter, *The Age of Reform: From Bryan to F.D.R.* (New York, 1955), 371.

14. New York *Times,* July 25 and November 19, 1915.

15. *Cong. Record,* 64 Cong., 1 Sess., 11379, 12825.

16. *Ibid.,* 4601.

17. Lawrence W. Levine, *Defender of the Faith; William Jennings Bryan: The Last Decade, 1915-1925* (New York, 1965), 42.

18. *Cong. Record,* 64 Cong., 1 Sess., 495.

19. *Ibid.,* 753.

20. *Ibid.,* 754.

21. New York *Times,* February 23, 1916; White House Executive Officer's Diary, 1916, in Wilson Papers.

22. New York *Times,* February 24, 1916.

23. *Ibid.,* February 25, 1916.

24. Wilson to Stone, February 24, 1916, in Wilson Papers.

25. New York *Times,* February 26 and March 3, 1916.

26. Gore to Charles A. Beard, September 28, 1926, in Gore Papers.

27. The complete text of the Gore resolution read:

"Whereas a number of leading powers of the world are now engaged in a war of unexampled proportions; and

Whereas the United States is happily at peace with all of the belligerent nations; and

Whereas it is equally the desire and the interest of the American people to remain at peace with all nations; and

Whereas the President has recently afforded fresh and signal proofs of the superiority of diplomacy to butchery as a method of settling international disputes; and

Whereas the right of American citizens to travel on armed belligerent vessels has recently received renewed guaranties of respect and inviolability; and

Whereas the right of American citizens to travel on armed belligerent vessels rather than upon unarmed vessels is essential neither to life, liberty, or safety, nor to the independence, dignity, or security of the United States; and

Whereas Congress alone has been vested with the power to declare war, which involves the obligations to prevent war by all proper means consistent with the honor and vital interest of the Nation:

Now, therefore, be it

Resolved by the Senate (the House of Representatives concurring),

That it is the sense of the Congress, vested as it is with the sole power to declare war, that all persons owing allegiance to the United States should, in behalf of their own safety and the vital interest of the United States, forebear to exercise the right to travel as passengers upon any armed vessel of any belligerent power, whether such vessel be armed for offensive or defensive purposes; and it is the further sense of the Congress that no passport should be issued or renewed by the Secretary of State or by anyone acting under him to be used by any person owing allegiance to the United States for purpose of travel upon any such armed vessel of a belligerent power." *Cong. Record,* 64 Cong., 1 Sess., 3120.

28. New York *Times,* February 25, 1916.

29. *Ibid.,* February 27, 1916.

30. Wilson to Pou, February 29, 1916, in Wilson Papers.

31. New York *Times,* March 3, 1916.

32. *Cong. Record,* 64 Cong., 1 Sess., 3410.

33. Compare Gore's remarks on March 2 with press reports of the February 25 conference in New York *Times,* February 26 and March 3, 1916.

34. The Gore Papers include a folder of material labeled "Sunrise Conference" containing letters which support this conclusion. Among them is a copy of a letter written by Gore to Charles A. Beard on September 28, 1926, in which the Senator gives his account of the circumstances leading up to the conference, the immediate results of it, and his part in the activity created by it. Although continuing to fuse the events of the two conferences, Gore's account of an afternoon and early morning conference agrees in general but not in detail with the newspaper stories relating events of the two White House meetings held on the afternoon of February 21 and the morning of February 25.

For a detailed account of the "Sunrise Conference" story and its historiography, see Monroe Billington, "The Sunrise Conference: Myth or Fact?" *Southwestern Social Science Quarterly,* XXXVII (March, 1957), 330-40.

35. *Cong. Record,* 64 Cong., 1 Sess., 3463.

36. *Ibid.,* 3465. The McLemore resolution in the House was tabled 276 to 142 on March 7. *Ibid.,* 3720.

37. *Ibid.,* 3410.

38. For a discussion of how the vote might have gone on the original Gore resolution, see Timothy G. McDonald, "The Gore-McLemore Resolutions: Democratic Revolt Against Wilson's Submarine Policy," *Historian,* XXVI (November, 1963), 70-71.

39. C. Hartley Grattan, *Why We Fought* (New York, 1929), 336.

40. Banner headlines in the Muskogee *Daily Phoenix,* March 4, 1916, read: "Senate in Uproar As Gore's Resolution is Decisively Cast Aside." The Tulsa *World,* March 4, 1916, reported Gore voting to table his own resolution without troubling to explain that the amendment completely reversed the resolution's meaning and purpose. The Hartshorne *Sun* observed with more asperity than understanding that "Senator Gore got so badly mixed on his resolution that on final roll call he voted against his own measure." Quoted in *Latimer County News-Democrat,* March 17, 1916.

41. E.g., Oklahoma City *Times,* March 3, 1916.

42. Quoted in New York *Times,* March 8, 1916.

43. Clifton James Child, *The German-Americans in Politics 1914-1917* (Madison, 1939), 94.

44. See New York *World,* March 7, 1916; New York *Times,* March 5, 1916; *Daily Oklahoman,* July 13 and 18, 1920, quoting Berlin *Vossische-Zeitung,* March 6, 1916, Frankfurter *Zeitung,* March 4, 1916, and New York *Staats-Zeitung,* March 4, 1916.

45. See Gore, "Basis for World Influence," 133.

46. Edwin Borchard and William Potter Lage, *Neutrality for the United States* (New Haven, 1937), 136.

47. *Cong. Record,* 64 Cong., 1 Sess., 7958.

48. Ray Stannard Baker and William E. Dodd (eds.), *The Public Papers of Woodrow Wilson* (New York, 1925-27): *The New Democracy,* I, 157-58.

VI

1. Gore to W. N. Redwine, April 4, 1916, in Redwine Papers.

2. Hopkinsville (Ky.) *Kentuckian,* October 2, 1916.

3. Link, *Wilson and Progressive Era,* 249.

4. Gore to John Easley, November 23, 1942, in Gore Papers.

5. Baker and Dodd, *Public Papers: New Democracy,* II, 426.

6. New York *Times,* March 5, 1917. The obstructionists were twelve: Norris (Neb.), La Follette (Wis.), Clapp (Minn.), Stone (Mo.), Cummins (Ia.), Kenyon (Ia.), Gronna (N.D.), Words (Calif.), Kirby (Ark.), Lane (Ore.), O'Gorman (N.Y.), and Vardaman (Miss.). Kenyon took no part in the Senate marathon, but he refused to place his signature on a manifesto which seventy-five others signed stating that they favored the armed-ship bill but were unable to vote for it because a small minority hindered them from expressing their support of the measure.

Gore was among the members listed as sick, out of town, or otherwise unavailable when the manifesto was hurriedly circulated. See *Cong. Record,* 64 Cong., 2 Sess., 4988-89.

7. Baker and Dodd, *Public Papers, War and Peace,* I, 9-14.

8. *Cong. Record,* 64 Cong., 2 Sess., 744, 863 ff.

9. E.g., Edward Everett Dale and Jesse Lee Rader, *Readings in Oklahoma History* (Evanston, Illinois, 1930), 756; Scales, "Political History of Oklahoma," 76. Most of this misunderstanding arose as a result of the bitter 1920 campaign when the opposition press grossly misrepresented Gore's stand on the war. *Supra,* 121-23.

10. *Cong. Record,* 64 Cong., 2 Sess., 2749. Personal interview with J. Roy Thompson, Jr., November 16, 1954; Gore to John Easley, November 23, 1943, in Gore Papers.

11. *Cong. Record,* 65 Cong., 1 Sess., 261.

12. Richard L. Neuberger and Stephen B. Kahn, *Integrity: The Life of George W. Norris* (New York, 1937), 125-26.

13. *Cong. Record,* 65 Cong., 2 Sess., 67.

14. For details of the preparation of the bill, see C. H. Cramer, *Newton D. Baker: A Biography* (Cleveland, 1961), 93-98.

15. *Cong. Record,* 65 Cong., 1 Sess., 6853.

16. *Ibid.,* 1485.

17. *Ibid.,* 65 Cong., 2 Sess., 9569-70.

18. Gore to Mrs. Robert Olds, October 27, 1942, in Gore Papers.

19. *Cong. Record,* 65 Cong., 2 Sess., 9573.

20. *Daily Oklahoman,* September 2, 1917. The papers apologizing for Gore were the Capron *Hustler* (which opposed both the declaration of war and the adoption of the selective draft), the Poteau *News,* the Weatherford *Booster,* the Hydro *Review,* and the Muskogee *Times-Democrat.* A few days after the results of the survey were announced, the *Times-Democrat* joined the bulging opposition to Gore. See *Harlow's Weekly,* XIII (September 12, 1917), 12.

21. Quotations from *Daily Oklahoman,* September 2, 1917; *Harlow's Weekly,* XIII (September 5, 1917), 13; XIV (April 10, 1918), 10.

22. October 22, 1917. The charge that Gore opposed Liberty bonds was without foundation. *Supra,* 93-94.

23. *Daily Oklahoman,* September 2, 1917.

24. Gore to Alger Melton, August 23, 1917, in Wilburn G. Cartwright Papers (University of Oklahoma Library).

25. Both telegrams printed in *Daily Oklahoman,* September 1, 1917; see also "Thomas P. Gore's Official Career," 1920 anti-Gore campaign pamphlet, in Gore Papers.

26. Gore to Melton, August 23, 1917, in Cartwright Papers.

27. *Cong. Record,* 65 Cong., 1 Sess., 6469.

28. Here are two typical petitions chosen from the many contained in the Gore Papers:

"We the undersigned citizens of this section have read with surprise your claim that you have acted upon the request of your constituency in obstructing the national programme and our president. We wish to say emphatically that we deplore the stand you have taken and denigh [*sic*] that you have acted under any instructions from us. We are loyal to our government our state and our flag. We demand that you either get in line or get out."

"We, the undersigned citizens of .... County, Okla., respectfully request that you do not resign your office of U.S. Senator, as you are being asked to do by the editors, capitalists and machine politicians of this state, but that you remain at your post of duty and continue to work and vote for the best interests of the common people, as you have done in the past."

29. Gore to W. N. Redwine, October 6, 1917, in Redwine Papers.

30. *Harlow's Weekly,* XIII (October 3, 1917), 12; (September 5, 1917), 14.

31. September 27, 1917.

32. Gore to J. Wesley Smith, October 18, 1917, in Cartwright Papers.

33. Williams to Gore, August 25, 1917, in Williams Papers. See also *Daily Oklahoman,* September 1, 1917.

34. Gore to Jesse Dunn, October 29, 1918, printed in *Cong. Record,* 65 Cong., 2 Sess., 11428.

35. *Ibid.,* 65 Cong., 1 Sess., 6852-53.

36. September 2, 1917.

37. Tulsa *Daily World,* September 24, 1918.

38. *Cong. Record.,* 66 Cong., 2 Sess., 5402.

39. *Ibid.,* 64 Cong., 1 Sess., 9914.

40. *Ibid.,* 9990.

41. *Ibid.,* 65 Cong., 2 Sess., 4631.

42. H. C. Peterson and Gilbert C. Fite, *Opponents of War, 1917-1918* (Madison, 1957), 216.

43. New York *Times,* May 28, 1917.

44. *Cong. Record,* 65 Cong., 2 Sess., 3443, 9094.

45. Gore to the Sovereign People of Oklahoma, Washington's birthday, 1920, in Gore Papers. To show that he was not deliberately trying to obstruct war efficiency by opposing these measures, Gore introduced a resolution providing for the purchase of the telephone system of the District of Columbia to insure the government complete control of this means of communication in safeguarding its military and executive affairs within the seat of government. *Cong. Record,* 65 Cong., 2 Sess., 274.

46. *Ibid.,* 65 Cong., 1 Sess., 2270-71; Gore to Melton, August 23, 1917, in Cartwright Papers.

47. *Cong. Record,* 65 Cong., 1 Sess., 6886; 2 Sess., 4004.

48. *Ibid.,* 65 Cong., 1 Sess., 6849.

49. *Ibid.,* 6850.

50. New York *Times,* June 10, 1917.

51. *Cong. Record,* 65 Cong., 3 Sess., 1996.

52. A typed copy of the manuscript of this speech is in the Gore Papers.

VII

1. David F. Houston, *Eight Years with Wilson's Cabinet, 1913 to 1920* (New York, 1926), I, 260.

2. Benjamin H. Hibbard, *Effects of the Great War upon Agriculture in the United States and Great Britain* (New York, 1919), 69.

3. Baker and Dodd, *Public Papers: War and Peace,* I, 42-44.

4. Hibbard, *Effects of the Great War upon Agriculture,* 100.

5. *Hearing before the Committee on Agriculture and Forestry, relative to proposals for increasing the production, improving the distribution, and promoting the conservation of food supplies in the United States,* U.S. Senate, 65 Cong., 1 Sess. (Washington, 1917), 1 ff.

6. *Cong. Record,* 65 Cong., 1 Sess., 5928.

7. *Ibid.,* 2239; Gore to Wilson, May 21, 1917, in Gore Papers.

8. Wilson to Gore, May 17, 1917, in Wilson Papers.

9. New York *Times,* June 15, 1917.

10. *Ibid.,* June 19, 1917.

11. *Daily Oklahoman,* July 6, 1917.

12. *Cong. Record,* 65 Cong., 1 Sess., 5272.

13. *Ibid.,* 3908.

14. *Daily Oklahoman,* June 27, 1917.

15. *Cong. Record,* 65 Cong., 1 Sess., 5996.

16. Frederic L. Paxson, "The American War Government, 1917-1918," *American Historical Review,* XXVI (October, 1920), 61.

17. New York *Times,* June 21, 1917.

18. C. B. Ames to Wilson, June 27, 1917, in Wilson Papers.

19. *Cong. Record,* 65 Cong., 1 Sess., 5197.

20. *Ibid.,* 65 Cong., 2 Sess., 4698.

21. New York *Times,* June 19, 1917.

22. Both quotes from *Harlow's Weekly,* XII (June 27, 1917), 12.

23. Gore to Secretary, Chamber of Commerce, Okmulgee, Oklahoma, July 29, 1917, in Wilson Papers.

24. W. E. Wood, M. C. French, and J. J. Moroney (Committee for Okmulgee Oil Producers) to Gore, n.d., in Wilson Papers.

25. *Cong. Record,* 65 Cong., 1 Sess., 3907.

26. *Ibid.,* 4459.

27. *Daily Oklahoman,* July 6, 1917; *Harlow's Weekly,* XIII (August 15, 1917), 13-14.

28. *Cong. Record,* 65 Cong., 1 Sess., 5833.

29. Wilson to Chamberlain, August 8, 1917, quoted in Baker, *Wilson,* VII, 209.

30. *Cong. Record,* 65 Cong., 1 Sess., 5834.

31. Frank M. Surface, *The Stabilization of the Price of Wheat during the War and its effects upon the returns to the Producer* (Washington, 1925), 11.

32. *Cong. Record,* 65 Cong., 2 Sess., 8488.

33. *Ibid.,* 3594.

34. *Ibid.,* 3831-32.

35. Thomas P. Gore, "The Wheat Farmers' Dilemma," *Forum,* LX (September, 1918), 257-58.

36. *Cong. Record,* 65 Cong., 2 Sess., 8488.

37. Wilson to Atlee Pomerene, March 25, 1918, in Wilson Papers.

38. *House Documents,* No. 1229 (ser. no. 7444), 65 Cong., 2 Sess., 3.

39. *Cong. Record,* 65 Cong., 1 Sess., 3180.

40. New York *Times,* June 14, 1917; *Cong. Record,* 65 Cong., 1 Sess., 1940, 3314.

41. New York *Times,* June 25, 1917.

42. *Ibid.,* June 26 and 27, 1917.

43. *United States Statutes at Large,* XL, Pt. I, 276-87.

44. Joseph P. Tumulty, *Woodrow Wilson as I Know Him* (New York, 1921), 412.

45. *United States Statutes at Large,* XL, Pt. I, 1046; Thomas Nixon Carver, *Governmental Control of the Liquor Business in Great Britain and the United States* (New York, 1919), 174.

46. *Cong. Record,* 65 Cong., 1 Sess., 197-98, 5666.

47. *Ibid.,* 2980.

48. New York *Times,* May 29, 1917.

49. *Cong. Record,* 65 Cong., 2 Sess., 2972.

50. See *The Depletion Allowance: What is it?,* a pamphlet prepared by Gore at the request of the General Depletion Committee for the Petroleum Industry, in Gore Papers.

51. *Cong. Record,* 65 Cong., 3 Sess., 1082.

52. *Ibid.,* 4399.

53. *Ibid.,* 4307.

54. *Ibid.,* 66 Cong., 2 Sess., 4674.

55. *Ibid.,* 951.

VIII

1. George A. Finch, "The Treaty of Peace with Germany in the United States Senate," *American Journal of International Law,* XIV (1920), 157.

2. Interview printed in *Cong. Record,* 65 Cong., 3 Sess., 4845.

3. *Ibid.* See also Denna Frank Fleming, *The United States and the League of Nations, 1918-1920* (New York, 1932), 147.

4. Quoted by Finch, "Treaty of Peace," 162. As presented to the Senate in July article 10 read: "The Members of the League undertake to respect and preserve as against external aggression the territorial integrity and existing political independence of all Members of the League. In case of any such aggression or in case of any threat or danger of such aggression the Council shall advise upon the means by which this obligation shall be fulfilled." *Cong. Record,* 66 Cong., 1 Sess., 2342.

5. *Senate Reports,* No. 176, part 1 (ser. no. 7590), 66 Cong., 1 Sess.

6. *Ibid.,* part 2.

7. *Ibid.,* part 3.

8. *Cong. Record,* 66 Cong., 1 Sess., 7953-57.

9. The irreconcilables voting for Gore's amendment were Borah, Gronna, Knox, La Follette, McCormick, Moses, Norris, Reed, and Sherman. Other affirmative voters besides Gore were Ball, Capper, Elkins, France, Jones (Wash.), and McLean. *Ibid.,* 8013.

10. *Ibid.,* 8134.

11. *Ibid.,* 8212, 8560.

12. *Ibid.,* 8730.

13. *Ibid.,* 8741.

14. Wilson to Hitchcock, November 18, 1919, *ibid.,* 8768.

15. *Ibid.,* 8800.

16. *Harlow's Weekly,* XVII (December 3, 1919), 1-2.

17. H. W. V. Temperley (ed.), *A History of the Peace Conference of Paris* (London, 1924), VI, 418.

18. Houston, *Eight Years,* II, 50.

19. New York *Times,* January 14, 1920.

20. *Cong. Record,* 66 Cong., 2 Sess., 4533.

21. *Ibid.,* 66 Cong., 2 Sess., 6276, 8134.

22. The charge that Gore opposed the League in the form advocated by Wilson because of his deep-seated antagonism to the President is impossible to substantiate by contemporary records. The only indication given by Gore which might lead one to believe that his opposition to the League was based on personal feeling was expressed nearly twenty years later when the Senator wrote, "Personally I have never doubted that his [Wilson's] ambition to be President of the League of Nations was the chief cause which resulted in our getting into the war." Gore to Sue McCollum, March 21, 1941, in Gore Papers.

23. Henry Cabot Lodge, *The Senate and the League of Nations* (New York, 1925), 164.

24. One authority has argued persuasively that the Treaty of Versailles failed to be ratified not because a two-thirds majority desired to reject it, but because the several groups favoring it were unable to agree on the conditions of ratification. He has pointed out that the leaders of the Senate did not understand the implications of their various positions and were in the end still thinking in terms of strategy rather than substantive results. See Clarence A. Berdahl, "Myths and the Peace Treaties of 1919-1920," *American Scholar,* XI (winter, 1941-42), 263-64.

25. Editorial, August 6, 1920.

26. Muskogee *Daily Phoenix,* February 6, 1920.

27. *Harlow's Weekly,* XIII (August 15, 1917), 8.

28. Scales, "Political History of Oklahoma," 212.

29. W. N. Redwine to J. J. Dennis, June 1, 1920, in Redwine Papers.

30. July 20, 1920.

31. Grundy Stevenson, editor of the Sulphur *Democrat,* quoted in *Harlow's Weekly,* XVIII (January 7, 1920), 2.

32. *Ibid.,* XVI (January 29, 1919), 10; (February 12, 1919), 24.

33. *Ibid.,* XVI (June 18, 1920), 12. Some of these uncashed checks are a part of the Gore Papers.

34. *Ibid.,* XVII (August 20, 1919), 1.

35. Gore to W. N. Redwine, October 14, 1919, in Redwine Papers.

36. See *Lest We Forget!*, a 1920 campaign pamphlet circulated by a veterans' organization against Gore, in Gore Papers.

37. *Cong. Record,* 64 Cong., 1 Sess., 9914.

38. The old French legal custom of *amende honorable* was a form of reparation for a crime or injury consisting of a formal and humiliating public acknowledgment of offense and apology which restored the injured or offended honor of the one wronged.

39. *Harlow's Weekly,* XIX (July 2, 1920), 2-3.

40. *Ibid.* (August 27, 1920), 1.

41. *Ibid.* (September 10, 1920), 2; *Daily Oklahoman,* August 31, 1920.

42. Tulsa *Daily World,* November 5, 1920.

43. Quoted in *Harlow's Weekly,* XIX (August 13, 1920), 6.

44. Quoted in *ibid.,* 4.

45. Gore to George H. White, August 10, 1920, in Hyde Papers.

46. *Daily Oklahoman,* August 6, 1920.

IX

1. 4 Wheat. 316 (U.S. 1819).

2. 11 Wall. 113 (U.S. 1871).

3. 285 U.S. 393 (1932).

4. A court is bound by its previous decision on the principle involved, its justification being that it secures social if not individual justice by adding stability, predictability, and permanence to the legal system.

5. 257 U.S. 501 (1922).

6. See especially 288 U.S. 508 (1933), 298 U.S. 587 (1936), 302 U.S. 134 (1937), 303 U.S. 362 (1938).

7. 303 U.S. 376, 387 (1938).

8. Personal letter from J. Roy Thompson, Jr., October 25, 1954.

9. For a detailed account of this dispute, see Monroe Billington, "The Red River Boundary Controversy," *Southwestern Historical Quarterly,* LXII (January, 1959), 356-63.

10. Wichita Falls (Texas) *Daily Times,* August 11, 12, and 18, 1919; November 8, 1919; January 26, 1920; Oklahoma City *Daily Oklahoman,* January 21 and March 18, 1919.

11. *Daily Times,* November 9, 1919; January 24, 1920; *Daily Oklahoman,* January 25, 1920.

12. *Daily Times,* January 28, 1920; *Harlow's Weekly,* XXI (December 23, 1922), 16; W. Clayton Carpenter, "The Red River Boundary Dispute," *American Journal of International Law,* XIX (July, 1925), 527.

13. *Daily Times,* April 1, 24, and 27, 1920; *Daily Oklahoman,* May 18 and 29, 1920.

14. 252 U.S. 372 (1920).

15. *United States Statutes at Large,* VIII, 252.

16. 162 U.S. 1 (1896).

17. 252 U.S. 372 (1920), 256 U.S. 70 (1921), 260 U.S. 606 (1923).

18. Oklahoma argued that since the river was navigable at one time it was still navigable in the sense that it *could* be navigated, but the Court rejected the novel contention that a river might be navigable in law although not in fact. 258 U. S. 574 (1922).

19. 281 U. S. 109 (1930). See also 272 U. S. 21 (1926), 273 U. S. 93 (1927).

20. 258 U. S. 574 (1922); Isaiah Bowman, "An American Boundary Dispute: Decision of the Supreme Court of the United States with Respect to the Texas-Oklahoma Boundary," *Geographical Review*, XIII (April, 1923), 165. *Daily Times*, January 20 and 28, 1920; *Daily Oklahoman*, January 21, 1919.

21. The original controversy between Oklahoma and Texas centered around Testerman, one of the most active oil explorers in the region. See *Daily Times*, January 22, 1919; August 12, 17, 21, and 22, 1919; November 9, 1919.

22. See the testimony of Gore, *Hearings before the Committee on the Public Lands, on H.R. 12233 and H.R. 13475, bills regarding the leasing of oil and gas lands in the Red River District, Oklahoma*, U.S. House of Representatives, 67 Cong., 4 Sess. (Washington, 1923), 374. See also Floyd E. Moore to Gore, August 31, 1939, in Gore Papers.

23. 265 U.S. 513 (1924).

24. Gore to C. H. Hyde, May 18, 1922 (letter and telegram), in Hyde Papers; W. N. Redwine to Gore, February 18, 1920, in Redwine Papers.

25. From a typed manuscript in the T. P. Gore clipping file (*Daily Oklahoman* Library). Senate bill no. 4197 was passed and approved in February and March, 1923. *Cong. Record*, 67 Cong., 4 Sess., 4806, 4818-20, 4879, 5600. See also *United States Statutes at Large*, XLII, Pt. I, 1448.

26. Testerman was one of eighteen claimants who received a total of $2,141,898 under this legislation. Forty-six applications for reimbursements were rejected. *Daily Times*, September 4, 1925; *Daily Oklahoman*, June 4, 1925; Oklahoma City *Times*, September 4, 1925.

27. Personal letter from J. Roy Thompson, Jr., February 7, 1955.

28. *Daily Oklahoman*, October 20, 1921.

29. *United States Statutes at Large*, XIV, 717.

30. *Ibid.*, XV, 581.

31. 258 U.S. 574 (1922).

32. *Cong. Record*, 68 Cong., 1 Sess., 29.

33. *Hearing before the Committee on the Public Lands, on H.R. 178, a bill authorizing payment of all money received as royalty from Red River oil lands to the Kiowa, Comanche, and Apache Tribes of Indians*, U.S. House of Representatives, 68 Cong., 1 Sess. (Washington, 1925), 83 ff.

34. *Cong. Record*, 69 Cong., 1 Sess., 7261, 10552, 10562; *United States Statutes at Large*, XLIV, Pt. II, 740.

35. New York *Times*, February 22, 1923; Thomas P. Gore, "Discussion of the Agricultural Credit Problem," *Proceedings of the Academy of Political Science*, X (January, 1923), 265-74.

36. T. P. Gore clipping file (*Daily Oklahoman* Library).

37. W. N. Redwine to Gore [July 19, 1921], in Redwine Papers.

38. *Ibid.*, August 27 [1921], *ibid.*

39. *Ibid.* [July 19, 1921], *ibid.*

40. Gore to George L. Bowman, July 12, 1921, in Gore Papers.

41. Miriam E. Oatman, "Oklahoma's Dramatic Year," *Southwestern Political and Social Science Quarterly*, IV (March, 1924), 327-31.

42. New York *Times*, October 13, 1923; *Harlow's Weekly*, XXII (October 20, 1923), 8-9.

43. Oklahoma City *Times*, quoted in *Harlow's Weekly*, XXII (October 20, 1923), 9.

44. Quoted in *Harlow's Weekly*, XXIII (March 22, 1924), 9.

45. Tulsa *Tribune* managing editor to Gore, March 29, 1924; Gore to Tulsa *Tribune*, March 30, 1924, in Gore Papers.

46. *Harlow's Weekly*, XXIII (April 5, 1924), 5. Oklahoma's former governor and Gore's long-time friend, Robert L. Williams, was encouraged to enter the senatorial contest, but Williams wanted Gore to make the race that year, asserting that the latter was needed in the Senate. Williams to Gore, March 5, 1924, quoted in Edward Everett Dale and James D. Morrison, *Pioneer Judge: The Life of Robert Lee Williams* (Cedar Rapids, 1958), 291-92.

47. C. H. Hyde to Gore, April 2, 1924, in Hyde Papers.

48. *Daily Oklahoman*, August 7, 1924.

49. Tulsa *Daily World*, August 3, 1924.

50. Scales, "Political History of Oklahoma," 265.

51. *Harlow's Weekly*, XXIII (July 26, 1924), 6. Dick Gore, Gore's brother and campaign manager, wrote to the candidate when the election returns were being completed, "Sorry we did not have the Standard Oil money, or Doheny money we were charged with having! One consolation we beat the millionaire . . . between three to 4 thousand." Dick Gore to T. P. Gore, August 9, 1924, in Gore Papers. An itemized but unnotarized statement in the Gore Papers indicates that Gore spent only $2,884.87 for the contest.

52. Gore to W. C. McAlester, August 11, 1924, in Gore Papers; *Daily Oklahoman*, August 7, 1924.

53. New York *Times*, July 12, 1924.

54. *Harlow's Weekly*, XXVII (October 10, 1925), 14.

55. Lawton *News-Review*, June 17, 1926.

56. Scott Ferris to M. Pruiett, February 23, 1928, in Gore Papers.

57. Houston (Texas) *Post-Dispatch*, June 29, 1928.

58. *Official Report of the Proceedings of the Democratic National Convention . . . 1928* (Indianapolis [1929]), 157.

59. *Ibid.*, 156; New York *Times*, June 29, 1928.

60. The votes of the sixteen delegates on the four ballots are recorded in a pamphlet in the C. N. Haskell Papers (University of Oklahoma Library).

61. New York *Times*, July 7, 1928.

62. *Ibid.*, October 18, 1928.

63. Scales, "Political History of Oklahoma," 316.

64. *Harlow's Weekly*, XXXVI (July 5, 1930), 12.

65. *Ibid.* (July 12, 1930), 10.

66. The 1930 race for the senatorial and the gubernatorial posts saw a total of five ex-governors of Oklahoma seeking the offices. Besides Gore's three opponents in the primary, ex-Governor J. C. Walton filed as an independent for the Senate though withdrawing before the November election, and ex-Governor M. E. Trapp was a candidate for governor in the Democratic primary. Walton and Johnston had been impeached and removed from Oklahoma's highest elective office for general incompetency.

67. Norman *Transcript*, quoted in *Harlow's Weekly*, XXXVI (June 28, 1930), 11.

68. Technically Gore did not keep his campaign promise. After the election victory, he moved his legal address to Oklahoma City, centrally located in the state, but a few miles west of the former Indian Territory boundary.

69. Quoted in *Harlow's Weekly*, XXXVI (August 9, 1930), 12.

70. Scales, "Political History of Oklahoma," 317.

71. *Harlow's Weekly*, XXXVI (August 16, 1930), 11.

72. Murray, *Memoirs*, II, 373-74.

73. *Ibid.*, 373.

74. Blackwell *Morning Tribune*, August 14, 1930.

75. E. P. Jones to "Buddy" (an ex-serviceman), October 10, 1932, in Gore Papers.

76. Gore to William H. Murray, November 19, 1930, *ibid.*

77. Tulsa *Daily World*, November 4, 1930.

78. Quoted in Scales, "Political History of Oklahoma," 318.

79. Gore to Postmaster General, October 22, 1930, in Gore Papers.

80. *Harlow's Weekly*, XXXVI (October 18, 1930), 8.

81. *Ibid.* (August 16, 1930), 12; (October 4, 1930), 10.

82. Italics supplied by the writer.

83. For an account of Murray's campaign for governor, see Keith Lynn Bryant, Jr., " 'Alfalfa Bill' Murray: Apostle of Agrarianism" (Ph.D. dissertation, University of Missouri, 1965), 347-69.

84. When Gore left the Senate in 1921 he wrote on two cards the date March 4, 1933, at which time he thought he would return to his old seat. One of these cards he placed behind the wainscoting in his office and the other he secreted in his desk in the Senate. He figured it would take a dozen years for the public mood to swing to his way of thinking again. Gore to John M. Holliman, December 16, 1941, in Gore Papers; Washington *Daily News*, December 16, 1936.

X

1. Harris Gaylord Warren, *Herbert Hoover and the Great Depression* (New York, 1959), 132-39.

2. *Cong. Record*, 72 Cong., 1 Sess., 1117.

3. Tulsa *Daily World*, June 25, 1931.

4. *Cong. Record*, 72 Cong., 1 Sess., 1090.

5. *Ibid.*, 1902.

6. *Ibid.*, 72 Cong., 1 Sess., 1705, 2641-45.

7. *Ibid.*, 3928, 3930.

8. *Ibid.*, 15598.

9. *Ibid.*, 72 Cong., 2 Sess., 2951-53.

10. *Ibid.*, 4398.

11. *Ibid.*, 72 Cong., 1 Sess., 15598.

12. *Ibid.*, 8379, 8481-82, 12448; *ibid.*, 72 Cong., 2 Sess., 3366, *passim.*

13. *Ibid.*, 72 Cong., 1 Sess., 11964.

14. New York *Times*, May 7, 1932.

15. *Hearings before the Committee on Banking and Currency, on S. 4632, S. 4727, and S. 4822*, U.S. Senate, 72 Cong., 1 Sess. (Washington, 1932), 166.

16. *Cong. Record*, 72 Cong., 1 Sess., 15596.

17. *Ibid.*, 1877.

18. *Ibid.*, 72 Cong., 2 Sess., 3465.

19. *Hearings before the Committee on Banking and Currency, on S. Res. 84*, U.S. Senate, 72 Cong., 1 Sess. (Washington, 1932), 274.

20. *Cong. Record*, 72 Cong., 2 Sess., 890.

21. *Hearings before the Committee on Banking and Currency, on S. 4627, S. 4755, and S. 4822*, U.S. Senate, 72 Cong., 1 Sess. (Washington, 1932), 60.

22. *Cong. Record*, 72 Cong., 2 Sess., 3379; New York *Times*, February 5, 1933.

23. *Hearings before the Agriculture and Forestry Committee, on Agricultural Conference and Farm Board Inquiry*, U.S. Senate, 72 Cong., 1 Sess. (Washington, 1931), 135-36.

24. *Cong. Record*, 72 Cong., 1 Sess., 15595.

25. Franklin D. Roosevelt to Gore, December 6 and 19, 1928, and January 22, 1929; Gore to Roosevelt, December 15, 1928, in Gore Papers.

26. Gore to John J. Raskob, December 15, 1928, *ibid.*

27. A copy of this speech is in the Gore Papers.

28. *Official Report of the Proceedings of the Democratic National Convention . . . 1932* (Washington [?], 1932), 288.

29. Personal letter from Johnston Murray (for his father, William H. Murray), March 7, 1955.

30. Gore to Franklin D. Roosevelt, July 25, 1932, in Roosevelt Papers.

31. Blackwell *Sunday Tribune*, October 2, 1932; *Daily Oklahoman*, October 16, 1932.

32. Robert Jackson to Gore, August 25, 1932, in Roosevelt Papers; Sioux City (Ia.) *Tribune*, October 24, 1932.

33. Oklahoma City *Oklahoma News*, November 15, 1932.

34. *Official Report of Democratic National Convention, 1932*, 364-65.

35. Gore to Friend [mimeographed letter to constituents], August 4, 1932, in Gore Papers. Gore encouraged Roosevelt to continue his appeal to the depression-ridden masses, when he telegraphed: "Stand by the forgotten man." Gore to Roosevelt, October 3, 1932, in Roosevelt Papers.

36. *Cong. Record*, 72 Cong., 1 Sess., 2418.

37. *Ibid.*, 14750.

XI

1. This chapter heading is also the title of a speech delivered by Senator Gore over the blue network of the National Broadcasting Company on January 24, 1932, sponsored by the Sentinels of the Republic. Printed copies of the fifteen-minute speech are in the Gore Papers.

2. At the end of the special session of Congress which lasted precisely one hundred days and after the passage of a large number of unprecedented reform measures, President Roosevelt invited guests to the White House to witness his signing many of the bills. At the occasion the President remarked, "More history is being made today than in [any other] one day of our national life." Gore amended, "During all time." Quoted in William E. Leuchtenburg, *Franklin D. Roosevelt and the New Deal, 1932-1940* (New York, 1963), 61. Roosevelt assumed what was being done was good; Gore had grave misgivings.

3. *Cong. Record*, 73 Cong., 1 Sess., 249.

4. Eric Manheimer, "The Public Career of Elmer Thomas" (Ph.D. dissertation, University of Oklahoma, 1952), 102, 108.

5. Joseph E. Reeve, *Monetary Reform Movements: A Survey of Recent Plans and Panaceas* (Washington, 1943), 154.

6. See "Papers Relating to Silver Question," in Elmer Thomas Papers (University of Oklahoma Library).

7. "A Statesman's Eyes," *Collier's*, XCI (June 24, 1933), 21.

8. New York *Times*, August 10, 1934.

9. *Cong. Record*, 73 Cong., 2 Sess., 11055.

10. *Ibid.*, 73 Cong., 1 Sess., 4922.

11. *Ibid.*, 73 Cong., 2 Sess., 11056.

12. Gore to J. E. Taylor, November 26, 1937, in Gore Papers.

13. *Hearings before the Committee on Banking and Currency, on S. 875*, U.S. Senate, 73 Cong., 1 Sess. (Washington, 1933), 205.

14. *Hearings before the Committee on Banking and Currency, on S. Res. 84 (72 Cong.) and S. Res. 56 (73 Cong.)*, U.S. Senate, 73 Cong., 1 Sess. (Washington, 1933), part 7, 3239.

15. "A Blind Man Eloquent" (editorial), New York *Times*, May 17, 1934.

16. *Cong. Record*, 73 Cong., 2 Sess., 8575.

17. *Ibid.*, 8577.

18. *Ibid.*, 73 Cong., 1 Sess., 1934.

19. *Ibid.*, 2562, 3121.

20. Gore to Henry A. Wallace, September 4, 1933, in Gore Papers.

21. *Cong. Record*, 73 Cong., 2 Sess., 10354.

22. *Ibid.*, 5710.

23. *Ibid.*, 74 Cong., 1 Sess., 9917.

24. *Ibid.*, 5763.

25. *Ibid.*, 74 Cong., 1 Sess., 6012.

26. *Hearings before the Senate Finance Committee on S. 1712 and H.R. 5755, bills to encourage national industrial recovery*, U.S. Senate, 73 Cong., 1 Sess. (Washington, 1933), 374.

27. *Cong. Record*, 73 Cong., 2 Sess., 6179-83.

28. *Ibid.*, 73 Cong., 1 Sess., 3308-3309; Gore to Franklin D. Roosevelt, October 20, 1934 (telegram), in Roosevelt Papers.

29. *United States Statutes at Large*, XLVIII, Pt. I, 200.

30. 293 U.S. 388 (1935).

31. Speech by Gore before the Governors' Oil Relief Conference, January 16, 1931, pamphlet in Gore Papers.

32. Gore to Charles Evans Hughes, May 28, 1935, in Gore Papers. Gore's blindness forced him to use a rubber stamp to sign his letters, but for some reason he laboriously signed this one with his own faltering hand. It is the only piece in the Gore Papers containing his actual signature. The writer has edited and published this letter in the *Chronicles of Oklahoma*, XXXII (winter, 1954-55), 429-31.

XII

1. For a study of this aspect of the New Deal, see Searle F. Charles, *Minister of Relief: Harry Hopkins and the Depression* (Syracuse, 1963).

2. *Cong. Record*, 74 Cong., 1 Sess., 3719.

3. Both telegrams printed in full, *ibid.*, 2611. For editorial comment see the Washington *Post*, February 25, 1935, and the Chicago *Daily News*, February 26, 1935. After the Works Progress Administration was established, Gore was not averse to channeling its funds into Oklahoma. Protesting the allocation of only

seventeen million dollars of W.P.A. funds to his state, he hoped the sum could be raised to thirty million. Gore and others to Franklin D. Roosevelt, November 14, 1935 (telegram), in Roosevelt Papers. For examples of Gore's requests for specific public works projects in Oklahoma see petition (July 26, 1933) and memo (November 17, 1933), *ibid.*

4. *Hearings before the Committee on Banking and Currency, on S. 3603,* U.S. Senate, 73 Cong., 2 Sess. (Washington, 1934), 270.

5. New York *Times,* January 26, 1935.

6. *Hearings before the Committee on Finance, on S. 1130,* U.S. Senate, 74 Cong., 1 Sess. (Washington, 1935), 133.

7. *Cong. Record,* 72 Cong., 1 Sess., 12964; Washington *Post,* June 18, 1934.

8. Gore to Oklahoma Constituents, May 7, 1932, in Gore Papers.

9. *Cong. Record,* 74 Cong., 1 Sess., 8074; Gore to Roosevelt, May 2, 1935, in Roosevelt Papers.

10. *Cong. Record,* 74 Cong., 2 Sess., 703, 1015.

11. *Ibid.,* 74 Cong., 1 Sess., 1134.

12. *Ibid.,* 1137.

13. *Ibid.*

14. Charles J. Tull, *Father Coughlin and the New Deal* (Syracuse, 1965), 75-78, 245.

15. The vote was 52 for and 36 against membership in the Court. Both Gore and Thomas of Oklahoma voted nay. *Cong. Record,* 74 Cong., 1 Sess., 1147.

16. Thomas A. Bailey, *Woodrow Wilson and the Lost Peace* (New York, 1947), 283.

17. Denna Frank Fleming, *The United States and the World Court* (Garden City, 1945), 136.

18. Oklahoma City *Times,* December 17, 1934.

19. *United States Statutes at Large,* XXXVII, Pt. I, 563.

20. *Senate Reports,* No. 1565 (ser. no. 9988), 74 Cong., 2 Sess.

21. Secretary of War (George H. Dern) to Roosevelt, February 19, 1934; Roosevelt to Gore, February 24, 1934; Gore to Roosevelt, January 7, 1936, in Roosevelt Papers.

22. *United States Statutes at Large,* L, Pt. I, 750.

23. *Harlow's Weekly,* XLVI (May 16, 1936), 6-7.

24. Oklahoma City *Times,* May 29, 1936.

25. New York *Times,* May 26, 1936; Miami (Oklahoma) *News-Record,* June 1, 1936.

26. *Harlow's Weekly,* XLVI (March 21, 1936), 8.

27. Interestingly, Gore attempted to woo Roosevelt to support his candidacy in the pre-campaign maneuverings. Gore to Marvin H. McIntyre, October 18, November 5, 7, and 15, 1935, in Roosevelt Papers.

28. Will Rogers to Gore, September 3, 1936, in Gore Papers.

29. This poem, appearing in the *Sequoyah County Times,* June 12, 1936, and reprinted in *Cong. Record,* 74 Cong., 2 Sess., 10394, was written by a gold-star mother and expressed the sentiments of many of the supporters of the Senator:

Tribute to Senator Gore

We're not so sore on Senator Gore
As we were back there in days of yore,

When he fought old graft and opposed the draft
And stood like a rock when thousands laughed.

But the war came on with its horror and noise
We lost our billions; we lost our boys,
And all we gained was a lesson of woe
That will haunt our lives wherever we go.
And the lesson teaches us more and more
That the safest thing is to vote for Gore.

30. Royden J. Dangerfield and Richard H. Flynn, "Voter Motivation in the 1936 Oklahoma Democratic Primary," *Southwestern Social Science Quarterly,* XVII (September, 1936), 97.

31. *Harlow's Weekly,* XLVII (July 4-11, 1936), 8.

32. Tulsa *Daily World,* July 7, 1936. To another candidate who had been defeated at the same time, Gore wrote, " 'As one ghost to another'—in the words of Robspere [*sic*] as he laid his head on the block—'goodbye and God bless you,' old top. I'll be seeing you—when we cross over the river—at the source of Salt Creek. In the meantime (and the time is mean) Your fellow cadaver, T. P. Gore." Gore to P. L. Gassaway, August 13, 1936, in P. L. Gassaway Papers (University of Oklahoma Library).

XIII

1. Gore to James A. Reed, December 31, 1936, in Gore Papers.

2. Jasper Saunkeah to Gore, January 2, 1947; Gore to Saunkeah, January 10, 1947, *ibid.*

3. Bound carbon copies of these particular briefs are in the possession of J. Roy Thompson, Jr., Washington, D.C. The three volumes specifically mentioned contain 177, 134, and 310 pages respectively.

4. See Gore's statement on percentage depletion in *Hearings before the Ways and Means Committee, on Revenue Revision of 1942,* U.S. House of Representatives, 77 Cong., 2 Sess. (Washington, 1942), 1011-27.

5. Gore to Joseph Tracy, January 9, 1937, in Gore Papers.

6. Gore to R. L. Patterson, May 27, 1937, *ibid.*

7. Gore to B. M. Anderson, Jr., August 19, 1937, *ibid.*

8. *Harlow's Weekly,* XLVIII (November 13, 1937), 8.

9. Gore to Mrs. Anna B. Korn, June 24, 1942, in Gore Papers.

10. Gore to Owen L. Cope, March 14, 1942, *ibid.*

11. Gore to William J. Armstrong, July 11, 1940; Armstrong to Gore, July 16, 1940; Gore to James A. Reed, February 4, 1937; Gore to Millard E. Tydings, August 11 and 20, and September 17, 1938; Gore to James F. Byrnes, February 25 and July 10, 1941, *ibid.*

12. Gore to Ed H. Moore, November 5 and 17, 1942, *ibid.*

13. Gore to B. M. Anderson, Jr., April 15, 1938, and December 9, 1939; Gore to Aldrich Blake, November 10, 1939, *ibid.*

14. Gore to Bob Landers, October 12, 1940, *ibid.*

15. Gore to Oren Root, October 17, 1940, *ibid.*

16. Gore to his sister, Mrs. Mary Wyatt, January 22, 1941, *ibid.*

17. Gore to his daughter, Mrs. Hugh D. Auchincloss, March 12, 1941, *ibid.*

18. Gore to Mrs. Mary Wyatt, April 4, 1941, *ibid.*

19. Gore to Roosevelt, December 10, 1941 (day letter), *ibid.*

20. Gore to Aldrich Blake, October 28, 1948, *ibid.*

21. *Daily Oklahoman,* March 17, 1949.

22. Gore to Weaver Gore, April 19, 1947; Gore to Mrs. Mary Wyatt, December 16, 1939, in Gore Papers.

23. *Journal of the Senate of the Twenty-Second Legislature of the State of Oklahoma, Regular Session, 1949,* 342-43; *Journal of the House of Representatives of the Twenty-Second Legislature of the State of Oklahoma, Regular Session, 1949,* 388-89.

24. J. William Cordell to Mrs. Thomas P. Gore, March 24, 1949, in Gore Papers.

25. During his last retirement, Gore made it a rule to listen over the radio "each and every Saturday night" to Colonel Robert R. McCormick, who, like the old Senator, was for "America first." Gore to F. E. Harkness, May 28, 1945, *ibid.*

26. Washington *Post,* June 18, 1934.

27. Gore to the editor of the Oklahoma City *Independent,* March 14, 1936, quoted in *Cong. Record,* 74 Cong., 2 Sess., 4378. One authority has argued that the pre-World War I progressives believed that "free enterprise" was the cornerstone upon which all other freedoms rest, and that it was therefore not difficult for them to become ardent conservatives during and following the New Deal without any sense of being inconsistent. See Hofstadter, *Age of Reform,* 226. Gore's career and his attitude toward it supports this thesis.

28. Gore's unusual ability helped him at other times too. Called upon to preside over the Senate on one occasion, he recognized without erring each Senator by his voice when he asked for recognition. *Harlow's Weekly,* V (March 28, 1914), 11.

29. Gore to R. L. Williams, June 6, 1908, in Williams Papers; Gore to E. W. Whitaker, May 28, 1915, in Gore Papers.

30. W. S. Couch, "Interesting People: Senator and Mrs. Gore," *American Magazine,* XLVIII (October, 1909), 555; New York *Times,* February 1, 1929.

31. Gore to J. Edgar Pew, October 11, 1945, in Gore Papers.

32. Gore to Robert Gandy, January 24, 1947, *ibid.*

33. Gore to T. L. Terry, October 3, 1945, *ibid.*

34. T. L. Terry to J. Edgar Pew, October 17, 1945, *ibid.*

35. Gore to Albert A. Barnhard, August 31, 1928, *ibid.*

36. Albert A. Barnhard to Gore, August 25, 1928; Gore to Barnhard, August 31, 1928, *ibid.*

37. Mrs. Thomas P. Gore to Woodrow Wilson, July 2, 1917; Wilson to Mrs. Gore, July 2, 1917, in Wilson Papers.

CRITICAL ESSAY ON AUTHORITIES

Manuscript Materials

The Thomas P. Gore Papers in the University of Oklahoma Library contain the principal manuscript sources available for a study of Gore's public career. Unfortunately, Gore destroyed most of his papers when he temporarily retired from public life in 1921, although the few pieces he retained relating to his public career before 1921 are quite helpful. Many of the letters written by Gore while he was in his last retirement after 1936 relate to his early activities, and these are particularly good for biographical data and his political philosophy. The bulk of the Gore Papers is composed of letters written to and by Gore in the 1930's and 1940's. Printed pamphlets and speeches are also included, with a few pertinent newspaper clippings.

Other manuscript collections in the University of Oklahoma Library which have occasional but important material relating to Gore include the papers of C. B. Ames, Wilburn C. Cartwright, Lee Cruce, P. L. Gassaway, C. N. Haskell, C. H. Hyde, Robert L. Owen, J. G. Ralls, W. N. Redwine, Elmer Thomas, and Jack C. Walton. The R. L. Williams Papers and the Fred S. Barde Papers in the Oklahoma Historical Society Library also supplement the Gore Papers. Several collections in the Manuscript Division of the Library of Congress supply information on the early years of the Senator's career which is not available from the extant Gore Papers. Especially important are the papers of Woodrow Wilson, A. S. Burleson, Josephus Daniels, and Maurice F. Lyons. The D. F. Houston Letter Books, Department of Agriculture Papers, National Archives, are useful for the period when Gore served as chairman of the Senate Agriculture and Forestry Committee. The Franklin D. Roosevelt Library with its tremendous amount of material on the New Deal has but a few specific references to Gore.

Government Documents: National and State

The *Congressional Record* for the Sixtieth Congress through the Seventy-fourth Congress (Washington, 1907-1936) provides an invaluable record for an understanding of Gore's senatorial career. The *Congressional Directory* for the same Congresses gives committee assignments and biographical sketches of all Congressmen. Senate and House *Hearings* of the Sixty-first Congress through the Seventy-seventh Congress (Washington, 1910-1942) also provide relevant material, as do Senate and House *Reports* and *Documents* for these Congresses. The *Statutes at Large of the United*

States of America and *United States Supreme Court Reports* are useful as records of legislation enacted during Gore's Senate years and while he was practicing law. Gore's official acts while he was a member of the Oklahoma territorial council are recorded in the *Journal of the Council Proceedings of the Seventh Legislative Assembly of the Territory of Oklahoma, Beginning January 13, 1903 and Ending March 13, 1903* (Guthrie, 1903).

Newspapers and Periodicals

The political career of Gore can be followed in the extensive collection of Oklahoma newspapers housed in the Oklahoma Historical Society Library. Available with the newspapers is an index of important persons and subjects mentioned in the papers held by the society, the index for Senator Gore, although incomplete, being an extremely valuable research tool. The most important newspaper in the state, the Oklahoma City *Daily Oklahoman,* should be singled out as an especially good source for the years 1903-1949. The T. P. Gore clipping file in this newspaper's library in Oklahoma City is far from complete, but much information concerning the Senator in the pages of this paper is readily accessible there. On the national level the New York *Times* (for the years 1907-1949) must not be overlooked. For Gore's years in Mississippi, a number of Mississippi newspapers are available. The Mississippi State University Library has on microfilm the best single collection of Mississippi newspapers for the 1890's, although the papers of the Mississippi State Department of Archives and History are also useful. The Walthall County courthouse has the best file of the Walthall *Warden,* from which Gore's Mississippi boyhood and early political activity can be partially reconstructed.

Sturm's Oklahoma Magazine (12 vols.; Tulsa, 1905-1911), published as *Sturm's Statehood Magazine* until June, 1906, is useful on the early politics of Oklahoma, but much more valuable for Oklahoma political history is *Harlow's Weekly* (49 vols.; Oklahoma City, 1912-1940), a political news weekly with a wealth of information. Periodical articles having useful information on Gore are W. S. Couch, "Interesting People: Senator and Mrs. Gore," *American Magazine,* LXVIII (October, 1909), 555-57, and Royden J. Dangerfield and Richard H. Flynn, "Voter Motivation in the 1936 Oklahoma Democratic Primary," *Southwestern Social Science Quarterly,* XVII (September, 1936), 97-112. Articles written by Gore include "Discussion of the Agricultural Credit Problem," *Proceedings of the Academy of Political Science,* X (January, 1923), 265-74; "The Foreign Policy of the United States," *Annals of the American Academy [of Political and Social Science],* LV (July, 1914), 277-81; "The True Basis for America's World Influence," *ibid.,* LXVI (July, 1916), 130-35; and "The Wheat Farmers' Dilemma," *Forum,* LX (September, 1918), 257-66.

Collected Works, Correspondence, and Convention Proceedings

Published readings, letters, and papers helpful in the preparation of this biography include Edward Everett Dale and Jesse Lee Rader (eds.), *Readings in Oklahoma History* (Evanston, 1930); Charles Seymour (ed.),

The Intimate Papers of Colonel House (4 vols.; Boston and New York, 1926-28); Ray Stannard Baker, *Woodrow Wilson, Life and Letters* (8 vols.; Garden City and New York, 1927-39); Ray Stannard Baker and William E. Dodd (eds.), *The Public Papers of Woodrow Wilson* (6 vols.; New York, 1925-27); and Elliott Roosevelt (ed.), *F.D.R.: His Personal Letters* (4 vols.; New York, 1947-50). *The Official Report of the Proceedings of the Democratic National Convention . . . 1912* (Chicago, 1912) contains material relating to Gore's public political activities, as do the official reports of the proceedings of the Democratic national conventions of 1908, 1928, and 1932.

Unpublished Works

James Sharbrough Ferguson, "Agrarianism in Mississippi, 1871-1900: A Study in Nonconformity" (Ph.D. dissertation, University of North Carolina, 1952), is a mine of material on the area in which Gore matured as a Populist politician. Only occasional references are made to Gore by Eric Manheimer, "The Public Career of Elmer Thomas" (Ph.D. dissertation, University of Oklahoma, 1952), and Keith Lynn Bryant, Jr., " 'Alfalfa Bill' Murray: Apostle of Agrarianism" (Ph.D. dissertation, University of Missouri, 1965). A mechanistic approach to Gore's oratory is made by Ralph Arden Wasson, "A Study of the Speaking Career and Speeches of Thomas Pryor Gore" (M.A. thesis, University of Oklahoma, 1941). Especially good for Gore's political campaigns is an excellent study brilliantly written by James Ralph Scales, "Political History of Oklahoma, 1907-1949" (Ph.D. dissertation, University of Oklahoma, 1949).

Studies Related to Oklahoma History

Numerous general histories of Oklahoma have been published. The following deserve mention here: Arrell M. Gibson, *Oklahoma: A History of Five Centuries* (Norman, 1965); Gaston Litton, *History of Oklahoma* (4 vols.; New York, 1957); Edwin C. McReynolds, *Oklahoma: A History of the Sooner State* (Norman, 1964); Edward E. Dale and Morris L. Wardell, *History of Oklahoma* (Englewood Cliffs, New Jersey, 1948); Grant Foreman, *History of Oklahoma* (Norman, 1942). For the territorial history of Oklahoma there are Roy Gittinger, *The Formation of the State of Oklahoma, 1803-1906* (Berkeley, 1916), and Dora Ann Stewart, *Government and Development of Oklahoma Territory* (Oklahoma City, 1933). Not to be overlooked for a study of Oklahoma politics are William H. Murray's *Memoirs of Governor Murray and True History of Oklahoma* (3 vols.; Boston, 1945), and Gordon Hines' *Alfalfa Bill: An Intimate Biography* (Oklahoma City, 1932). *Pioneer Judge: The Life of Robert Lee Williams* (Cedar Rapids, 1958) by Edward Everett Dale and James D. Morrison contains much political history of the state. Although Gore and his first colleague had few activities in common, this list would be incomplete without mention of Edward Elmer Keso's *The Senatorial Career of Robert Latham Owen* (Gardenvale, P.Q., Canada, 1938).

217

General Studies and Monographs

For the best general account of the South during the last quarter of the nineteenth century, there is C. Vann Woodward's *Origins of the New South, 1877-1913* (Baton Rouge, 1951). An excellent volume on Mississippi politics including the period in which Gore served his political apprenticeship is Albert D. Kirwan's *Revolt of the Rednecks; Mississippi Politics: 1876-1925* (Lexington, 1951). Volumes helpful for an understanding of the period when Gore was active in national politics and in the Senate include: George E. Mowry, *The Era of Theodore Roosevelt, 1900-1912* (New York, 1958); Harris Gaylord Warren, *Herbert Hoover and the Great Depression* (New York, 1959); Richard Hofstadter, *The Age of Reform: From Bryan to F.D.R.* (New York, 1955); William E. Leuchtenburg, *Franklin D. Roosevelt and the New Deal, 1932-1940* (New York, 1963). Finally, the published works of three multi-volume studies still in progress give much general and some specific material relating to Gore or his times: Arthur S. Link, *Wilson: The Road to the White House* (Princeton, 1947), *The New Freedom* (Princeton, 1957), *The Struggle for Neutrality, 1914-1915* (Princeton, 1960), *Confusions and Crises, 1915-1916* (Princeton, 1964), *Campaigns for Progressivism and Peace, 1916-1917* (Princeton, 1965); Frank Freidel, *Franklin D. Roosevelt: The Apprenticeship* (Boston, 1952), *The Ordeal* (Boston, 1954), *The Triumph* (Boston, 1956); Arthur M. Schlesinger, Jr., *The Age of Roosevelt: The Crisis of the Old Order, 1919-1933* (Boston, 1957), *The Coming of the New Deal* (Boston, 1958), *The Politics of Upheaval* (Boston, 1960).

INDEX

106, 151; on foot-and-mouth disease, 59; on grain standards, 60; on rural credits, 60, 61, 63, 151; on Smith-Hughes Act, 61; on Smith-Lever Act, 61; and wheat amendment, 102-04; resolution to muster farmers from army, 108; on Agricultural Adjustment Act, 163-64; on Bankhead Cotton Control Act, 164; on plan to abolish tenancy, 164-65; on loans to agricultural corporations, 165
—Blindness: in childhood, 3; inspiration to blind people, 27, 190; and personal habits, 26; and political career, 187-88; advises the blind, 188-89; on facilities for the blind, 189
—Conference with: W. F. McCombs, 45; A. S. Burleson, 51; Josephus Daniels, 51; A. M. Palmer, 51; Edward House, 53; W. Wilson, 53; W. J. Bryan, 70; Herbert Hoover, 102; F. D. Roosevelt, 156
—Criticized by: Democrats, 8; Oklahoma newspapers, 18-19, 85-86, 117; Methodist bishop, 87; Oklahoma oil producers, 99-100; George Chamberlain, 101; veterans' groups, 122, 144
—Criticizes: Democratic party, 19; J. P. Morgan, 22; John D. Rockefeller, 22; W. H. Taft, 25; N. W. Aldrich, 30; Agricultural Advisory Committee, 98; W. Wilson, 100, 109; John C. Walton, 136; Daily Oklahoman, 138; Calvin Coolidge, 140, 156; Herbert Hoover, 140, 156; Republicans, 49, 140; New Deal, 159, 182-83; F. D. Roosevelt, 159, 180-81
—Economic conservatism: on deficit spending, 92; on war debt, 93; resolution on economy and retrenchment, 93; on social work, 148-49; on welfare state, 149; on balanced budget, 150; on government expenditures, 150, 169, on socialism, 170; mentioned, 68-69, 79
—Indians: lands, 21, 195n24; on McMurray contracts, 39-40, 40-42; on Five Civilized Tribes, 40; on Indian schools, 42; on Choctaw Indians, 43; on Indian claims, 133-34; and opening of Indian rolls, 195n25; mentioned, 42, 179
—Lawyer: enters Law School, Cumberland University, 5; receives Bachelor of Law degree, 5; admitted to Mississippi bar, 5; father's assistant, 5; establishes office in Texas, 6; establishes office in Lawton, Oklahoma, 11; establishes office in Washington, D. C., 127, 179; practice, 127-34, 139, 179
—League of Nations: interview on, 111; and article 10, 111, 117; amendment to democratize war, 111, 113-15, 118; speech on, 117
—Letter from: W. Wilson, 66, 96; Robert L. Williams, 88; D. F. Houston, 102; F. D. Roosevelt, 154

—Letter to: Daily Oklahoman, 84; Alger Melton, 87; Oklahoma oil producers, 99; Tulsa (Oklahoma) Tribune, 137; F. D. Roosevelt, 156; Charles Evans Hughes, 168
—Oil: and discovery depletion allowance, 107; and oil industry, 107-08, 137, 167, 177; and Coronado Oil Company, 127-29; and Red River boundary dispute, 129; and Edward L. Doheny, 137
—Personal life: born, 2; childhood, 2-4; school years, 3-4; first public speech, 4; schoolteacher, 4; migrates to Texas, 6, 8; lawsuits, 9, 65-66; and wife, 9-10, 188; moves to Oklahoma Territory, 10; physical description, 27; financial condition, 127; lecturer at National University, 134; wit and humor, 153; moves to Oklahoma City, 166, 208n68; automobile accidents, 181, 184; diabetic, 184; death, 184; burial, 185
—Political activity, Democratic: joins party, 9; attends national convention, 1900, 9; attends Oklahoma convention, 1902, 11; nominee for territorial council, 11; elected to territorial council, 12; contributions to territorial legislation, 12-13; desires Senate seat, 13; favors single statehood bill, 15; addresses statehood convention, 16; at Oklahoma constitutional convention, 16-17; political platform, 1907, 18; senatorial candidate, 18-19; elected to Senate, 20; addresses national convention, 1908, 25; nominated for second term, 24; re-elected, 1908, 25; praises W. Wilson, 1912, 44, 46; and presidential campaign of 1912 in Oklahoma, 46-48; compromises with Champ Clark supporters, 47; speech in Oklahoma City, 1912, 47; speaker at 1912 national convention, 48-49; chairman of Bureau of Organization, 1912, 52; re-elected, 1914, 67; presidential campaign of 1916, 80, 81; election of 1920, 121-26; defeated, 124; views defeat, 126; retires from Senate, 127; senatorial nominee, 1924, 137; defeated, 138; 1926 election, 139; delegate to national convention, 1928, 140; campaigns for Senate, 1930, 141-46; re-elected, 147; delegate to national convention, 1932, 154; campaigns in Oklahoma, 1932, 155-56; and Oklahoma primary, 1936, 175; defeated, 177; with draws as candidate for Congress, 180, 181; desires Senate seat, 1938, 181; end of political ambitions, 181-82. See also Elections
—Political activity, Populist: nominated for Mississippi legislature, 4; nominated and defeated for presidential elector, 5; campaigns in Texas, 6; nominated for state representative, 1895, 6; popular

speaker, 7-8; defeated, 8; attends Populist national convention, 1896, 8; nominated and defeated for Congress, 1898, 9. *See also* Elections
—Tariff: and Payne-Aldrich Tariff, 29-32, 38; and reciprocity, 36; and Underwood Tariff, 54; on oil tariff, 137, 168; and barriers, 152, 153
—Taxes: and war profiits, 92; and liquor tax, 92-93; and federal gasoline tax, 127, 137, 150, 167, 169; and oil taxation, 129
—Treaty of Versailles: speech on, 113-15; opposes Hitchcock reservations, 115; supports Lodge reservations, 118; votes on, 116, 119
Gore, Thomas T., 2
Gore, West, 4
Gore and Gore law firm, 8
Gore-Bond controversy, 65-66
Gore-Ferris Agreement, 47
Gore Resolution of 1916: not introduced in Senate, 72; introduced in Senate, 73; debated, 73-77; defended by Gore, 74-75; amended by Gore, 75; Gore's motives for amending, 76; tabled, 76; and W. Wilson, 76-77; reaction to tabling of, 77; and National German-American Alliance, 77; complete text of, 199n27
"Gore Volunteers," 121
Grain: grading of, 60. *See also* Wheat
Grasshopper plague, 59
Great Britain, 118
Greer County case: and Texas boundary, 130
Gregory, T. W., 50
Grenada, Mississippi, 5
Gronna, Asle J., 83
Guthrie, Oklahoma, 12, 16
Guymon (Oklahoma) *Herald:* criticizes Gore, 18-19

Haileyville, Oklahoma, 170
Hamon, Jake L., 41
Harding, Warren G., 125
Hardwick, Thomas W., 91
Harmon, Judson, 50
Harp, E. A., 65
Harper's Weekly, 46
Harreld, John W., 125, 139, 140
Hartshorne, Oklahoma, 170
Harvey, David A., 14
Harvey, George, 46
Haskell, Charles N., statehood convention leader, 17; praised by W. J. Bryan, 19; gubernatorial inaugural address, 20; supports Champ Clark for President in 1912, 46
Hayes, Samuel W., 66, 128, 144
Hay-Pauncefote Treaty, 1901, 57
Healdon (Oklahoma) *Hearld:* criticizes Gore, 86
Hearst, William Randolph, 173

Helvering, Commissioner of Internal Revenue v. *Mountain Producers,* 129
Hepburn Act, 1906, 32
Heyburn, Weldon B., 23-24
Hill, Ira, 146
Hill, Robert P., 180
Hitchcock, Gilbert H.: and Treaty of Versailles, 112, 116, 119; and League of Nations, 115, 117
Hoffman, Roy, 17, 18, 19
Hog cholera, 59
Hollis, Henry F., 64
Hollis-Bulkley bill, 62-63
Hoover, Herbert: wartime foor administrator, 98; and Lever food control bill, 99-100; conference with Gore, 102; ridiculed by Gore, 140, 141; criticized by Gore, 145, 156, 187; and moratorium plan, 149; economic policies, 149; on prohibition, 157; and farm distress, 163
House, Edward, 53
House of Representatives Foreign Affairs Committee, 72
House of Representatives Public Lands Committee, 133
Houston, David F.: on Hollis-Bulkley bill, 62; and conference on food, 95; and food proposals, 95; letter to Gore, 102; mentioned, 59, 94, 98
Howard, E. B., 138
Hudspeth, R. S., 52
Huerta, Victoriano, 67
Hughes, Charles Evans, 80, 81, 168
Hughes, William, 50
Hutchings, William T., 17

Immigration: Gore's position on, 30; restrictions on, 56
Income tax: supported by Gore, 21; resolutions for constitutional amendment, 31, 32; and tariff, 53; and oil, 107
Indian Claims Commission, 179
Indian lands: and Gore, 21; sale of, 40; mineral wealth in, 39, 42, 129
Indians: and Gore, 39, 42, 179, 187; taxation of, 42; and treaties, 132; and oil, 132-34. *See also* Apache, Chickasaw, Choctaw, Comanche, Creek, Kiowa, Osage, and Seminole Indians; Five Civilized Tribes
Indian schools: appropriations for, 39, 42
Indian Territory: statehood bills in Congress, 14; Democratic party in, 15
Industrialists: and disarmament, 68
Industry: and Oklahoma depression, 141
International Institute of Agriculture, 62
Interstate Commerce Act, 32
Interstate Commerce Commission, 33
Ireland, 118
Irreconcilables: and Treaty of Versailles, 115, 116, 119
Irrigation: study of, 60